USAF
Phantoms

USAF Phantoms

Anthony M. Thornborough

ARMS & ARMOUR PRESS

London New York Sydney

First published in Great Britain in 1988 by Arms & Armour Press Ltd.,
Artillery House, Artillery Row, London SW1P 1RT.

Distributed in the USA by Sterling Publishing Co. Inc., 2 Park Avenue,
New York, NY 10016.

Distributed in Australia by Capricorn Link (Australia) Pty. Ltd.,
P.O. Box 665, Lane Cove, New South Wales 2066.

British Library Cataloguing in Publication data:
Thornborough, Anthony M.
USAF Phantoms.
I. McDonnell Douglas F-4 aeroplanes,
to 1986
I. Title
623.74'64

ISBN 0-85368-887-7

Edited and designed at Little Oak Studios.
Typeset by Typesetters (Birmingham) Ltd.
Reproduction by M&E Reproductions, North Fambridge, Essex.
Printed and bound in Great Britain by Adlard & Sons Ltd.,
Letchworth, Herts.

Title-page illustration: Three Missouri Guard F-4Es are fitted with a
new, one-piece cockpit windshield, as seen on the sharkmouthed
aircraft to the right of this photograph. The Phantom on the left carries
the standard screen. (McDonnell Douglas)

CONTENTS

FOREWORD

A history of aviation, especially any dealing with its military aspects, could not be called complete unless it contained an extensive detailing of the McDonnell Douglas F-4's development and utilization. No other modern day jet fighter has had such a lasting effect on the free world's air forces. Beginning as a naval project in 1953, its production spanned nearly 25 years and over 5,000 aircraft. This is particularly impressive when viewed alongside the fighter numbers and production rates of today.

Previous fighters had not been called upon to perform in such varied roles. The Phantom began as a naval air superiority aircraft which – because of political considerations, budget constraints and a very successful flight test program – quickly became the USAF fighter of the '60s. The large rugged airframe rapidly found other uses. A relatively easy modification soon resulted in a capable and long-lasting reconnaissance vehicle for many air arms. As more thrust was provided by engine upgrades and further airframe modifications were accomplished the F-4 continued to grow in capability. Along with air superiority and reconnaissance its roles include the very demanding Wild Weasel (electronic radiation suppression) mission, and anti-shipping, air defense, interdiction and close air support tasking. The modifications also included use of the so-called 'smart munitions' and the latest versions of both the AIM-7 and AIM-9 air intercept weapons. These modernization initiatives resulted in continued utilization and procurement of the Phantom. Perhaps not an ideal aircraft for many of its assigned tasks, it certainly became a 'jet of all trades'.

The varied requirements for its many missions and the divergent thinking of its many users are best illustrated through the different uses of its rear cockpit. Originally it was a Naval Flight Officer who, not being pilot-qualified, was provided with numerous duties but no means of flying the aircraft. The USAF quickly changed that concept. They not only provided the rear seat occupant with a control stick and the means of controlling nearly all of the normal pilot actions, but they filled that seat with a rated pilot. The GIB (guy in back) was not the most sought after pilot spot in the system. It soon became apparent this was a very expensive and wasteful means of employing pilots. The Air Force then recognized the backseater as a separate profession, called them various names until finally settling on Weapons Systems Operator (WSO) or 'Wizzo', allowed them to become experts at the various tasks required of that position, and provided a short course in flying the aircraft in emergency situations. Indeed, the F-4 was the last of the USAF two-seat tactical fighters until the advent of the F-15E.

My personal experience with the Phantom has left me with two lasting impressions. First, it is an easy aircraft to fly – in fact, perhaps the easiest of the modern jets I have flown. Secondly, however, when you begin to explore the boundaries of its flight envelope it becomes extremely difficult to employ to its *maximum* without venturing into loss of control situations. But to those who have expended the time and effort necessary to explore and master the F-4, it becomes not only a formidable weapon system but a worthy adversary to those you may chance to encounter under a hostile situation.

'Double Ugly' and 'Rhino' are but two of the better-known nicknames it has been graced with in the past. With love by some, with ridicule by others, those names were bestowed by many of the same aircrews who owed their lives to the reliability and ruggedness of the F-4. There are others who (having suffered the indignity of being ridiculed by their peers for their handling of some of the F-4's idiosyncrasies) provided more colorful names to the Phantom's repertoire!

Who can forget the overwhelming noise, the black smoke from the engines mixed with the white smoke of the show, and the very size of the aircraft as they came over singly and in formation? They were the 'Blues' and the 'Birds' – America's military aerobatic masters. The shows they put on with the F-4 will never be matched for sheer sensationalism. It was truly a heartstopping event that had the children gasping in awe and the adults vowing to return again and again. It is not the same today: the small, graceful and quiet aircraft used presently by the Thunderbirds and the Blue Angels has eliminated some of the pizzazz of their past performances.

What lies in the future for this past master of the skies? Will it be the Israel Aircraft Industries 'Phantom 2000' or some lesser upgrade that will lead the F-4 into the twenty-first century? Will it be destined to live out its life in third world air forces or will the US, UK, FRG or Israel, among others, recognize the span left in that airframe? Given the costs of today's aircraft and the fiscal restraints being imposed on the military, the future of the Phantom II, already having spanned four decades, may well see its time measured not in years or even decades but in generations!

Alexander P. MacDonald
Major-General, NDANG

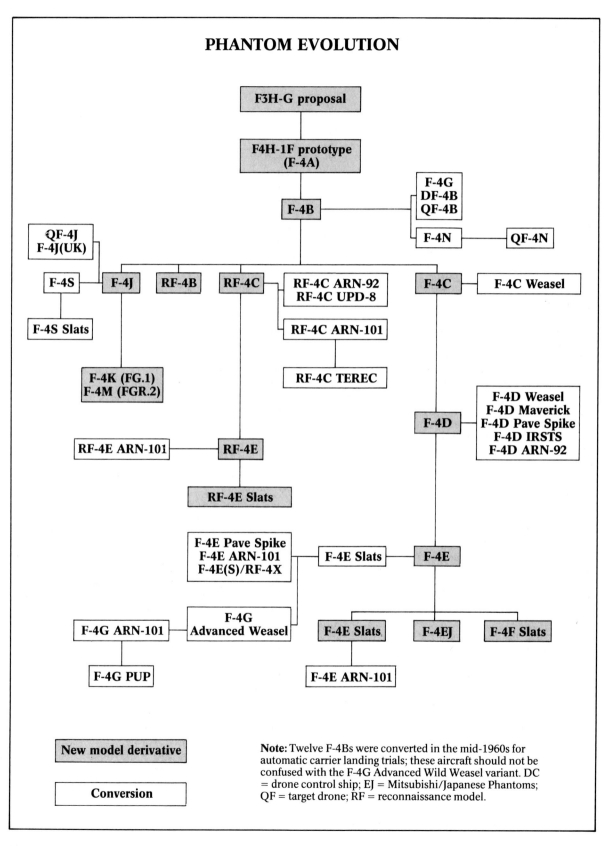

PHANTOM EVOLUTION

F3H-G proposal

F4H-1F prototype (F-4A)

F-4B

F-4G
DF-4B
QF-4B

F-4N — **QF-4N**

QF-4J
F-4J(UK)

F-4S — **F-4J** — **RF-4B** — **RF-4C** — RF-4C ARN-92 / RF-4C UPD-8 — **F-4C** — F-4C Weasel

F-4S Slats

RF-4C ARN-101

F-4K (FG.1)
F-4M (FGR.2)

RF-4C TEREC

F-4D Weasel
F-4D Maverick
F-4D Pave Spike
F-4D IRSTS
F-4D ARN-92

F-4D

RF-4E ARN-101 — **RF-4E**

RF-4E Slats

F-4E Pave Spike
F-4E ARN-101
F-4E(S)/RF-4X

F-4E Slats — **F-4E**

F-4G ARN-101 — F-4G Advanced Weasel — **F-4E Slats** — **F-4EJ** — **F-4F Slats**

F-4G PUP — F-4E ARN-101

New model derivative

Conversion

Note: Twelve F-4Bs were converted in the mid-1960s for automatic carrier landing trials; these aircraft should not be confused with the F-4G Advanced Wild Weasel variant. DC = drone control ship; EJ = Mitsubishi/Japanese Phantoms; QF = target drone; RF = reconnaissance model.

INTRODUCTION

McDonnell's F-4 Phantom II will always be considered one of the aviation greats of all time, not just on account of its proven records of performance and versatility over the past two and a half decades, but also because of its extraordinary commercial success. When the first prototype Phantom II took to the air on 27 May 1958, McDonnell foresaw a requirement for a mere 376 fighters. This figure grew over the years, until in May 1981 the 5,201st airframe was rolled out,* the last of a long line of models that in US service alone by this time had accumulated some 10 million flying hours – the equivalent of one F-4 staying airborne for over a thousand years!

It comes as no surprise, therefore, that much has been written about the F-4 – its development, the Navy/Marines record-breaking era and its entry into operational fleet service, together with the type's subsequent adoption by both the USAF and many foreign customers (some eleven countries to date), and more still on the Phantom II's impressive combat record in South-East Asia and the Middle East. However, little has been done to document the role of the F-4 with today's military air powers. To do this properly, covering the diverse career of the Phantom across the globe since the start of the 1970s, would require several volumes; this book concentrates on the evolution of the models flown by the United States Air Forces.

The USAF fleet today is still the largest single Phantom force, with a current inventory strength exceeding fourteen hundred aircraft in five major marks, and it is one which is unlikely to dwindle substantially before this decade rings out. The force accumulates an average of over 300,000 flying hours each year, greater than any other USAF fighter aircraft. All USAF F-4 types, missions and upgrades are included in the book, while special attention is given to three comparatively new missions assigned to the Phantoms, 'Wild Weasel' defence-suppression, ARN-101 24-hour strike and 'real-time' reconnaissance gathering. These particular roles epitomize the adaptability of the Phantom II to new technology and requirements, for it would have taken an aircraft the size of a B-47 successfully to perform any of these tasks when the F-4 first entered service. Other interesting topics include the massive transition that has converted the Air National Guard and Air Force Reserve fighter inventories from well-loved but aged 'Century Series' jets to the F-4. This process, which started in 1971 and continues to this day, has been a huge undertaking that has embraced more than 800 Phantoms,

forming a vital link in USAF's Total Force concept. Third-generation fighters entering the active inventory are, however, squeezing the Phantoms out from front-line duty at an accelerated pace, but the newcomers currently lack some of the ingredients that let the F-4s hold their own in many mission areas. Both F-4 superiority and inferiority are charted. Also discussed are the dramatic effects of the Arab-Israeli Yom Kippur War of October 1973 upon the art of electronic warfare, particularly in the areas of self-defence and defence suppression systems.

Throughout the book there will also be found a clear trend in the nature of USAF F-4 operations – a re-steering towards specialization, spurred on by new technology and potential enemy counter-technology, away from the multi-role Phantoms of earlier days. This shift reflects the fact that the USAF has now written a more modern philosophy on tactical fighter operations, under which readiness is deemed far more important than comparatively crude multi-capability. So sophisticated has modern warfare become that aircrews and their machines must be honed on very specific mission tasks, and as the backbone fighters during this period of change, the USAF F-4s are an excellent yardstick with which to measure these ever-evolving new developments. As always, however, increased specialization brings about a higher requirement for better co-ordinated teamwork, so many of the Phantoms' various tasks are inextricably intertwined both with each other and with those of other aircraft. For this reason some of the other USAF aircraft and roles must be discussed, at least briefly.

Finally, the book closes with a look at forthcoming upgrades currently 'in the pipeline'. Some of these have been developed specially for the USAF; others have been proposed for foreign countries but may nonetheless find their way on to the USAF service models. Surrounding the most extensive of these potential updates is a fierce controversy over the future of the F-4 within the USAF: should some of them be refurbished for service through to the twenty-first century or should they be retired to make room for newer, more expensive fighters?

Whatever the outcome of this heated argument, the very dispute itself underlines the faith that is still widespread on one side of the camp in the ability of the F-4 to adapt still further to future threats.

---

*A Mitsubishi licence-built F-4EJ.

Acknowledgements

I am sincerely indebted to all those people who gave up so much of their valuable time to help supply components for this long-term assembly project. Their generosity and patience as I continued to bombard them with request after request, month after month (in some cases year after year), was outstanding. I thank them for bearing with me.

Special thanks go to Jerry Stiles, Director of *The Leading Edge*, and to John J. Harty, Phantom Program Support Manager at McDonnell Douglas, for always being on hand to solve the major problem areas; Major General Alexander P. MacDonald, Adjutant General of the North Dakota Air National Guard's 'The Happy Hooligans', for his generous assistance; Major Mike 'Crash' Cassidy, for his considerable time and energy; SSgt. Michael D. Dugre, for his help and enthusiasm; Jack Cressman of Lear-Siegler, who was instrumental in getting the important ARN-101 show on the road; Don Flamm of Ford Aerospace, Vincent Vinci of Rockwell International, Brian E. Lynch of Loral and Alec J. Molton of Mil-Slides, for their patience; Ben Knowles, for coming up with some terrific rare photographs; the Magazines/Books and Public Affairs Offices in Virginia, Ohio and Georgia; and the California, Kansas, North Dakota, Nevada and Texas Air National Guards.

Many thanks are also due to the following commanders, aircrewmen, ground crewmen, public affairs specialists, historians, subsystem suppliers, photograph archivists and friends, who tied up the 'loose ends': Donna B. Anderson, Maj. William H. Austin, Luisa C. Bailey, Capt. John L. Barry, Timothy Beecher, Bill Belew, August H. Bickel, Maj. Donald Black, R. S. Blake, C. W. Blaney, Helen Box, Lt. Michael Braun, Paul Brown, C. Bushey, Dave Caldwell, Michael J. Carney, TSgt. Genelle Clifton, TSgt. Stephen Q. Cox, Mary Ann Cox-Terrell, P. R. Craven, Capt. Peggy C. Cuellar, Peter E. Davies, SSgt. S. B. Diehl Jr., Maj. Daniel Donohue, P. Dusseault, Lt. Antonino Fabiano, Brig. Gen. Eugene Fischer, TSgt. Larry B. Fountain, Norma L. Gibson, Chip Glissom, Dorine M. Goss, Ann Grizzel, Sgt. Rebecca Haight, Don Haley, D. J. Harper, Lt. Col. Jerry Hicks, Dan Hogan, R. E. Hollingsworth, Thomas K. Horton, SMSgt. Theodore T. Huston III, Elizabeth Lane-Johnson, Arthur H. Jungwirth, Charles M. Kenny, Lt. Terry L. Kopish, Leon Levitt, Nancy Litzau, Robin Loving, Lt. Col. Clayton B. Lyle, Lt. Philip S. McCarthy, MSgt. Mike McCoy, J. D. McGilvray, Ken Mackintosh, Larry Martinson, Lt. James G. Mohan, Capt. Randal E. Morger, Maj. Moscatelli, Pat Muldrow, Thomas J. Mullican, Kevin Mulligan, P. J. O'Connell, Michael D. Pefley, Brian Pickering, Gen. Piotrowski, Gary Pounder, Scott Rayburn, TSgt. Philip F. Rhodes, SSgt. Tessie L. Richardson, Wayne Riendeau, Dave Robinson, Capt. Gerald K. Robinson, Maj. Ronald W. Saeger, John Savage, SSgt. Merie Schileer, Stephen Schofield, TSgt. Robert E. Scott, Lou Sharp, MSgt. Frank E. Shirar, Marilyn S. Silcox, Sgt. Charles Silva, Maj. Thomas Skypeck, Lt. Col. Eric Solander, Capt. Robert E. Staal, Mary Stuetzer, Richard D. Sukey, D. Suslik, Z. Joe Thornton, Capt. Mike Turner, Carl L. Tuttle, Lt. Col. Joseph Wagovich, Bill Warden, Hal Watkins, TSgt. Leland H. Weppler, Walter F. Werner, SSgt. Scott White, Jim Williford, Lt. Col. Joseph Winsett, and Lucille Zaccardi.

Finally, special thanks to my wife and sweetheart Maggie for all the hours she spent going through the manuscript with me, and for putting up with my obsession with the project over the past few years!

Author's note

Throughout the book I have endeavoured to provide accurate figures relating to numbers of aircraft currently operational, in terms of their allocation and configuration. Readers should note that the figures may have altered slightly as aircraft go in and out of depot-level maintenance, while several units are on the brink of swapping their Phantoms for F-15 and F-16 'Teenagers'.

Anthony M. Thornborough
Bristol, England, June 1987

1. THE EARLY YEARS

Adoption and Adaptation

On 30 March 1962 the USAF officially adopted the McDonnell Phantom II, the Navy's new baby. That day, a letter of intent was received by the manufacturers for one F-110A and two YRF-110s, subsequently redesignated F-4C and RF-4C respectively in the Department of Defense's number reshuffle in September of that year.

There was no question that the F-4 was a good all-round performer: it had just recently outflown the Air Force/Convair F-106 Delta Dart during comparative flight tests at Edwards AFB, California, and looked destined to do the same with several other US Air Force fledgeling aircraft. A remarkable series of record-breaking manoeuvres by the US Navy and Marine Corps capped this series of events, which ultimately brought pressure on the Air Force from Secretary of Defense Robert McNamara. He was keen to maintain US service modernization rates while capitalizing on longer production runs and lower joint-service life-cycle costs to reduce unit prices and keep the budget watertight, and an order that would eventually total 47 F-4As and 651 F-4Bs* was well under way for the Navy. But although the F-4 outflew the F-106 (the USAF's newest air defence interceptor), had 25 per cent more radar range and consumed 33 per cent fewer maintenance man-hours per flight-hour (MMHFH), the Air Force was still sceptical, concerned particularly about shortcomings in the F-4's ability to perform effective tactical ground attack sorties, including the then almost sacred nuclear bombing role. This point was aggravated by the fact that McNamara had set his sights on terminating the production of the Republic F-105 (the USAF's newest fighter-bomber) while allowing only small areas of permitted change to the F-4B in the USAF's adaptation of the jet fighter to strike work.

While the reconnaissance YRF-4C progressed as a separate venture (see Part 4), the USAF squeezed as much mileage as it could from those areas of permitted change, and issued Specific Operational Requirements (SOR) 200 in August 1962, requesting an expanded ground-attack capability, dual flight controls (the Navy used the rear-seat crewman purely as a Radar Intercept Officer), and forward air base operability. The go-ahead, after some finalizing of requirements, was settled on 31 December under contract NOw(A)63-0032, and thus emerged the F-4C. This new version took to the air on 27 May 1963 – precisely five years after the original XF4H-1 prototype – and joined hands with the USAF when the first operational deliveries began later that November.

The changes made to the aircraft included a number of minor but important variations over the Navy model. First, the General Electric J79-GE-15 power-plant replaced the Navy J79-GE-8. These new engines obviated the requirement for an external air hose starting trolley, by incorporating a facility for cartridge starts. Provision for the cartridges – charges to start the engines turning pneumatically – was made in the lower wheelcase, accessible via hatches in the aircraft belly between the wings. This is a sooty but effective means of launching aircraft at forward bases without the need for extensive support equipment. In turn, the 20kVA electrical generators were moved to an extended, bullet-shaped centre-body at the front of each engine.

Other modifications included larger, softer, lower-pressure main gear landing tyres, increased in width by 3.8in, so that a fully loaded F-4C could better distribute its weight over thinner paved concrete runways; similarly, commensurate with the higher gross operating weights of USAF aircraft, more powerful brakes and an anti-skid system were also added. All these main undercarriage modifications required the wing roots to be enlarged in order to accommodate the bulkier landing gear assembly.

Several items were retained from the F-4B, notably the arrester hook (useful for short-runway landing or for emergencies), the outboard wing hydraulic fold facility, and the nose cone ventral fairing (though without its infra-red seeker). Additionally, the F-4C retained the F-4B's AN/ASA-32 Automatic Flight Control System (AFCS), which is used to provide a number of mach/altitude automatic-pilot relief modes, especially useful for the USAF, which regularly deploys its fighters on long and arduous overwater flights. On the other hand, the catapult bridle hooks were removed, and the retractable probe arm used by the Navy's probe-and-drogue in-flight refuelling system was deleted in favour of a 'pop-up' receptacle in the spine aft of the cockpit, compatible with KC-135 Stratotanker 'flying boom' fast jet-petrol transfer, but dropping the potential for fighter-to-fighter 'buddy' refuelling.

However, the greatest changes came in the internal black box and instrument configuration, necessary because of the requirements for an expanded ground attack capability and for dual flight controls. These introduced an extensively reworked 'office' for the

---

*Including two F-4Bs converted into YRF-4Cs and handed over to the USAF.

back-seat Weapons Systems Operator (WSO, or 'Wizzo'), complete with two new side consoles, a lowered front panel for better forward vision over the Aircraft Commander's (AC's) shoulders, and a re-located radar tracking handle, attack switches and other refinements. In line with the expanded attack provisions, the Westinghouse AN/APQ-72 fire control radar in the nose was modified to APQ-100 standard for ground mapping, and came with a range strobe for manual bombing. The AN/AJB-3 nuclear bombing package was replaced by the superior AJB-7 all-altitude nuclear bombing system, for the release of 'special weapons' on a timed basis from target or offset aimpoint in level and loft modes at various established angles. Innovations included the Litton AN/ASN-48 inertial navigation system (INS), which when tied through the ASN-46 navigation computer provides a continuous calculation of aircraft position, height and airspeed, all of which are correlated with the other black boxes for more accurate navigation, autopilot relief and ground attack. Extra wiring was also added for the command-guided AGM-12 Bullpup missile, while the Navy's LAU-17 inner wing pylons were modified to incorporate tougher MAU-12 racks in a new curved pylon, though the Navy pylons were used for several years.

Despite these improvements, the F-4C's conventional bombing provisions were more or less a copy of the F-4B's, a manual system relying heavily on a crew's individual expertise to hit targets with any precision. For example, in dive-bombing, there are a number of dive angles – usually between 15 and 45° – each with its optimum weapons release height above ground. The crew either memorize these heights or refer to charts which they carry with their other flight paraphernalia. In practice, during the bomb run, the pilot will first depress the gunsight aiming reticle in his line of sight (preset by twisting the 'MILS' knob for a specific dive angle to be used on to the target) so that, with the target in his sight, he has the aircraft properly pitched at the moment of weapons release to compensate for

cannon shell, rocket or bomb ballistics. The pilot will then line up and dive on to the target, and attempt to hold the aircraft as precisely as possible at the chosen dive angle and required air speed, while the WSO in the rear continuously calls out their descending height over the intercom. At the proper weapons release height over the target the WSO calls for a 'pickle' (for the pilot to press the bomb release button) and, with the gunsight on target, the ordnance should fall along the predicted trigonometric path and smother the enemy with explosives.

As an alternative, the F-4C did incorporate a new bombing feature, the SST-181X Combat Skyspot. This equipment was used extensively in Vietnam where cloud or other cover effectively prohibited accurate visual bombing. An antenna, sprouting off-centre just behind the rear cockpit fairing, would transmit signals to ground receiving radars, which in turn could readily identify the F-4C's position. The ground station then vectored the crew on to preselected target co-ordinates and commanded bomb release at the right moment. This method of level bombing – often conducted in formation – was fairly accurate against sprawling targets, and was frequently used against enemy vehicle parks or ammunition caches. The last F-4C, number 583, came off the St. Louis lines on 4 May 1966, to be followed by the second USAF attack variant, the F-4D.

Getting nearer the mark

Looking the same in most respects to the F-4C – not surprisingly, since it shared a common structure and embodied a large number of F-4C subsystems – the F-4D was in fact a vastly superior strike machine.* The reason for this lay in two new devices: the AN/ASG-22 Lead Computing Optical System (LCOSS), replacing the old fixed gunsight; and the AN/ASQ-91 automatic Weapons Release Computer System (WRCS), moving

*The No. 1 fuel tank behind the cockpit was reduced from 314 to 231 US gallons to make room for extra avionics, the generators were up-rated to 30kVA capacity and the inertial navigator was updated to the ASN-63 model. The F-4D also introduced the superior APQ-109 radar.

the Phantom's conventional strike capabilities to a much higher level of precision, with the added bonus of automating much of the crew's workload. A look into the methodology behind a typical ground attack best explains how these systems work.

With bomb stations, mode of release (either in pairs or singly in rapid succession) and fuses set, the pilot switches on the master arm, priming the chosen weapons ready for use. Target run-in and visual acquisition are conducted by a belly-wrenching pop-up manoeuvre, hauling the jet up from a ground-hugging profile to between 2,000 and 5,000ft, the height varying with the kind of bomb to be used, the method of attack employed and target height. After rolling inverted to acquire the target visually through the canopy glass, the pilot will push the nose of the Phantom down, roll the wings level, and centre the target in his gunsight.

The most accurate method of bomb attack available to the F-4D using the WRCS package is the automatic 'dive–toss' delivery mode. Using this, the WSO will lock the radar on to the ground, which involves caging the dish in a fixed forward alignment ahead of the Phantom's flight path 'ready for pickle'. With the gunsight pipper superimposed over the target, the pilot presses the bomb release button, thereby telling the WRCS to ingest and hold the radar-generated slant-range information to target. This data is computed with inputs from the INS to determine automatically the optimum bomb release time. Still keeping the button pressed, and with the WSO calling out the descending height for good measure, the pilot pulls the Phantom up out of the dive, and the WRCS, sensing when all the release parameters have been met, lets the bombs go (sometimes up to ten or more seconds after the initial pickle) to put a pattern of explosives along the target.

The chief advantage of 'dive–toss', unlike the other ground-attack modes available, is that the pilot needs not meet all the attack requirements – airspeed, dive angle, altitude, etc. – precisely. Instead, using a mixture

Above left: The fourth 'real' F-4 for the USAF, F-4C-15-MC 63-7410, seen at Edwards AFFTC in 1963. The aircraft wears Navy camouflage and has LAU-17 inner wing pylons; the Air Force trim on the tanks, wing leading edge and intake lips is aluminium coloured. The first USAF unit to receive F-4C Phantoms was the 4453rd Combat Crew Training Wing at MacDill AFB, Florida, in November 1963. (USAF via Lucille Zaccardi)

Above: F-4C-25-MC 64-0887 in early 1972 when assigned to the 92nd TFS, 81st TFW, in England. This machine was later handed over to the Spanish Air Force and was re-coded C.12-33. (MAP via Peter E. Davies)

Below: Phantom ground-attack techniques. The upper diagram illustrates an attack with either rockets or gun pods and the lower the technique of loft bombing.

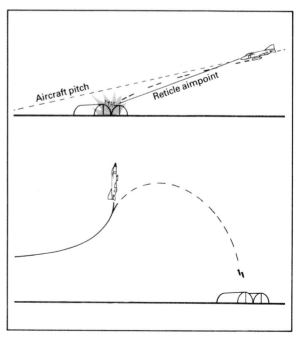

of radar- and INS-furnished data, the WRCS will automatically compensate for any height or speed variations, giving the pilot more freedom for evasive manoeuvring during the particularly hair-raising attack run. Accuracy with the 'dive–toss' mode varies according to the height above target at which the bombs are let loose. As a general rule, at around 1,000ft above ground level, average bomb miss (more correctly termed circular error probable, or CEP) is usually around 75–100ft. This figure degrades by about 20ft for every 1,000ft of altitude at bomb separation, and as most weapons releases are conducted at higher altitudes, the figure invariably degrades to about 150ft – a negligible CEP if as many as eighteen bombs are let loose on the aimpoint!

In other modes of bomb attack the radar is not locked on the ground but rather provides a sector scan of the terrain ahead, a continuous sweep of radar imagery on the cockpit radarscope. WRCS-generated crosshairs appear on the scope and can be placed over the target either automatically, by calling up stored target co-ordinates in the nav-attack computer, or manually, by the WSO moving them about with the aid of the right console thumbwheel cursor controls. With the 'freeze' button pressed, the inertial system will track the designated spot and keep the crosshairs in place. This is used to help navigate to target and assist the WRCS preparatory to a visual strike; if visibility is bad, the crew can pickle the bombload manually purely on the basis of the displacement of the crosshairs, though this is a very crude method. As an alternative, the WRCS features an offset mode. Because the radarscope imagery is fuzzy at the best of times, it is far easier to place the crosshairs over an offset identification point (a prominent landmark or beacon) instead. With the true target's co-ordinates keyed-in on the right-hand console, the WSO presses the 'target insert' button. The computer then compares the relative positions of the initial point and the target and furnishes the pilot's gunsight with a comprehensive set of roll-steering commands, to take the crew to the target. Meanwhile, the radarscope crosshairs will have repositioned themselves over the target imagery automatically to assist the WRCS in computing the correct moment for automatic weapons release. Having used the LCOSS steering tabs to line up with the target, the pilot presses the pickle button and keeps it depressed all the way up to bomb release.

Also available from the WRCS are the automated 'dive laydown' and 'laydown' modes. In 'dive laydown', the pilot puts the F-4 into a dive and presses the bomb release button when the target is in his sight. He then pulls back on the stick to decrease the rate of dive to deposit a bundle of weapons in a comparatively long, sequential pattern. In 'laydown', the pilot presses the pickle button when the target moves into his gunsight reticle which, following initial designation, will not only move in traverse (which it does in all bombing modes) but also in elevation, to help the pilot compensate for aircraft drift *and* pitch. High-drag Snakeye bombs with pop-out airbrakes are generally

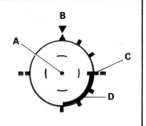

Key
A. Centre pipper (aiming mark for weapons)
B, C. Zenith and roll indexes. Tabs outside reticle move to provide roll steering cues to pilot.
D. Analogue bar, serving to illustrate range to target (furnished by nose radar). Unwinds as range decreases.

Above: F-4D/E LCOSS (Lead Computing Optical Sight System). This imagery is presented on the pilot's gunsight glass to assist in navigation, air-to-ground and air-to-air attack.

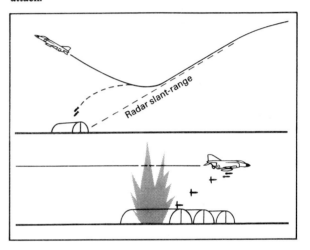

Above: Ground attack using the 'dive–toss' (upper drawing) and 'laydown' techniques, the latter with Snakeye bombs.

used during 'laydown'-type attacks – as they are in low-altitude dive-bombing – to avoid any risk of the Phantom getting caught in the bomb blast.

But, with the exception of 'dive–toss', all these bombing modes have their limitations: it is crucial that the pilot holds the aircraft as precisely as possible at the prescribed airspeed and attack profile, or, as one WSO put it, 'Whoops, you bomb the wrong piece of real estate!' As such, bombing accuracy can be severely degraded if the crew are forced to take evasive action against enemy anti-aircraft fire during the critical attack run. An INS or WRCS failure will demand that the crew revert to the methods used in the F-4C, which is as dependent on crew skill as darts.

In spite of some of its minor shortcomings, the WRCS-aided F-4D represented a quantum jump over the F-4C, and put the Phantom into a new class, paving the way for vast international sales. For this reason, as will be seen later, no USAF upgrades were to be incorporated into the F-4C, save for one highly specialist role.

The 793rd F-4D allocated to the USAF (32 were supplied directly to Iran, making a total of 825 built) was delivered on 28 February 1968, after which time

McDonnell diverted their efforts into the near-definitive strike model, the F-4E. This aircraft retained the best features of the F-4D, including the WRCS and an upgraded LCOSS, but it also went several steps further, incorporating new technology as it became available in the course of its fourteen-year production run. It also without doubt came the closest of any of the attack models to what the Air Force had wanted all along – within the constraints of contemporary technology and available funds.

Originally, the F-4E was to have carried an advanced radar system known as the coherent-on-receive doppler system (CORDS), featuring a pulse-doppler radar with magnificent clutter-free, look-down marriage potential with newer models of Sparrow air-to-air missiles, and excellent ground mapping capabilities for all-weather radar bombing. Unfortunately, development problems plagued the system, creating two production slippages and the eventual cancellation of the programme – a factor which prompted the massive continued procurement of the F-4D in Fiscal Year (FY) 1966 and which very nearly caused the demise of the F-4E altogether.

The DoD put the F-4E programme on a financial 'drip-feed', while heads were scratched in an attempt to come up with a solution. Eventually, Westinghouse saved the day and came forward with their AN/APQ-120 radar. This is a more compact solid-state version of the older 32in radars, packing an elliptical antenna dish 5in narrower than its predecessors. Some argued that the Navy F-4J's APG-59/AWG-10, a bigger but more effective pulse-doppler radar and fire control

system with superior air-to-air capabilities, should have been fitted, but the Air Force disagreed – their new APQ-120 was compatible with a slim 33in nose extension, a modification introduced so that the F-4E could house the General Electric M61A-1 20mm 'Gatling' gun. If the F-4J radar package was to go in, the F-4E would be another short-nosed model with no room for such a weapon. The Navy were not desperate to have an internal gun and proceeded to build 522 F-4Js; they also sold the idea of the pulse-doppler radar to Britain, which went on to buy 170 similarly equipped F-4K/Ms and fifteen modified F-4Js* and was the only foreign customer not to buy models derived from USAF Phantoms. The Air Force dug in its heels, and along came the gun and new 640-round, linkless-feed ammunition drum, the dream of so many F-4 pilots who had encountered continuous frustration with the unreliable missile-only air-to-air armament of the F-4C/D. An additional fuel tank was made possible by the added weight of the gun in the nose, and this was incorporated as a welcome counter-

---

*Called the FG.1, FGR.2 and F-4J(UK), respectively, by the British Ministry of Defence. McDonnell Douglas have termed the F-4J(UK) variant the FGR Mk. 3.

Below: The first production F-4Ds went to TAC's 33rd TFW at Eglin AFB and USAFE's 36th TFW at Bitburg AB. Seen here is F-4D-25-MC 64-0963, a Bitburg example, with the clean nose radome standard on F-4Ds prior to the introduction of the Bendix AN/APS-107 RHAWS. (Via Peter E. Davies)

balance in the aft fuselage, above the engines. Another boost for the F-4E was the replacement of the General Electric J79-GE-15s with more powerful J79-GE-17 powerplants, something no pilot would complain about.

Deliveries commenced with an initial production batch of 99 F-4Es, the first of which touched down at Nellis AFB, Nevada, in October 1967; 904 more followed, the last of which was handed over in August 1977.* This marked the end of Phantom production for the Air Force, but a number of deficiencies, mostly legacies from the early Navy-orientated design (and

---

*Of the 1,003 total, ten FY75 aircraft were bought on behalf of the Luftwaffe and 44 FY68 aircraft on behalf of the Israelis, making a grand total of 949 exclusively for USAF use, the last of which was delivered on 10 December 1976.

Above: F-4D-29-MC 65-0795 at Nordholz, West Germany, in August 1977. The unit was on deployment from Hill AFB. Note the deployed flaps and open drag 'chute door. (Ben Knowles)

Below left: A 'hard-wing' F-4E with the old-format, short gun muzzle, photographed in 1970 when serving with the 336th TFS, 4th TFW. The 'Fourth but First' Wing flew 8,000 combat missions in SEA between April and September 1972 and between March and September 1973, and 'bagged' a MiG-21 on 15 August 1972. Its primary duty was chaff-carpet laying. On 9 May 1974 the 336th TFS became the first fighter squadron in TAC to log 50,000 accident-free hours. (MAP)

Below right: F-4E-32-MC 66-0312, 4530th TFTS, 1st TFW, at MacDill AFB, Florida. The aircraft is a 'hard-wing' Phantom but has the revised, longer 20mm gun muzzle. (CWM via Peter E. Davies)

argely overshadowed by problems with another joint-service machine, the F-111) still persisted.

Stall-spin problem

The worst of these headaches related to the F-4's wing. The original aerofoil, as used by all models prior to 1972, employs boundary layer control (BLC). This comprises leading- and trailing-edge high-lift flaps, with air piped from the seventeenth stage of the engine compressors and blown out over the flaps to increase the lift properties of the wing. The flaps are deployed during launches and recoveries to shorten take-off runs and reduce landing speeds – so essential to practical carrier operations. After take-off, as speed builds up, the flaps are retracted to form a clean, low-drag wing optimized for high-speed point interception work.

This worked well for the Navy – so well that Block 26 F-4Bs and subsequent Navy Phantoms had the immediate inboard leading-edge flaps deleted. F-4s configured for carrier combat air patrol, the role for which the type had been designed, normally flew at weights well below their gross 54,000lb level, carrying only full internal fuel, a maximum of three external tanks (which were expended and then jettisoned) and six or eight air-to-air missiles. But, unlike their sea-faring counterparts, USAF strike Phantoms were in-variably flown with full fuel and stores at weights approaching their gross 58,000lb figure, and even higher when combat demands relaxed these limits. Drawing sine waves through the air to avoid anti-aircraft artillery (AAA), throwing the aircraft down to under 500ft to dodge surface-to-air missiles (SAMs) and then pulling the heavy jet up again too sharply often caused the Phantom to start buffeting, yawing and then to depart from controlled flight into a flat stall spin, to plummet back to earth like an uncon-trollable rotating fire bomb. Many USAF officers commented that if they ever got caught in such a spin, the only way to get out was literally to do that – eject. McDonnell were aware of the problem, and so too

were the Marines, who similarly operated their F-4B/J Phantoms loaded to the hilt with cumbersome iron bombs in hard manoeuvres.

By 1970, it was estimated that the US Air Force and Marines had lost well over 100 Phantoms because of this problem (the Navy figures, which have been released, cite the loss of 83 aircraft and 43 crewmen between 1962 and 1980). Extensive re-education pro-grammes were set up for all services (it takes about twice as long to learn to fly the F-4 as compared to the new F-15), but the USAF went one step further, invest-ing over $100 million in McDonnell's Agile Eagle programme. This introduced a new wing designed to overcome the stall-spin hazard. Funds were made available after hearings concerning the losses had taken place before the Defense Appropriations Com-mittee in August 1971.

The new wing, using leading-edge slats (LES), provide an immense improvement in manoeuvrability and low-speed control. A lieutenant-colonel who had flown with both types of wing – 'hard' and 'slatted' – on the F-4E commented that he had seen heavily laden F-4Es perform manoeuvres 'which they would not have dared to do prior to the LES modifications'. Maj. Cassidy from the Kansas Air Guard similarly com-mented: 'In the [LES] F-4E you can slap the stick around with no problems; if you did the same in the F-4C/D you can snap it out of control'. The F-4E's hydraulic slats deploy automatically at high angles of attack (AOA), the resultant slot preventing airflow separation near the leading edge so that the aerofoil can perform its job and provide sufficient lift and stability. A manual override allows the pilot to deploy them for heavyweight low-speed control. At above 600kts, or AOAs of 10.5 units or less, the slats retract, closing the slot and cleaning up the wings – less 'baby smooth' than the old BLC configuration, but the marginal increase in drag is a small price to pay for the enormous benefits in control and safety.

F-4Es that had already come off the production lines were modified with the LES while undergoing pro-

grammed depot maintenance (Technical Order 1F-4E-566), together with a wing-stiffening strap. Block 50 F-4Es on the St. Louis lines, starting with number 803, 72-0121, introduced built-in slats with a thicker, redesigned wing skin.* All models received new or reworked outboard mainwing sections, which necessitated removing the hydraulic wing-fold mechanism (the wings must be manually cranked up to the folded position). F-4C/Ds never received the upgrade, even though the Navy later applied the technology to some 215 ostensibly similar F-4J Phantoms under their F-4S 'S-for-slats' Project SLEP (Service Life Extension Program), conducted at Naval Air Rework Facilities North Island, California, and Cherry Point, North Carolina.

External vision
Another problem related to the rearward visibility from the Phantom's cockpit. As early as the Navy F-4B of 1960, the rear portion of the canopy glazing was re-faired in a raised style so as to give the second crewman better forward visibility, which was further enhanced on the dual-control F-4C by lowering the rear dashboard. It is acknowledged, however, that the rear view is not very good, and when one considers the well-established fact that over 80 per cent of air-to-air kills are achieved by an unseen enemy, normally from the rear quarters, it comes as no surprise that the F-4's 'six o'clock' was a vulnerable blind spot which was regularly exploited by hit-and-run MiG pilots. To get around this, the F-4 was fitted with small segment mirrors attached to the interior cockpit canopy bow frames, but it was later agreed that an external fitting would be much more effective. This was to be installed for the WSO's use only – he performs the bulk of 'checking six' while the pilot is busy keeping the jet clear of the surrounding terrain or is glued to an enemy out in front.

The first solution that emerged, in 1972, was a twin set of mirrors which overlapped the metal arch separating the two canopy hoods. Although this did provide a much better rear view, extending coverage to the rear ventral quarters, at speeds above 350kts the

Above: An F-4E on its way to the target with a cumbersome load of 'iron' and cluster bombs, ALQ-87 ECM pods and external fuel. F-4E-32-MC 66-0313 became a MiG-19 killer on 6 October 1972 in the hands of AC Clouser and WSO Brunson but was later destroyed. (MAP)

mirrors played on the airflow around the canopy, creating a terrible low-frequency rumble which fed through to the cockpit intercom, effectively 'jamming out' communications between the two crew members. The back seat of the F-4 provides a very rough ride at low level, so one can imagine the problems faced by the WSO in a hot climate, trying to do his job while the aircraft performs high-speed, heavy jinking, with the irritating noise and poor F-4 air conditioning. Not surprisingly, F-4 WSOs are often referred to as 'iron stomached'. Many units removed the mirrors (especially the training squadrons, where time-urgent commands between instructor and student must never be interfered with), but in the end the aerodynamic shielding was redesigned to great effect. A single mirror was attached to the top of the bow frame and the result was, as one navigator commented, 'amazing – I don't recall a problem with noise since'.

Furthermore, for air-to-air combat, another improvement was necessary. The reason for this lay behind the all-missile armament of the early F-4C/D models, and a number of related problems. Too many Sparrow radar-guided missiles were fired at enemy fighters at much too high a closing speed or below the missile's effective minimum range. This occurred because, during MiGCAP sorties flown over North Vietnam, F-4 air crews were prohibited from using their Sparrows in a counter-MiG role without having first positively identified a target as an enemy. 'Red Crown' radar picket ships and airborne EC-121 'Disco' assistance was often unable to provide detailed enough stand-off information on the identity of

---

*Block 48 aircraft were actually the first to introduce the LES, starting with F-4E No. 756, 71-0237, using 'out of station' kits which were applied after production but prior to delivery. These had the retrofit-style ventral steel strap as opposed to the new lower torque box skin.

ghters – particularly during the major multiple air-
raft strikes when the MiGs came out – often because
iendly aircraft were unable to provide a reliable IFF
dentification Friend or Foe) signal. The result was
at F-4s, with little fuel left, had to go and 'mix it' with
e more manoeuvrable MiGs, often with unfavour-
ble results. One technique used in an attempt to get
ound this problem was to get a brace of F-4s from a
iGCAP flight to dart ahead and report back to the
thers over the radio; the second pair would then
unch missiles. Break-off timing, the lack of surprise
d stray missiles still caused problems, however.

The solution came in the form of Northrop's Target
dentification System Electro-Optical (TISEO), a
ackage first tested in combat by the 366th TFW
Gunfighters', flying late-block, 'hard wing' F-4Es, and
ased at Da Nang AB, South Vietnam. Officially
nown as the AN/ASX-1, TISEO is essentially a long-
nge, high-resolution, closed-circuit TV system.
troduced on the Block 48 F-4E production line as a
andard feature in the summer of 1972, the TISEO
mprises four line replaceable units (LRUs), the main
ortion of which protrudes from the port wing's
ading edge, just above the inner wing pylon, like a
lephoto lens. Once selected, it can be slaved on to a
rget either automatically by the nose radar, or
anually by the WSO, providing a long-range stand-
ff TV image on the F-4E's radarscope CRTs. Two
elds of view (FOV) are provided, each for different
agnification levels, enabling the crew to pick up
rgets the size of a Tu-95 'Bear' at over 40nm and

aircraft as small as a MiG-23 'Flogger' at ranges of over
10nm, weather permitting – both well outside normal
'eyeball' limits. Once the target is identified, the crew
are then free to use stand-off medium-range tactics for
a kill, at which both the Sparrow missile and Phantom
excel.

Due to the timid nature of the MiGs in the late
stages of the Vietnam war, the 'Gunfighters' were
unable to put the system to actual combat use, though
Israeli Phantoms have reportedly used the package to
great effect in clashes with the Syrians in the clear
skies of the Middle East. According to several USAF
officers, the package is also used nowadays in the air-
to-ground mode. Those F-4Es actually flying with
TISEO – the AN/ARN-101 digital attackers, described
in the next chapter – use the device to pick up and
check on navigational waypoints. In this respect, it is
ironic that no air defence Phantoms actually carry the
TISEO, but only the dedicated strike models.

Precision munitions
Although the visual, computed 'dive–toss' delivery
technique available to the F-4D/E is quite accurate,
the accuracy was insufficient for some of the pin-point
attack requirements in South-East Asia (SEA). To
attack the Ho Chi Minh Trail – the thin umbilical
logistics lifeline supplying the guerrillas in South

Below: 'Wizzo' Joe Johnson near his 'office'. The noisy,
twin, external rear-view mirror fitting is evident. (Peter E.
Davies)

Above: An F-4E with the new TISEO protruding from its port wing leading edge. Early TISEO trials aircraft were all 'hard-wings'. The white pod is an SUU-20 practice rocket/bomb dispenser. (Northrop)

Below: 'Zot' (laser designator) F-4D-31-MC 66-7693 with the distinctive Pave Knife AVQ-10 pod installed. The pod contained a laser gun and an LLLTV sensor which were used for target-acquisition, tracking and 'sparkling' for LGBs. It was used in combat by the 433rd TFS, 8th TFW, during the famous bridge-busting missions of 1972. Twelve F-4Ds were so equipped. (Ford Aerospace)

ietnam – there was a requirement for absolute precision. Similarly, some of the more rewarding targets in the inner city zones of North Vietnam were left alone because of fears of large civilian casualties. Instead, throughout the 1968–72 stand-down the F-4 largely concentrated on a close air support (CAS) role, providing back-up for US ground troops and downed airmen; others provided flak-suppression for the giant 'Stingers', 'Shadows' and 'Specters' (converted cargo aircraft rigged as gunships) which sprayed the 3,500 known miles of the Trail with gun and howitzer fire.

But the potential of the Phantom as a precision bomber was not abandoned: in fact, a number of weapons delivery efforts were under way which would enable the F-4 to put bombs on targets with improved accuracy. Part of this new package comprised two new weapons, the first models of which arrived in SEA in 1967. Known as the laser-guided bomb (LGB), these were introduced as converted M-117 750pdrs, but the equipment soon became standardized as the Paveway, built and supplied by Texas Instruments, and designed to be plugged on to either Mk. 84 2,000lb or M-118 3,000lb 'iron' bombs (with smaller versions following soon afterwards). Quite simply, these LGBs homed on to targets illuminated ('sparkled') by a laser designator. Laser marking in turn came from a friendly gunship, which could use a forward looking infra-red (FLIR) device tied to the laser for night-time marking, or from an F-4 in daylight when visibility was reasonably good.

Two designators were utilized by F-4Ds during the war in SEA: the Martin Marietta AN/AVQ-9 Paveway, and the Ford Aerospace AN/AVQ-10 Pave Knife.

Paveway was a 75lb cockpit-mounted designator which was plugged on to the rear dashboard and optically slewed on target by the WSO using an eyepiece while the aircraft was in a pylon turn. A 'Buddy Phantom' then lobbed in LGBs which were guided to the target. Pave Knife was a longer-range laser gun packaged in a banana-shaped pod which provided the crew with the option of marking targets for its own bombs as well as those of its colleagues, in an autonomous laser bombing operation. Pave Knife employed a Dalmo Victor low-light-level TV (LLLTV) sensor, boresighted with the laser, in a head that could be swivelled on to the target by the WSO by use of a slew stick. With the LLLTV imagery in his new Sony TV cockpit display as a reference, the WSO would manoeuvre the sensor head about until the imagery was centred under the video crosshairs; the laser could then be fired for target marking. The Pave Knife-equipped 433rd TFS ('Satan's Angels') were the first successfully to demonstrate the self-contained laser bombing concept in 1972, a typical 'Knife mission load comprising a centreline and a starboard wing fuel tank, electronic countermeasures (ECM), the Pave Knife pod and two 2,000lb KMU-351 LGBs.

Another weapon, known as the electro-optically guided bomb (EOGB) was also fielded at this time, first as a spin-off from the Navy/Martin Marietta

Below: On 25 May 1972 8th TFW F-4Ds hit six of the eleven spans of the Lang Giai bridge, 65 miles outside Hanoi and the key link between North Vietnam and the People's Republic of China. Bombs used were Paveway I Mk.84s and M-118s. (USAF via Texas Instruments)

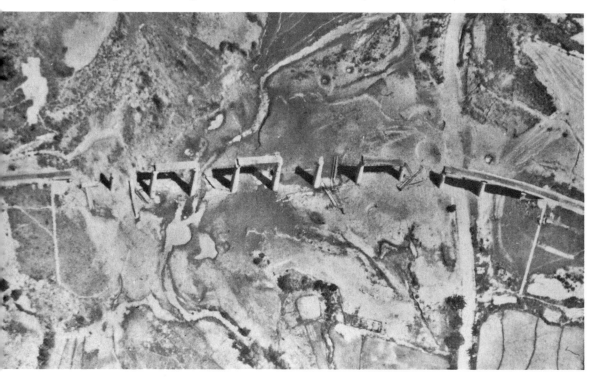

AGM-62 Walleye, and then in its near-definitive form as the Air Force homing bomb system (Hobos) GBU-8. Manufactured by Rockwell International, the Hobos, like the Paveway system, came as a kit to be attached to regular Mk. 84 or M-118 'iron' bombs, but its operation was fundamentally different from that of LGBs. Rather than using laser homing, the Hobos had its own TV seeker which fed pictures on to the F-radarscope CRTs. Using these as a reference, the pilot would line up on the target, the WSO would then position the seeker so that the crosshairs were centred on the desired impact point, and the bomb would then be released. It followed the preselected contrast point within its FOV until impact – the launch aircraft meanwhile, having departed from the area for its own safety.

Paveway and Hobos radically improved F-4 CEP. Targets were routinely struck with accuracies measured to within 15ft, as demonstrated time and time again in the late stages of the Vietnam War particularly against tanks during the spring 1972 invasion and against bridges during the famed 'Linebacker I' raids over North Vietnam later that summer. In fact, a total of 106 bridges were successfully put out of commission in 86 days – including the hitherto seemingly indestructible Paul Doumer and Thanh Hoa bridges, the curse of so many raids during the 'Rolling Thunder' campaign of the 1960s.

By August 1973, when the last war sortie had been

Top: A GBU-8 Hobos EOGB-I on a bomb dolly.
(Rockwell International)

Above: A GBU-8 Hobos installed on F-4D-31-MC 66-8698 at Eglin AFB, Florida. Note the clamps, to tighten and hold the Hobos guidance kit to the Mk.84 2,000lb bomb.
(Rockwell International)

Below: MiG-killer F-4D (a MiG-17 on 26 October 1967 when flown by AC Capt. John D. Logeman and his GIB McCoy) sits on the ramp in West Germany with its later Pave Phantom Loran 'towel bar' retrofit clearly visible. This jet was written off in an accident on 16 November 1976. It is one of the subjects featured in the Monogram F-4C/D model kits, and on Microscale decal sheet 48-72. (MAP)

own, over 30,000 of these 'smart' (as opposed to 'dumb' or unguided) bombs had been used, showing a consistent direct hit rate of over 50 per cent. Not only did the 'smart' weapons allow much smaller strike forces to perform a given mission (it took two Pave-Ways as opposed to 40 WRCS or 200 manually released bombs to guarantee a 'shack' or first-pass bull's-eye at realistic release heights), but the devices also helped placate a good number of anxious ordnance men, who had been moaning to the press about major bomb shortages'.

However, although these 'smart' weapons helped curtail both aircraft losses and ordnance shortfalls, they offered the desired accuracy only under day and clear-weather conditions; at night, pilots had to revert to regular bombing methods and use strong moonlight to put their gunsight pippers on target, or, during flak-suppression sorties, memorize the source of gun flashes on the ground and cue the gunsight reticle on to the spots whirling about in front of their eyes! Quasi-blind bombing using the existing offset or range-line techniques were demonstrating appalling miss distances of several hundred feet, totally inadequate for the missions at hand – 'We scared a lot of parrots, monkeys and snakes and levelled a lot of foliage!' – and only secondary explosions were a positive indication that something had in fact been hit.

To close the gap the USAF inaugurated Project 'Pave Phantom', a serious effort to give the F-4 a genuine blind-bombing capability. The heart of Pave Phantom, applied to some 70 F-4Ds drawn from pro-

Above: The mysterious experimental Pave Fire II laser system seen attached to F-4D-31-MC 66-7700 of the 13th TFS, 432nd TRW at Udorn AB, Thailand, in September 1971. The exact function of this 'one-off' pod remains uncertain, with published reports claiming it to be part of a project initiated in 1969 to use laser scanning as an aid to optical target lock-on – presumably a laser-ranging device to compute weapons release. (USAF)

duction Blocks 32 and 33, was the ITT Avionics AN/ARN-92 Loran C/D, a hybrid nav-attack system comprising the receiver and a new computer married to the existing Litton INS, and fielded on black-bellied Phantoms of the 25th TFS and 497th TFS 'Night Owls' based at Ubon, Thailand. Long-range navigation techniques had their origins back in the Second World War as the Loran A, and the new Loran C/D worked on similar principles, using a series of ground transmitters to assist in navigation to target and back.

Prior to a sortie, after having plotted the intended course, the WSO fed in up to eight desired route way-points, rendezvous or target co-ordinates into the onboard ARN-92 computer; these keyed-in 'destinations' could be used in conjunction with the autopilot for automatic flight to target. Once airborne, the WSO pressed the 'M' or start button, thereby telling the system to seek and then lock on to the ground transmitters. In South-East Asia the long-range Loran C chains employed a master and three slave transmitters: the master was located at Sattahip, Thailand, the X slave at Lampang, Thailand, the Y slave at Con Son off the south-east coast of South Vietnam, and the Z slave

at Tan My on the north-east coast. Loran D, which supplemented and eventually superseded Loran C as a bombing aid, used shorter-range (200-mile) mobile tactical master and slave transmitters. The ARN-92 picked up the signals of the master and any two slaves and, as the slaves were triggered off by the master at regular intervals, the ARN-92 was able to compare the time differences (TDs) between the incoming signals and automatically deduce the F-4D's TD co-ordinates; by cross-referring these to onboard maps and tables, they could also, if required, be converted into geographical latitude/longitude co-ordinates.

These Loran positional fixes helped keep the F-4D on course by updating the inertial computer, which in turn provided steering cues – 'precise, easy-to-follow left and right commands to the pilot', as ITT described it at the time – to take the Phantom along the pre-planned route with much greater accuracy than un-aided INS navigation. Bombing could then be conducted 'blind' over the target, using a comparison of continually monitored aircraft positions with the known Loran TD or geographical target co-ordinates. Bomb-release itself could be effected on the basis of those co-ordinates, or by using radar, by placing cross-hairs over the aimpoint and getting the ARN-92-updated inertial system to help the ballistics computer perform automatic weapons release. (In fact, in South-East Asia many ARN-92 F-4Ds were tasked to drop flares as well as bombs in the 'Night Owl', 'Fast FAC' pathfinding mission, to dispense leaflets as part of America's 'psy-war' or 'bull**** bombing' effort, and to seed traffic sensors along the Ho Chi Minh Trail under the 'Igloo White' programme.) Twenty RF-4Cs, from production Blocks 40 and 41 and assigned to the 14th TRS, 432nd TRW, were rigged with a similar package, enabling their crews to haul the jets out of Udorn, Thailand, and accurately perform their mission at night and in all weathers, with precision annotation of co-ordinates on the camera and sensor film.

In general, the ARN-92 worked well, but it was never fitted on to F-4s on a larger scale because of a few 'bugs' which persisted from the outset of its operational combat début. Originally, the aircraft carried the receiving aerials in an aerodynamic design faired into

Above: An 8th TFW 'Wolfpack' F-4D, toting a pair of GBU-10 Paveway I LGBs, two Sparrow radar-guided missiles, two fuel tanks and a pair of ALQ-87 jamming pods, about to do some bridge-busting 'up North' in 1972. (USAF via Texas Instruments)

the dorsal spine and fincap. Unfortunately reception difficulties, caused by the recurring electrical anomalies associated with the F-4, prevented the jets from picking up the signals under a number of conditions. To overcome this problem Pave Phantoms were fitted with a distinctive 'towel bar' antenna on the spine, but even then, after the 'M' button was pressed it would frequently take up to a quarter of an hour before the ARN-92 became firmly locked on to the ground transmitters. Evasive jinking manoeuvres often caused the system to break lock altogether. A 'no Loran' light would shine up on the control panel, and the WSO would have to direct the ARN-92 to start searching all over again. Breaking lock would also occur during aerial refuelling with KC-135s, because of static electricity 'burst noise' discharges between the aircraft momentarily jamming the receivers.* Consequently the USAF sought a newer, more reliable system before undertaking the expense of refitting the F-4 fleet, but in the end this took some seven years to develop and it came too late for work in Vietnam.

Since 1972, as second- and third-generation smart and ARN nav-strike technology has become available, overcoming all the troubles of those early pioneering developments, the Phantom has been through many significant upgrades. Developed as part of the Pave Strike programme, the bulk of these enhancements became operational between 1972 and 1975, but a number of additional weapons and avionics improvements have also been introduced since the spring of 1978, extending the precision strike-reconnaissance capabilities of the Phantom into night and all weathers. In the mid-1980s, alongside the more self-contained F-111 'Aardvarks', these aircraft provide the USAF's entire 24-hour tactical strike force.

*A myriad of newly developed static dispensers retrofitted to the tail and wings helped cure this problem in the mid-1970s.

2. INTO THE EIGHTIES

'We Handle It'

The overall effect of the Pave Strike programme has been to create a number of separate and quite distinct configurations from the generic F-4E. Although, with one or two exceptions, there exists a high degree of interoperability with these new devices on all strike Phantoms, for the purpose of analysis the various weapons-sensor upgrades can be said to have divided the 1960s-vintage F-4E into three main mission streams: the largely unchanged aircraft, built between 1967 and 1970 and used in training or for the Pave Spike and Maverick daylight precision attack mode; the ARN-101/Pave Tack-equipped night and bad weather bombers, coming from F-4E stocks built between 1971 and 1976; and an extensively rebuilt derivative, the F-4G 'Wild Weasel', modified from FY69 production aircraft and detailed later in the book.*

Training

The early-build 'vanilla E', equipped with the strike package discussed earlier, is the starting point for all newcomers on to the type. Training with this basic 'plain Elaine' comes within the jurisdiction of the 35th Tactical Training Wing (TTW), 831st AD, at George AFB in California. Located in the Mojave Desert some 50 miles outside Los Angeles, George has come to be popularly referred to as the 'high desert, big business base', spending well over half a million dollars on each air crewman going through its Phantom courses. West German air crews also undergo basic and advanced instructor training with the 35th TTW – the WGAF currently owns eight of the 35th's 54 F-4Es, specifically bought for this purpose. Squadrons assigned to the training role are the 20th Tactical Fighter Training Squadron (TFTS), concentrating more on the West German contingent, and the dual-committed 21st TFTS 'Cheetahs', which trains USAF pilots and WSOs while maintaining a secondary operational capability.

New arrivals at the base from the Lead-In Fighter Training (LIFT) course at Holloman AFB, New Mexico, usually spend 30 weeks sharpening their new skills on the F-4E.† George is Advantageously placed for grasping 'Phantom basics', with modestly short flying times to nearby ranges in California and Nevada, and 360 blue-skied flying days a year. The course is fairly extensive, reflecting both the multi-role capability of the F-4E and its higher-than-average demands on pilot skill, particularly for pure air combat. Ground training consumes over 150hrs (and much homework), including up to 65hrs' simulator time. This academic background course is managed by the 35th

Tactical Training Squadron, which teaches both American and West German crews the theory behind flying the F-4 before the trainees are let loose on the expensive Phantoms parked in chevrons out on the flightlines. Typically, a pilot will clock up 58 sorties and a WSO around 41 sorties before receiving their operational assignments. Weapons training on the F-4E – for the USAF air crews alone – involves getting to grips with the aircraft's AJB-7 nuclear weapons capability (though the lofted delivery of Douglas-devised 'training shapes' is performed at an operational level). Other sorties include aerial refuelling practice, two on air intercept and another eight on air combat tactics. Live weapons training is carried out over the Cuddeback weapons range, located just to the north of the nearby Edwards Air Force Flight Test Center (AFFTC) and manned by some twenty personnel who travel out there from George by bus and monitor strike runs with target practice ammunition. More advanced CAS tactics can be perfected at the Army's Fort Irwin training centre, 75 miles distant.

For USAF air crew with prior experience in the F-4, there are shorter refresher and model transition courses. For example, whereas a newcomer will fly anything up to 60 sorties to qualify, an ex-F-4D pilot might only have to notch up a mere two sorties; ex-RF-4C pilots, even 'high time' air crew, usually spend at least 23 sorties converting to the F-4E and the strike mission.

Some six months after having first set foot into George, the newly qualified crews are posted to one of the many active F-4E squadrons scattered across the world for 'fine tuning'. Air crews serving their first fighter tour are allocated a higher proportion of the unit's authorized flying time under a programme originally designated 'Gold Flag'. They use this to work on their new specialization, aiming towards the goal of attaining flight lead status – that is, the ability to plan, lead and hold together a strike mission made up from four or more Phantoms. This normally takes a full tour of around 24 months. The more experienced flyers will help the juniors hone their mission skills,

---

*At the time of writing, the USAF operated a total of 109 F-4Es with no special capability, 192 compatible with Pave Spike and Maverick, 156 ARN-101 models, and 102 F-4Gs. Eighteen FY69 Pave Spike F-4Es are presently being 'demodified' and converted to F-4G status under Class V Mod 3177 (TCTO 1F-4E-670).

†These are invariably college graduates, in their early to mid-twenties, who have undergone basic and advanced flying training on Cessna T-37s, Northrop T-38s, Boeing T-43s and specially modified AT-38Bs. Refer to the Appendices.

while selected envoys, drawn from the weapons and tactics instructor cadre at the squadron, will undergo periodic assignment to the McConnell Kansas Air Guard's Fighter Weapons Instructor Course (FWIC) – held at Nellis AFB, Nevada, until 1985 – or Weapons Systems Evaluation Program in Florida, to keep the entire unit up to date with new developments in systems and tactics.

Precision daylight strike

Contrary to the popular opinion that the F-4 is a 'fighter', the mission assignments George graduates are likely to encounter are precision daylight attack along the forward edge of the battle area (FEBA) and inter-diction. The former mainly involves anti-tank and anti-truck work, while the aim of the latter is to destroy hardened targets behind the FEBA, such as command bunkers, supply depots and enemy airfields; this may include a standby nuclear strike role. The chief exponents of this work are the 347th TFW based at Moody AFB, Georgia, with 84 F-4Es.

Aside from their normal bombing capabilities, one of the chief weapons they carry is the Hughes AGM-65A TV-guided Maverick missile, first intro-duced in 1972. Up to six can be carried at a time, in two triple clusters on the F-4E's inner wing pylons; this creates relatively high drag, but the package is extremely potent. Its use is also fairly straightforward. In practice, after Maverick has been selected, the pilot will pop the Phantom up to between 500 and 1,000ft and peer our of the windshield to acquire a target. He will then put the jet on course, and relay a verbal description of the target over the intercom to the WSO. With the missile activated, its TV seeker will be transferring video imagery of the outside world, within its 5-degree FOV, on to the cockpit radarscopes. At this stage in the proceedings, the WSO will use his right console tracking handle to slew the seeker about until the target image is centred precisely in the middle of his radarscope crosshairs. Releasing the tracking switch, the missile becomes firmly locked and, after a quick confirmation of the target between the crew, may be fired with a press of the trigger button. Maverick will shoot off its support rail, and will then follow the selected image autonomously, in a 'fire and forget' mode, until its 125lb warhead hits the target.

Meanwhile, the crew set up another launch or else fly off.

Improvements to the 'A' model Maverick came when the Scene Magnification AGM-65B version was introduced in 1975. This retains the same method of attack as the original type, except that the WSO uses greater image magnification via a sharper, 2.5-degree FOV, which enables targets to be acquired, positively identified and locked on to at much greater ranges. At these distances – as much as ten miles in exceptionally clear skies – the workload shifts more to the WSO, who will have to perform a good deal of seeker slewing to compensate for misalignment between aircraft and target. This is now assisted by what Hughes call 'quick draw' capability: by slaving a second Maverick to the first, and a third to the second, two or more can be fired rapidly at a particularly difficult target or the others can be quickly adjusted to lock on to other nearby objects. In this mode, for example, all three can be directed into a concrete bunker, or a triple cluster can be despatched in rapid sequence, to pulverize a series of trucks in a convoy.

The other main device used by the daylight strike units is the Westinghouse Pave Spike, an updated version of a late-Vietnam-era prototype system which superseded Pave Knife and added a new combined laser transmitter/receiver, computer and 'fast track' facility; it was put into series production in 1974 for some 300 selected F-4Ds and Es. Phantoms adapted to carry the pod also received a digital scan radar modification enabling video or radar to be displayed on the one scope.

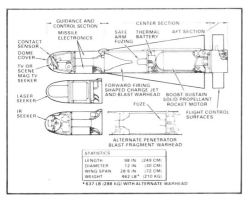

GUIDANCE AND
CONTROL SECTION
MISSILE
ELECTRONICS

CONTACT
SENSOR
DOME
COVER
TV OR
SCENE
MAG TV
SEEKER

LASER
SEEKER

IR
SEEKER

CENTER SECTION

SAFE   THERMAL
ARM   BATTERY
FUZING

AFT SECTION

FORWARD FIRING
SHAPED CHARGE JET
AND BLAST WARHEAD

FUZE

BOOST SUSTAIN
SOLID PROPELLANT
ROCKET MOTOR

FLIGHT CONTROL
SURFACES

ALTERNATE PENETRATOR
BLAST FRAGMENT WARHEAD

STATISTICS		
LENGTH	98 IN	(249 CM)
DIAMETER	12 IN	(30 CM)
WING SPAN	28 5 IN	(72 CM)
WEIGHT	462 LB*	(210 KG)

* 637 LB (288 KG) WITH ALTERNATE WARHEAD

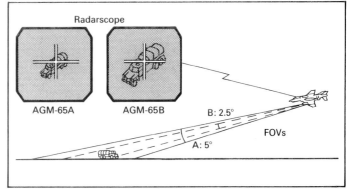

Radarscope

AGM-65A

AGM-65B

B: 2.5°

FOVs

A: 5°

Above: A Moody-based F-4E demonstrates its remarkably clean ventral paintwork. The Phantom carries six Mk.82 500lb 'slicks' on a centreline MER, two live Sidewinder AIM-9Js on the starboard wing, a GBU-10 Paveway II LGB on its left wing station and Pave Spike under the forward port Sparrow missile well. Moody's biggest deployment to date was to Cairo West, Egypt, from 15 June to 23 October 1980, during Operation 'Proud Phantom'. Twelve F-4Es and 520 base members deployed to familiarize crews with operations in the Middle East and to assist the Egyptian Air Force in improving the operational readiness of its F-4E fleet. (USAF)

Like Pave Knife, the ASQ-153* uses a TV sensor in a gimballed head which transfers video imagery of the outside world on to the WSO's radarscope CRT. Taking his tracking handle, the WSO can swivel the entire sensor head about for target acquisition and tracking, in front, to the sides and behind the Phantom – in fact just about anywhere under the aircraft and a few degrees above the wings. The 'fast track' feature enables the head to move from one extreme of its viewing limits to the other in about a second, while the WSO can select one of two FOVs, a wide one providing 3× magnification for a general look outside, or a narrow FOV providing 12× magnification to help track individual targets more clearly. Once a target has been located, the WSO will maintain the sensor manually on target throughout a bombing manoeuvre, keeping it firmly in the video crosshairs. Derotation will ensure that the TV image is not upside down if the pod is looking aft, and there is an indicator on the top right-hand side of the pilot's front console so that he does not climb, bank or dive beyond the viewing parameters of the pod.

The reason for all this TV tracking is to cue a neodymium YAG laser transmitter boresighted with the TV sensor on to a visually acquired target. This may be used to mark a target for LGBs, as before, but another possibility exists: by firing the laser and using the receiver to pick up reflected laser pulses from a marked target, the pod can calculate slant-range from the enemy, which can then be used by the onboard WRCS to produce ballistics computations for automatic lofted or 'spike toss' iron bomb deliveries – or for a level, automatic 'release on range' bomb drop – with much greater accuracy than that possible with regular radar-ranging.† This precision capability can be used to create choke points in enemy lines of communication (LOCs), such as bridges and tunnels, and the subsequent chaos can then be exploited by other strike aircraft.

LGBs used in conjunction with Pave Spike, just like the Paveway I series, are supplied by Texas Instruments as kits designed to be plugged on to the existing range of 'iron' bombs. Specific modules – a tail section and a nose seeker called 'groups' – are available for each of the major 'iron' bomb types, and since 1973, when TI started production of the Paveway II follow-on series, the kits have come with a refined tail group employing large 'pop-out' fins for greater glide range and increased bomb manoeuvrability. One of the chief advantages of LGBs is that the launch aircraft need not carry out the laser marking. Instead, another lighter, less vulnerable Phantom can perform this while a heavily laden 'buddy' lobs its bombs from behind the cover of masking terrain. Because in a large

---

*Otherwise known as the AN/AVQ-23 designator.
†In the ROR mode the pilot sets the required slant-range release for the chosen delivery height and air speed into the 'range indicator' on his top left front console. Bomb release then takes place on cue automatically when pod laser slant-range to target corresponds to the setting.

multiple aircraft strike many LGBs may be launched at any one time, earmarked for different targets, the F-4Es WSOs enter a laser code into a small panel on the right console. This will ensure that each bomb is guided by a specific designator, and, above all, makes enemy jamming or diversionary tactics (such as marking a spot of ground to lead the bomb astray) more difficult. Laser marking is always done near the end of Paveway's ballistic trajectory, no more than eight or so seconds before impact. Premature designation for LGBs lofted at long range would cause the seekers which cue the aerofoil wings to look down too soon, causing the bomb to lose momentum and fall short of the target.

Training with both Maverick and Pave Spike is a

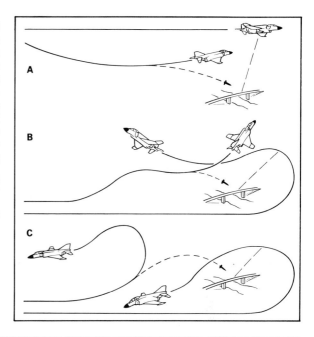

Right: Laser-bombing techniques. A. Bombing from a steep dive while designating from high altitude. B. Low-altitude ingress, pop-up and shallow dive-bomb while designator pops up to lase target. C. Loft bombing from low altitude as designator pops up for lasing.

Below: Prinicpal features of the Paveway II Mk. II laser-guided bomb. (Texas Instruments)

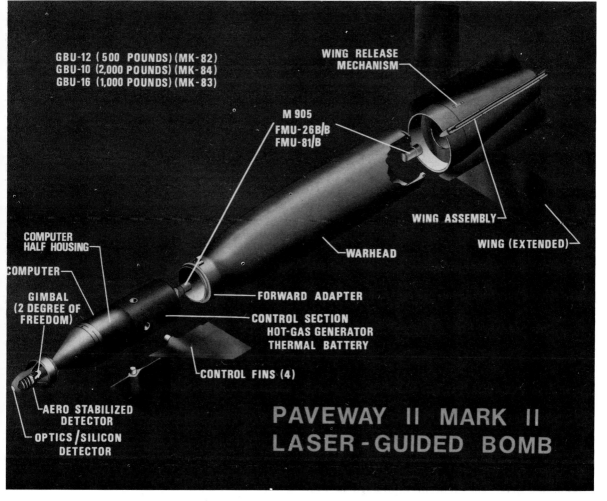

GBU-12 (500 POUNDS) (MK-82)
GBU-10 (2,000 POUNDS) (MK-84)
GBU-16 (1,000 POUNDS) (MK-83)

WING RELEASE MECHANISM

M 905
FMU-26B/B
FMU-81/B

WING ASSEMBLY

WING (EXTENDED)

WARHEAD

COMPUTER HALF HOUSING

COMPUTER

GIMBAL (2 DEGREE OF FREEDOM)

FORWARD ADAPTER

CONTROL SECTION
HOT-GAS GENERATOR
THERMAL BATTERY

CONTROL FINS (4)

AERO STABILIZED DETECTOR

OPTICS/SILICON DETECTOR

PAVEWAY II MARK II
LASER-GUIDED BOMB

continuing business for all crews assigned to the task and is usually interspersed between fairly lengthy periods using the more basic F-4D/E auto and F-4C manual bombing techniques (the latter being practised as often as possible so that crews are familiar with the techniques required to press home an attack in a 'systems out' situation). The 'fire and forget' Maverick is comparatively easy to master, taking between five and fifteen seconds to set up for launch at long range. The manual tracking required with Pave Spike, however, takes much longer to learn, the co-ordination between pilot and WSO occupying most of the time. According to Capt. Michael R. Turner, former Flying Training Officer with the 68th TFS ('Lightning Lancers'), immediately upon F-4E check-out at Moody AFB the crews begin training with both Maverick and Pave Spike. Each programme takes from two to three weeks to complete and normally consists of around ten hours of academics on each system before the first sortie, with the flying portion taking up between thirteen and fifteen flights. Upon completion of their initial check-out on the systems, each crew is required to maintain its skills via a refresher course held every six months. This is called 'continuation training', and involves at least three hours of academic revision on each device, plus twelve Pave Spike and fifteen Maverick deliveries per period. The Pave Spike flying portion employs BDU-33 25lb 'dumb' bomb rounds as well as laser bombs since they possess the same ballistic characteristics, while it is safely assumed

that laser homing would produce better accuracies if such homing were used – the remarkable precision of Paveway LGBs is legendary. Sensor tacking and laser-computed methods of 'iron' bomb attack in level, lofted and toss modes are equally important parts of the syllabus. Routine Maverick training employs inert, tailless TGM-65 rounds which can be used to practise seeker lock-ons. According to Capt. Turner, it is expected that at least 75 per cent of the Pave Spike deliveries and 40 per cent of the Maverick 'shoots' are 'hits'. Hughes claim that in over 2,900 live Maverick launches to date, more than 85 per cent have in fact achieved direct hits: the Israelis, who have used Maverick in combat, claim that some 87 per cent struck their intended targets, some of these results having been achieved during the heat of attacks on SAM sites!

Digital attackers
Another derivative of the Vietnam-era F-4E which has emerged over the last decade has been created by integrating the Lear Siegler AN/ARN-101(V) digital nav-attack system. First defined in 1971, specifying 'blind' weapons/sensors capabilities for the F-4 at least to the standard of Pave Phantom and the ARN-92, the

Below: AIM-9P Sidewinder-equipped, ARN-101-modified F-4Es in formation over the 'home-drome'. Leading is the 'Fourth but First' CO, accompanied by the Wing's squadron ships. (USAF)

requirements were formalized in April 1972 under Tactical Air Command's ROC 12-72. A three-year head-to-head fly-off ensued at the Eglin Armament Development Test Center (ADTC), in Florida, with Lear Siegler and ITT Avionics flying their competing systems on F-4D test-beds. Lear Siegler emerged as victor, and 333 kits have been supplied to the USAF since 1978 for installation in F-4E/G and RF-4C Phantoms. With the addition of just these few wires, black boxes and cockpit controls (including a new multifunction tracking handle), the Phantom's precision attack and reconnaissance capabilities have been extended into night and all weathers. This has been achieved by incorporating a brand new, hybrid, digital nav-attack and Loran system, aided further by the ability to carry a large external strap-on sensor pod supplied by Ford Aerospace, the AN/AVQ-26 Pave Tack. The major operators of the dual package are the 4th TFW, based at Seymour-Johnson AFB, North Carolina, and equipped with 78 Phantoms.

Strike F-4Es retrofitted with the ARN-101 – some 170 machines in all – were drawn from later production runs, coming from the survivors of Blocks 50–62 delivered between 1972 and 1976. These are newer, more trustworthy airframes that, theoretically, will be structurally sound through to the end of the century and beyond. Additionally, one privileged foreign air force, Israel's *Heyl Ha'Avir*, has bought and is fielding the ARN-101 on 140 of its F-4Es. As Capt. John L. Barry, Aide to the Commander of TAC's 12th Air Force, put it, 'The sizeable investments in these improvements will dictate keeping the F-4E around for awhile, well into the '90s'.

Major tasks assigned to the USAF ARN-101 squadrons are similar to those performed by the daylight Pave Spike/Maverick F-4E teams, except that there is a much greater emphasis on night operations and, more particularly, on interdiction behind the FEBA, against second-echelon armoured forces, fuel and supply depots, airfields, anti-air defences, other support bases and LOCs. A look into the ARN-101 equipment itself is informative.

Part of the AN/ARN-101 includes a Loran module, a navaid described earlier. Loran antennae are located on the dorsal spine and in the fin-cap, in a streamlined, faired-in design. The Loran provides co-ordinates for navigation updates in three styles – latitude/longitude, Universal Transverse Mercator (UTM) and Loran Time Difference. A Kalman filter also ensures that spoof signals, designed to jam the Loran, are cut out of circuit and not sent on to erroneously update the inertial platform (providing a momentary cut-out which does not cause it to break lock from the Loran transmitters – ARN-92 Phantoms revert to the INS and dead reckoning when their system reports a 'jam'). The ARN-101 Phantoms can, moreover, be flown aggressively without causing the system to break lock.

Prior to take-off, for navigation purposes the WSO will plan the course, taking the aircraft through a series of waypoints and targets – anything up to sixty in all, though a typical flight will embrace only a handful. He

ACTIVE 'VANILLA' F-4E OPERATORS

Squadron	Wing	Base	Type	Tail-code
20th TFTS 21st TFTS	35th TTW	George AFB, California 12th AF, TAC	F-4E	GA
36th TFS 497th TFS*	51st TFW	Osan AB, South Korea 7th AF, PACAF	F-4E	OS
68th TFS 69th TFS 70th TFS	347th TFW	Moody AFB, Georgia 9th AF, TAC	F-4E	MY

ACTIVE ARN-101 DMAS-MOD F-4E OPERATORS

Squadron	Wing	Base	Type	Tail-code
3rd TFS 90th TFS	3rd TFW	Clark Field, Philippines 13th AF, PACAF	F-4E/G	PN
334th TFS 335th TFS 336th TFS	4th TFW	Seymour-Johnson AFB, North Carolina 9th AF, TAC	F-4E†	SJ
561st TFS 562nd TFTS 563rd TFS	37th TFW	George AFB, California 12th AF, TAC	F-4E/G	WW
23rd TFS 81st TFS 480th TFS	52nd TFW	Spangdahlem AB, West Germany 17th AF, USAFE	F-4E/G‡	SP

*The 497th TFS operates from Taegu AB, South Korea, with the code 'GU'. †To F-15E 1989. ‡To F-16C/D and F-4G.

feeds all these co-ordinates into the operations room computer, which in turn pops out a pre-programmed data transfer module (DTM), which is about the same size as a video game cartridge. This can then be plugged into the rear cockpit to tell the ARN-101 exactly where the crew intend to fly. The pre-planned course may involve some deviations to avoid known 'hot spots' of enemy anti-air activity and to take advantage of radar-masking terrain. Prior to 1979, as on the ARN-92, this required a lengthy button-pushing process to feed in all the data piece by piece, but the DTM only requires the WSO to press one button, and may be removed after the mission to show a complete flight course for rapid post-mission debrief.

During the course of the flight, the Loran and inertial systems work together automatically to keep track of the aircraft's position and keep the crew on the intended flight path. Errors in the ARN-101 may in turn be updated by the crew, using optical TV sensors such as the wing-mounted TISEO during daytime, or the Pave Tack pod FLIR imagery at night. By placing the sensor video crosshairs over a prominent terrain feature along the route, and inserting its co-ordinates into the navigation panel, the ARN-101 can be manually updated; this is done by correlating the co-ordinates, the angular geometry of the sensor, and other available data such as laser range information. Typical features used for these updates might include a bridge or a bend in a river. Radar and 'overflight' can also be used to update the navigation systems. However, all these methods are said to be fairly time-consuming for the WSO, and are only used if the F-4E has deviated from the flight plan because of fighter opposition forcing the crew way off course, or some other unforeseen circumstance.

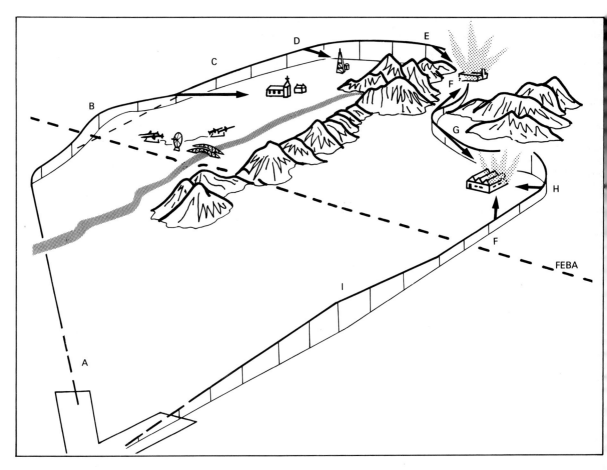

Throughout the sortie, as the WSO continually monitors the aircraft's position, the pilot uses the ARN-101 navigation data to fly to the target area. The ARN-101 ties in with the Automatic Flight Control System (AFCS, or autopilot) to fly the aircraft in a 'hands off' mode. Using this, the ARN-101 will provide lateral steering commands to the AFCS, while the pilot monitors the instruments and stays ready to haul the aircraft manually up and down over obstacles. If he chooses to fly the aircraft himself, he can use Loran-updated roll and steering commands displayed on his gunsight, presented by the reticle which points to the 'current steer destination'. A new leg along the route will suddenly cause the reticle to start swinging to the left or right, depending on the next turn to be made.

The remainder of the ARN-101 Digital Modular Avionics System (DMAS) consists of the all-essential strike avionics, replacing the old F-4D/E ASQ-91 WRCS and several other black boxes and providing a vast upgrade in the aircraft's ability to deliver weapons automatically. As mentioned briefly in the previous chapter, apart from the more flexible 'dive–toss' method of ground attack, the other strike approaches used by basic F-4D/Es are 'canned', requiring the pilot to fly the aircraft within very carefully defined parameters of air speed, dive angle and altitude. Any deviation will cause inaccuracies, and this is almost

certain to happen because of the necessity for at least some degree of evasive action during an attack run. The ARN-101 makes the F-4 a true 'uncanned' strike jet, giving the pilot much greater freedom during bomb runs and allowing the crew to develop tactics which increase their chances of survival with no compromise to bombing accuracy: the ARN-101 will automatically compensate for height, dive angle and air speed deviations in every single attack mode. The pilot simply keeps his aircraft pointed in the right direction while the ARN-101 computes the optimum bomb release time, a calculation which even encompasses the type of bomb being used and the time it takes for the weapons ejection racks to respond! The net increase in accuracy offered to a good crew conducting visual bomb deliveries at just over 1,000ft above target is said to be in the order of a factor of five, reducing the old F-4D/E CEP of about 150ft to as little as 30ft. This is comparable to the capabilities of the modern-generation F-16 and F-18 attack fighters. To further mitigate CEP, the ARN-101 F-4Es from the 4th TFW have been utilizing larger 750lb bombs instead of the more routine 500pdrs, the larger bomb-blast radius compensating for any inaccuracies.

All the regular F-4D/E bombing, missile and rocket/gun modes of attack are retained on the ARN-101 F-4E, but because of the new flexibility they fall under ewer headings – Continuously Computed Impact Point (CCIP), whereby 'the bombs fall where the pilot designates his pipper'; trusty old 'dive–toss'; blind; air-to-ground missile; rocket/gun; and AJB-7 nuclear. The most important of these, arguably, is the all-weather blind bombing capability which uses target co-ordinates stored in the ARN-101 memory. When

Left: ARN-101/Pave Tack interdiction mission – night/bad weather. A. F-4E departs on its mission. B. Concentrated enemy anti-air defences just behind the FEBA force the F-4E crew to deviate from their intended flight path. C. The WSO uses Pave Tack to provide a positional update by checking their position relative to a known landmark. D. The intended course is resumed, and a target of opportunity crops up: the WSO uses Pave Tack or the radar to feed its co-ordinates into the ARN-101 memory. The target may be attacked at a later date, on another mission. E. Using the local terrain to hide their attack, the crew perform a blind-bombing manoeuvre on their pre-planned target, and a bomb release is effected automatically by the ARN-101 on the basis of radar or Loran data. F. Pave Tack FLIR imagery is recorded on tape for post-mission damage assessment. G. The Pave Tack laser/receiver provides slant-range data to the ARN-101 to compute weapons release time over target no. 2. H. Pave Tack illuminates the target with laser energy to assist any LGBs employed. I. With the aircraft back over friendly territory, the ARN-101 provides navigation and landing glidescope data to the pilot for a neat return to base. The ARN-101 cartridge is removed for post-mission analysis.

Below: A pilot performs the pre-sortie 'walk-around', checking that the 'flying portions' of the Phantom are looking healthy. The clip-board appears attached to a painful location! (USAF)

'blind' is selected on the weapons delivery selection dial, the gunsight reticle serves to provide roll, dive and steering commands to the pilot so that he can perform the attack manoeuvre without an external visual reference. A pull-up cue will tell him when to haul the aircraft up out of the dive, during which time the bombs will be released automatically by the ARN-101. The optimum attack profile is very similar to a 'dive–toss' manoeuvre, calling for a dive and 4g pull-up designed to lob the bombs forward on to the target. Automatic weapons release is computed by the ARN-101 on the basis of either Loran co-ordinates or radar information, as on the ARN-92.

The Ford Aerospace AN/AVQ-26 Pave Tack pod, developed from 1974 and first delivered in August 1979, is a complementary strike aid for use by USAF ARN-101 F-4Es. The first Phantom unit to achieve Initial Operational Capability (IOC) with Pave Tack was the 4th TFW in April 1983. For non-ARN-101 Phantoms, Ford Aerospace has developed a special digital-to-analogue interface, and this is being fielded on South Korean F-4Es, which have eight of the pods on standby.

Pave Tack replaces the centreline ventral fuel tank and performs much like Pave Spike, except that, in place of the TV sensor, it uses a USAF common modular FLIR, enabling the WSO to identify and track targets not only during daytime but in the dark and through haze as well, at ranges of anything up to 12nm. As with Pave Spike, a video image is flashed up on the WSO's radarscope when the pod is activated, and may be set to one of two FOVs – a wide, 10° setting for target searching, or a narrow, 2.5° FOV for

individual target tracking and laser marking. Again, the WSO uses his sidestick control to steer the sensor head about, and a laser transmitter and receiver bore-sighted with the FLIR can be used for more accurate weapons release, by supplying slant-range data to the ARN-101. If LGBs are employed, the laser can be used to mark targets for homing purposes.

Aside from allowing the crew to see outside the aircraft at night and through limited bad weather, the Pave Tack FLIR sensor has a number of other useful functions. The hot and cold 'see through' qualities of FLIR enable the WSO to discriminate between a dummy target and a real one, or, for example, the quantity of fuel in an oil storage hold, thereby avoiding the problem of wasting bombs or missiles on worthless targets. Targets of opportunity, such as a cluster of tanks hidden under the leafy canopy of a wood, would also be visible to a well-trained WSO. Even if the target is not attacked, its position can be fed into the ARN-101 memory for later reference. FLIR imagery can also be used to provide visual warning of low-level obstacles. The F-4E, unlike the other AVQ-26 Pave Tack users (the RF-4C and the F-111) does not have

a terrain-following radar for automatic or manual vertical steering, and so the FLIR can be used to great effect to provide visual warning of hills and high ridges, not to mention towers and chimneys. A feature soon to be incorporated into Pave Tack will provide another important advantage over Pave Spike: with this new facility, the sensors can be stabilized in place

Below: Zip! The flagship of the 4th TFW shakes off a clip of 20mm Gatling gun ammunition. Despite the new 'smart' weapons, the old gun remains a favourite with the pilots. (USAF, 4th TFW)

Bottom: F-4E-48-MC 71-0237, from the 3rd TFS 'Peugeots', 3rd TFW, runs up its turbojets on take-off at Clark Field in the Philippines. The aircraft is configured with full external fuel and a baggage pod. The 3rd TFW has earned three US Presidential Unit Citations, three USAF Outstanding Unit Awards with combat 'V' devices, four USAF Outstanding Unit Awards, the Philippine Presidential Unit Citation, the Republic of Korea Presidential Unit Citation, and three Republic of Vietnam Gallantry Crosses with Palm. It also possesses ten Korean Conflict Campaign Streamers and eleven Vietnam Campaign Streamers! (USAF)

instead of the WSO having to maintain them on target manually throughout a laser-aided manoeuvre.

Using co-ordinates stored in its memory – those fed in either before or during the course of the mission – the ARN-101 is able to cue Pave Tack on to the target automatically. This saves a great deal of time in target acquisition, and has two great advantages. First, 'pop-up' to acquire the target can be performed at the last minute to minimize exposure; second, the WSO can immediately use the narrow FOV for longer-range target identification – he merely refines the sensor alignment after Pave Tack has been slewed on to the right area. Similarly, imaging infra-red (I^2R) weapons like the new Maverick AGM-65D can be locked on to targets at maximum stand-off ranges.* This D-model night and bad-weather Maverick can be slaved to both Pave Tack and the ARN-101 for rapid target lock-on.

The ARN-101/Pave Tack also works this way with TI's new Paveway III 2,000lb low-level laser-guided bombs (LLLGBs). These Paveways have greater glide range and more manoeuvrability than the old I and II series; furthermore, they need not be pointing toward the target when released – they can use midcourse autopilot to get to the target area. By comparing the aircraft's position with the stored target co-ordinates, the ARN-101 can compute and perform bomb release before the F-4E picks up height to mark the target with laser energy from Pave Tack, so that, again, exposure to enemy defences is minimized. The ARN-101 interacts totally with the onboard radar, radar cursors, TISEO, gunsight LCOSS, Pave Tack and weapons seekers, so just about anything is possible!

If these tricks were not enough, the ARN-101 has even been slaved to outside control. In a joint test with a Pave Mover F-111 (an airborne platform designed to detect enemy ground traffic), the Pave Mover fed pulsed, coded messages through an F-4E's Loran antenna and flew the jet, via the autopilot, on to the

*The AGM-65C was a laser-homing model which did not go into production, although the USMC has since fielded a derivative model, the AGM-65E, which employs a bigger, 300lb warhead.

Below: 'Pair-O-Dice' 90th TFS Phantoms prepare to top-up with fuel. An F-4E is nearest, and an F-4G Wild Weasel variant lurks below. (USAF)

target for automatic weapons release – a remarkable development. Newly reconfigured 707 airliner stock, to be redesignated E-8A, is scheduled to carry similar equipment operationally, as part of America's Joint Surveillance and Target Attack Radar System. J-STARS provides 'real-time', computer-enhanced graphics showing the size, disposition and movement of enemy ground forces, and relays target data to suitably equipped strike aircraft like the ARN-101 F-4E for the purpose of stand-off attack. The package is due to enter full operational trials in 1989.

New equipment for the ARN-101 F-4E comes in the form of Rockwell International's 2,000lb GBU-15 cruciform and short-chord winged, TV-guided glide bombs. First delivered to active units in 1982, the weapon is now operational, although it has been used by Israeli F-4Es since 1977. The GBU-15 (EOGB-II) works on very similar principles to the Hobos EOGB-I, using radarscope video imagery for target lock-on, except that this bomb can be released at supersonic speeds for greater glide range. Furthermore, the crew can perform seeker lock-on either before release, where there is line-of-sight (LOS) to the target, or later, in the mid or terminal phases of bomb flight, using a data link pod to pass on commands and relay video images back for seeker lock-on adjustment. The data link communication between bomb and aircraft is provided by the AN/AXQ-14, a small centre-line store built by Hughes Radars. Not only does the data link allow lock-on to be conducted after launch,

but it can also enable the WSO to fly the bomb manually all the way to target.

Survivability is greatly enhanced when two or more aircraft co-operate with each other, one performing bomb release, and one or both using a data link. In this way the 'bomber' may launch the weapons behind the cover of masking terrain, while the other F-4E stands well out of the range of enemy anti-air defences and communicates via the data link; in one such test using this technique the data link F-4E was over 45nm away at 500ft. Launch aircraft usually must be within 8nm of the target, although, as with all optically guided weapons, this varies according to the prevailing weather and other factors affecting visibility, such as smoke or clouds.

Coupled to the TV seeker, distance-measuring equipment can be installed in the GBU-15. This relies on a previously known target position, but has the advantage that the launch aircraft need never come into LOS with the target; instead, after launch, radio commands tell the bomb where to fly. During the terminal phase of bomb flight, as the GBU-15 dives towards the ground, the WSO can switch over from DME to the TV function on the data link control panel, acquire video communication and check up on target line-up in his radarscope, making corrections if required. Developments with the GBU-15 include combinations of the night-Maverick I^2R instead of daylight TV seeker, the SUU-54 cluster munition canister, and even a rocket motor (turning the glide bomb into the AGM-130 missile).

Self-defence

Stand-off weaponry alone, or 'minimum engagement' as the USAF puts it, is not enough to ensure survival, so over the years the F-4E has enlisted the help of several electronic countermeasures (ECM), both passive and active, designed to foil anti-aircraft defences. Although optically sighted medium- and small-arms fire can pose a significant danger by force of numbers, the ECM are aimed primarily against the more accurate ground and airborne threats. Most of these employ radar (pulsed or continuous-wave) or optical systems in the form of TV or infra-red homing, or both. These weapons are more effective at altitudes of 500ft and more, so if they can be countered the F-4 crews

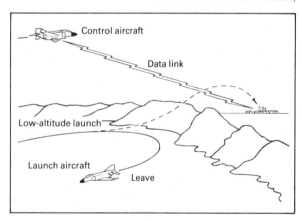

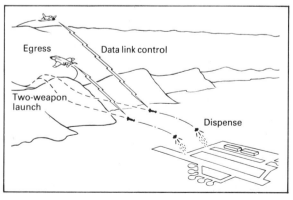

Left, top: Mission profile for F-4 high-altitude, two-aircraft indirect attack using GBU-15(V)1/B (TV data link).

Left bottom: Mission profile for airfield attack using GBU-15(V)N/B TV/IR and data link SUU-54 plus submunition.

Right, top: Rockwell International GBU-15 glide bombs installed on an F-4E. These 'smart' bombs pack a 2,000lb warhead and may be fitted with either TV or imaging infra-red optical seekers. (Rockwell International)

Right, bottom: A close-up view of the GBU-15 and AXQ-14 systems. The inner faces of the air brake and auxiliary air doors are painted glossy red. (Rockwell International)

can fly at these heights relatively unmolested and avoid taking their aircraft down into the concentration of small-arms fire.

The passive part of the ECM package is the threat warning system, the radar warning receivers (RWRs, formerly known as RHAWS, for radar homing and warning systems). At present equipping the F-4E and its Phantom colleagues is the Applied Technology AN/ALR-46, upgraded to ALR-69 status under the Compass Tie programme of the mid-1970s and under replacement by the new ALR-74. Their receiver antennae listen for enemy radars operating in the 0.5–18GC frequency range or C- to J-bands, within which most Soviet-built radar-controlled SAMs, AAA, fighter and back-up radars operate. The RWRs have the ability to sense both pulsed and continuous-wave radars in that range of the spectrum, the CW sensing capability having been added after the Israelis experienced heavy losses in the initial stages of the Yom Kippur War – many of the 33 F-4Es lost were felled by systems their RWRs could not detect, particularly the 'Straight Flush' tracking radar of the deadly SA-6 'Gainful'. Incoming signals are amplified and analyzed by the RWRs so that radar type, threat status and azimuth can be displayed on the cockpit indicators – small screens looking like dartboards which each crewman has in his '2 o'clock' position. Radar information is displayed in simple alphanumerics: for example, a '6' represents an SA-6 radar, 'A' denotes AAA radars, and enemy fighters appear as miniature aircraft symbols. Priority threats – those radars directing a missile or guns – will be surrounded by a flashing circle, the warning cue to take evasive action. Sounds rumbling through the headsets, which are tied through to the RWRs with an adjustable volume level, also bring attention to the opposition.

Although all this is useful in itself (with good pilot reflexes, SAMs can often be physically outmanoeuvred), the ECM suite makes further use of the information by passing it on to the jammers. This equipment can work independently, by comparing the RWR data with its own analyses and providing automatic spontaneous disruption, or the WSO can intervene and select countermeasures which he considers more appropriate. Two types of countermeasures are used on the F-4E, a jamming pod and a chaff/flare dispenser.

Jamming pods used by the current strike forces are the Westinghouse AN/ALQ-119(V) – being upgraded to ALQ-184 status by Raytheon – and its successor, the ALQ-131(V) modular pod. Both can jam in up to three radar-operating bands, while the more advanced ALQ-131 has the potential to be expanded into a five-band system, able to cope with a larger number of radars operating in many different frequencies. Power management enables the pods automatically to apportion valuable electrical power to the priority threats. This energy is used to foil enemy radars in one of two ways – by noise- or deception-jamming. Noise-jamming can be performed against all radar types by blasting them with either spot-jamming signals across a narrow range of frequencies or broad-barrage coverage across a number of bands, the net effect being either partially or wholly to 'white out' the enemy radar screens, or to swamp an automatic system's 'brain' with signals, so that the position of the Phantom is obscured from view. The problem with this technique, even with power management, is that the small electrical generating capacity of strike Phantoms limits their power

Right: F-4E-58-MC 73-1173, complete with Westinghouse '3-band' AN/ALQ-131 ECM pod strapped to the port missile well adapter. The 20mm gun hatch is open. (Westinghouse)

output, so that when they are forced to jam a number of bands, spreading out their available power, the enemy controller can boost his power level and 'see' the Phantom through the 'fog'. The new ALQ-184 has been designed to cope with this problem. An electronic, scannable antenna is aimed directly at the enemy emitter to increase the ALQ-119's effective radiated power (ERP) by as much as ten times, and a flight of Phantoms, each aircraft carrying one or two of the new ALQ-184s, could play havoc with the enemy emitters. Even so, broad-band barrage noise disruption is better left to dedicated jamming aircraft such as the Grumman EF-111A Raven, which can draw on

greater power supplies and work against a larger number of radars, leaving the F-4s to concentrate upon their strike work.

Within deception jamming there are a number of techniques available. The first is range deception, or the 'transponder mode'. By taking in the enemy radar pulses, analyzing them and then transmitting them back at the radar alongside the echoes, the enemy radar's automatic gain control (AGC) will more often than not lock on to the ECM signals, as these are stronger and more clear. Once the AGC has locked on to the ECM signals and has begun to ignore the true returns, all that is required is gradually to introduce

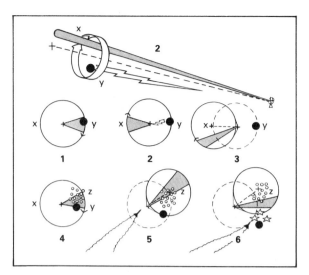

**Above: Fooling a conical-scan radar and related SAMs.
A. Using a jamming pod: 1. The aircraft's receiving systems listen to and analyze the enemy radar emissions so that onboard ECM can later respond with convincing fake echoes (i.e. at the same frequency and pattern). 2. The ECM pod replies with modulated output. When the radar beam is off the aircraft at point *x* (as depicted) the pod sends out strong fake echoes, and when the beam is on or near the aircraft at point *y*, weak or non-existent signals are transmitted by the ECM. This modulated output is repeated over several conical scans. 3. The radar dish now swings its axis over to scan the sky around point *x*, believing the aircraft to be there. It has now been 'walked off' the aircraft, which will disappear from the enemy radarscope. B. Using chaff: 4. The crew release a series of chaff cartridges which blossom into a distracting cloud of radar-reflective particles around point *z*, aft of the Phantom. 5. The large reflective cloud overdrives the enemy radar gain control. The dish swings its axis over to scan the sky around point *z*, believing the cloud of chaff to be the target aircraft. Command-guided SAMs and radar-directed AAA are directed on to the wrong spot, and semi-active homing missiles will be attracted to the radar-painted chaff cloud. C. Using flares: 6. Infra-red heat-seeking missiles (or radar-guided SAMs with terminal infra-red guidance) may not be fooled by the chaff or jamming pods. Instead, these anti-air weapons must be distracted by flare cartridges, which burn to provide a strong IR source and attract the cool, heat-seeking sensors of certain weapons.**

and increase a time delay between receiving a radar pulse and transmitting back a spurious echo. As time of return relates to aircraft range, the increasing delay in the 'echoes' put out by the jammer will cause the radar computer to think the aircraft is further away than it actually is, throwing SAM and AAA lead-firing angles off the Phantom. To provide false azimuth and elevation data, the ECM pod replies out of phase. This works very well against fighter, SAM and AAA conical-scan fire-control radars, which use a narrow beam, quickly and repeatedly scanning a tract of sky (often in a helical, conical mode). Their return echoes are strong when the beam hits the aircraft and weaker or non-existent when it misses. The whole radar dish

turns towards the last known position of the aircraft, as indicated by the strongest echo at any point within the conical scan. ECM pod 'repeater mode' signals matching the radar's output, but out of phase, can be used to throw the radar off the aircraft. This works because the ECM signals copy the radar but are time-phased so that when the beam is off the aircraft the ECM pod transmits strong fake echoes, and when hitting the aircraft weak signals are sent out. As the whole radar dish is swivelled on to the last known aircraft position, here a false one, it can gradually be 'walked off' the F-4 completely. In the next moment, enemy guns should be shooting at clouds and SAMs fired off in the wrong direction, chasing targets as elusive as the F-4's name.

However, these techniques do not fully counteract the threat. Early-model SAMs, such as the SA-2 'Guideline', are flown to the target by ground stations which track the relative positions of both the missile and the aircraft under attack and attempt to 'merge the dots', relaying radio commands to the SAM for a direct impact or a proximity-detonated blast of shrapnel. Thus if the jammer is successful in deceiving the anti-air systems, the missile will be directed on to 'ghosts'. The newer missiles have their own semi-active seekers, and only rely on the ground radars to 'paint' the target for them. Even if the radars are fooled into directing their dishes away from the target, the beam might still be wide enough, or might cover a large enough volume of sky, to show up the aircraft so that the SAM can home in. If a SAM launch warning flashes up on the radar-warning scope, the WSO must release chaff and flares and hope to lead the missile astray.

The Westinghouse pods can perform noise and deception jamming, though the exact methods used are, for obvious reasons, classified. The ALQ-131, designed in 1972 as a replacement for the ALQ-119, went into production by late 1976 and first entered operational service with the F-4E/G fleet in 1979. Its chief advantages over the earlier models include increased speed to analyze and respond to enemy radar threats, an improved power management facility and a new reprogramming feature. This reprogramming can be performed prior to missions using air base support equipment for the pod's Centrally Integrated Test System (CITS). A specific 'jamming strategy' can be fed in in about half an hour to counter radars anticipated *en route* to the target and back, based on radar information supplied by TEREC RF-4Cs or other electron-sniffing 'Ferret' aircraft. The ALQ-119, -131 or -184 pods can be carried on the Phantom using a small adapter fitted under the port forward missile well. Pave Spike bombers which use this hardpoint for their laser pods usually carry the ECM gear either under the starboard forward Sparrow well or, sometimes, on the starboard inner wing pylon.

Backing up the jamming pods is Tracor's AN/ALE-40 chaff and flare dispenser, developed after experience in Vietnam. Chaff itself has been in use since the Second World War, when it was originally introduced on strategic bombers, in the form of metal

Above: Tracor AN/ALE-40 'Square Shooter' dispensers installed. At left is the cartridge dispenser; the downward tilting module is used for flares. (Tracor)

Below: A glossy grey 178th FIS, 119th FIG North Dakota Guard F-4D, 64-0976, taxiing out for a Sidewinder drone kill sortie at 'William Tell' 1984. The aircraft was assigned to AC Capt. Goltz, WSO Capt. Arnold and crew chief MSgt. Stuhr. Early 'non-smart' F-4Ds assigned to the air defence mission received the ALE-40 chaff/flare retrofit, but retain the older Bendix APS-107E RHAWS and were not modified with the digital scan radar fitting (designed to facilitate the use of Pave Spike and Maverick video on the radarscope display). (Mil-Slides)

strips cut to dipole lengths matching the wavelengths of the radars that were to be jammed. Once disgorged, they create false aircraft return echoes or, if used in quantity, partly or wholly blot out the enemy radars. This compounds the difficulties of target acquisition and tracking and, by overdriving the AGC, may even cause the radar to slew off the aircraft and on to the chaff cloud, while a radar-painted cloud of chaff is a distraction for semi-active homing missiles. The ALE-40 is carried on the rear of both sides of the F-4E's inner wing pylons in four modules, each of which can be packed with up to thirty 8in RR-170 cartridges composed of aluminized glassfibre or aluminium strips. The chaff is usually employed during actual strike runs, or when a missile launch warning has been received. The WSO is also able to pre-select a number of release modes – for example, a chaff cartridge every three seconds from any or all of the dispensers – or the system can react to specific incoming warnings from the RWR on its own. Also available for use on the ALE-40 via a special downward-tilting adapter are flare blocks, housing up to fifteen MJU-7 cartridges each. These are designed to foil infra-red homing missiles, such as the shoulder-launched SA-7 'Grail' or the vehicle-mounted SA-9 'Gaskin'. Flares, too, are selected as a precautionary measure during low-level attack, particularly during the dangerous climb-out, when the Phantom's twin jet exhausts are exposed. WSOs will 'hit the chaff and flares' with full force during this part of the strike run. Active 'mini-decoy' jammers, which can be dispensed from

these modules, may also be available: Israel uses such devices on its F-4Es, along with bigger, Brunswick 'maxi-class' Samson decoys, which are about the size of a 500lb bomb with huge 'pop-out' glide fins.

General ECM training is conducted at the very strictly controlled ranges available at Nellis AFB's Tactical Fighter Weapons Center (TFWC) in Nevada, under the 'Red Flag' and 'Green Flag' efforts. The less well known 'Green Flag' programme concentrates on ECM and Command, Control, Communications and

Above: A Brunswick 'Samson' decoy. Used by Israeli F-4Es, up to three of these may be carried on a regular triple ejection rack (TER). (Brunswick)

Below: A 36th TFS WSO climbs into the cockpit of F-4E-39-MC 68-0421 as ground crew connect the air starter. Electrical earthing leads are also attached. (MAP)

Intelligence (C^3I) training, under which strike crews get to use full ECM and learn to communicate with their ground and airborne commanders through the 'electronic thicket'. In a typical 'Green Flag' training exercise, spread out over six weeks, 600 or more aircraft will fly some 3,000 sorties over the ranges, opposed by simulated 'Smokey SAMs', AAA strobes, radar emissions and communications jamming. Studies indicate that most strike forces would be unable to communicate with each other within a radius of at least 5nm from a mobile Soviet ground force, so the training also emphasizes aircraft co-operation with minimum radio ties. To reduce the effect of Soviet 'comjam', USAF Phantoms are receiving the 'Have Quick' Vinson secure UHF upgrade and, aboard RF-4Cs, Parkhill secure HF radio modifications as well, though these are to be supplemented by the Joint Tactical Information Distribution System (JTIDS), which will relay data to and from AWACS (Airborne Warning and Control System), Comfy Levi and other airborne co-ordinators. More importantly, 'Green Flag' allows the USAF's many and varied electronic warfare aircraft to learn to work together alongside the strike force, and to evolve joint tactics that do not interfere with each other. The effectiveness of onboard ECM over this range against simulated threats had been a great confidence-booster to F-4 crews. Outside Nellis, ECM are rarely used in the same integrated fashion. In US Air Forces Europe (USAFE), an irate lobby of farmers recently caused the use of chaff to be suspended when it was discovered that several dairy cows took a liking to the metal strips after they fell to earth!

Maintenance and Overhauls

Those F-4s still flying today are a hotchpotch of technologies – containing both valves and microchips, analogue and digital systems, sheet metal and composites – spanning thirty years of industrial know-how. More than any other USAF aircraft, save perhaps the SR-71, Phantoms require the best from their ground crews. This is compounded by the fact that even the newest F-4 is really a 1950s design, possessing only modest amounts of built-in test (BIT) equipment and LRUs, which means that a great deal of the maintenance work has to be done out on the flight lines or in confined, theatre air base vulnerability (TAB-V), hardened aircraft shelters. This puts a great burden on the ground crews, who are unable to unplug an unserviceable LRU and replace it with a good one; if something goes wrong, an aircraft might well be grounded until the problem is fixed.

Combat Orientated Maintenance Organization

Some 'downtime' is unavoidable, owing to the inability nowadays to pool inter-Wing resources as was common when F-4s were deployed at forward bases in large numbers during the 1970s. Current F-4 maintenance requirements call for just under 30 MMHFH; during 1972 (according to McDonnell Douglas) F-4s demanded an average of around 24 MMHFH. However, although, on balance, the required maintenance hours have increased, and in spite of the age of the aircraft, the actual availability of the Phantoms has improved markedly. This is credited to the organizational changes that have taken place since 1977.

In June 1972 Wings were completely recentralized. Although maintenance teams had been organized this way for a long while, the final blow came when ground crews and 'their' aircraft lost all trace of squadron identity. Bland Wing markings replaced all squadron insignia as aircraft were pooled and became Wing property, and specialists would wander around the base fixing specific quirks as and when they received notification from ground and air crew write-ups.

The apparent shift of responsibility from people on the flight line to higher levels in the centralized organization seriously eroded *esprit de corps*. Vandalism was on the increase, which, along with some straightforward carelessness, led to several thousand dollars' worth of damage a week, quite apart from the adverse effects on aircraft availability.

An investigation was launched in 1974 to look at causes behind aircraft disablement. One typical example cited in the resultant 1978 report was deliberate damage to the compressor blades of an F-4 J79 turbojet powerplant, which cost $65,000 to fix. Higher up the USAF Commands, an uneasiness was growing. The psychological ramifications of the collapse of South Vietnam played some part in this deterioration of morale, while, at the same time, TAC was suffering a drain of experienced ground crews. Better pay and perquisites helped to alleviate the latter problem by the close of the 1970s, but the single most important factor in reversing the downward trend was one of TAC HQ's famed 'Flag' projects.

Termed 'Black Flag', and formally implemented by the 56th TFW in October 1977 at MacDill AFB, Florida (at the time flying four squadrons of F-4Es), the new concept aimed at putting ground crews on a wartime organizational footing by decentralizing them back on to a squadron basis, as had proved so successful in Thailand and South Vietnam a few years beforehand. Squadron identity returned, as crews were reassigned to specific squadrons and flights. With this came subtle but important changes such as the readoption of aircraft fin-top squadron colours, the application of squadron badges on the port intake ducts, and the painting of air crew and individual crew chief names on the Phantoms' canopy rails – all of which added a more personal involvement with specific aircraft and led to a stronger sense of identity in general.

The organizational change itself involved two related concepts, Production Orientated Maintenance Organization (POMO) and Production Orientated Scheduling Technique (POST). Under POMO, Wings took on three core squadrons. First, there is the Aircraft Generation Squadron (AGS). This is split up into Aircraft Maintenance Units (AMUs), one for each of the F-4 squadrons and each responsible for keeping its batch of Phantoms airworthy with a good bill of health. Identity is enhanced as the AMUs each take their own squadron colour in line with their TFS, TRS or training squadron. The new arrangement has also led to a reduction in deployment time during emergencies, when Wings split up and deploy to various foreign locations (often these are 'bare bases' with the minimum of a runway, taxiways, parking areas and a water supply), because the small cohesive teams are 'ready to go'.

The functions of the AMUs include organic flight-line maintenance – anything, in fact, from repairing wheel leg hydraulics to 'cotton picking' (collecting spent drag 'chutes). The greatest benefit reaped from the AMU arrangement has been that ground crews become familiar with the requirements and idiosyn-

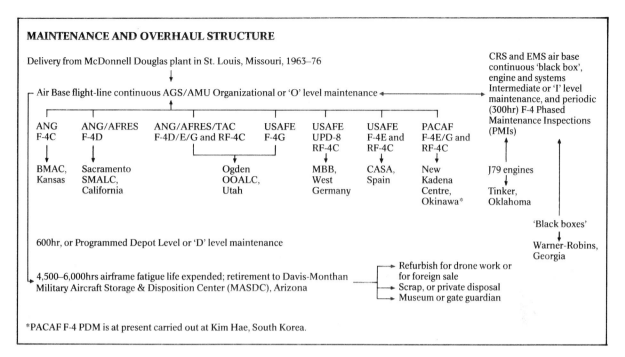

MAINTENANCE AND OVERHAUL STRUCTURE

Delivery from McDonnell Douglas plant in St. Louis, Missouri, 1963–76

Air Base flight-line continuous AGS/AMU Organizational or 'O' level maintenance ←

CRS and EMS air base continuous 'black box', engine and systems Intermediate or 'I' level maintenance, and periodic (300hr) F-4 Phased Maintenance Inspections (PMIs)

ANG F-4C	ANG/AFRES F-4D	ANG/AFRES/TAC F-4D/E/G and RF-4C	USAFE F-4G	USAFE UPD-8 RF-4C	USAFE F-4E and RF-4C	PACAF F-4E/G and RF-4C
BMAC, Kansas	Sacramento SMALC, California	Ogden OOALC, Utah		MBB, West Germany	CASA, Spain	New Kadena Centre, Okinawa*

J79 engines

Tinker, Oklahoma

'Black boxes'

Warner-Robins, Georgia

600hr, or Programmed Depot Level or 'D' level maintenance

4,500–6,000hrs airframe fatigue life expended; retirement to Davis-Monthan Military Aircraft Storage & Disposition Center (MASDC), Arizona

→ Refurbish for drone work or for foreign sale
→ Scrap, or private disposal
→ Museum or gate guardian

*PACAF F-4 PDM is at present carried out at Kim Hae, South Korea.

Left, top: Crew chiefs from the 37th TFW give the thumbs-up to the cameraman. Their charge, the F-4E behind, is an ex-Spangdahlem ARN-101-Mod aircraft. The device near the nose is a portable fire extinguisher. (USAF photo by SSgt. M. Dugre)

Left, bottom: An ARN-101 F-4E receives some specialist treatment on the flight line at George AFB, California. Flight-line servicing is performed by Phantom Wings' Organization Maintenance Squadrons. (USAF photo by SSgt. M. Dugre)

cracies of individual aircraft, so that not only can spares requirements be predicted, but malfunctions can be repaired much more quickly. The AMUs all pool their skills within each group, so that the old problem of having one-task specialists perhaps doing nothing while other specialists work overtime no longer applies today. As pioneered under 'Black Flag', the two other maintenance squadrons consist of the Component Repair Squadron (CRS), and the Equipment Maintenance Squadron (EMS), providing the back-up shop facilities for work that cannot be achieved on the flight lines for want of special repair or troubleshooting equipment, or because of safety factors.

The POST philosophy complements the POMO organizational changes by ensuring that aircraft are readied for specific missions as and when required. This entails pre-positioning fuel, ordnance and spares, ready for an impending mission or for returning aircraft, to reduce 'ground time' between missions. POST thus enables surge sortie levels to rise dramatically, putting the Wing on a flying schedule preparing it for levels for activity which it might face should it be required to fight (on average each aircraft would be expected to fly at least 2.3 combat sorties a day).

Following TAC, the first Wing in USAFE to employ the changes was the 50th TFW at Hahn AB, West Germany (at the time flying three squadrons of F-4Es), with the aim of putting the new techniques to the test under European conditions. The 50th had been gear-

ing up for the new system since January 1977, but the true test came on 10 April 1978 under the surge sortie exercise 'Salty Rooster'. This put the Wing's seventy F-4Es on a wartime footing. This was no routine, weekly surge sortie exercise of two days, but rather a full fortnight of maximum effort.

Hahn's POST/POMO went under the name of Tactical Aircraft Maintenance System (TAMS), though it, too, comprised the familiar three squadrons and AMUs. In spite of some dreadful weather, the 2,771st F-4E sortie was safely recovered on 22 April, equating to a 2.7 sortie rate per aircraft per day for the full twelve-day exercise. One F-4E flew nearly 70 consecutive sorties without missing a scheduled take-off (several Phantoms flew 60 consecutive sorties), while even the more aged 'high-time' F-4s were getting airborne for as many as 50 sorties in a row without having to abandon a take-off.

Hahn also introduced further refinements to the 'Black Flag' concept, called Integrated Combat Turnaround (ICT), under which an F-4 could undergo several simultaneous ground tasks, further cutting aircraft 'ground times'. For example, simulated chemical scrubbing, re-arming and systems check-out could all be done safely at the same time. Before ICT it took two hours to turn around a strike configured F-4E, but this is now down to an average of just over thirty minutes.

All these procedures have now become standard and, within TAC, POST/POMO has been merged and

renamed COMO, for Combat Orientated Maintenance Organization. Estimated maintenance savings on the active F-4 strike fleet run at about 50 per cent, cutting average maintenance time on any given task from two hours to less than 60 minutes. Sortie levels have also risen annually by about 10 per cent since 1978, giving strike crews much more valuable air-time. Currently, F-4Es generate 0.87 sorties per aircraft per day, increased to an average of 2.9 during surge drives. F-4Es have some of the best figures for aircraft 'down-time' – only 12 per cent of their time – while 'canni-balization' is as low as 7.5 events per 100 sorties. PACAF F-4E availability, one of the best in the USAF, is now running at over 80 per cent.

Ogden – Phantom life-line

After four or so years of flying 'on the clock', most F-4s start to get fairly tired, their bodies in need of some surgery, their electrical and hydraulic nervous systems often partially broken or leaking, and their patched-up paintwork faded, chipped and washed out. They are then sent from their operational and training squad-rons to one of the many Programmed Depot Mainte-nance (PDM) centres for a major refit, easing the burden from the base maintenance ground crews. At the PDM centres the Phantoms receive several new pieces of equipment or modifications, under various Technical Orders (TOs) or Time Compliance Tech-nical Orders (TCTOs), bringing them up to date with

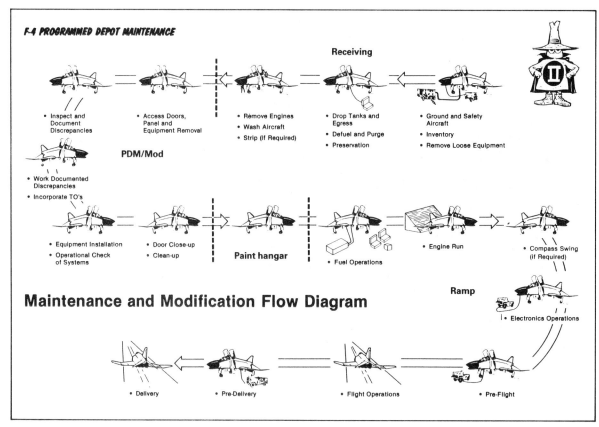

F-4 PROGRAMMED DEPOT MAINTENANCE

Receiving

- Inspect and Document Discrepancies
- Access Doors, Panel and Equipment Removal
- Remove Engines
- Wash Aircraft
- Strip (If Required)
- Drop Tanks and Egress
- Defuel and Purge
- Preservation
- Ground and Safety Aircraft
- Inventory
- Remove Loose Equipment

PDM/Mod

- Work Documented Discrepancies
- Incorporate TO's

- Equipment Installation
- Operational Check of Systems
- Door Close-up
- Clean-up

Paint hangar

- Fuel Operations
- Engine Run
- Compass Swing (If Required)

Ramp

- Electronics Operations

Maintenance and Modification Flow Diagram

- Delivery
- Pre-Delivery
- Flight Operations
- Pre-Flight

the latest operational requirements. A look at Ogden Air Logistics Center (OOALC), the biggest F-4 PDM centre, and one which is qualified to perform major or 'Class V' modifications, provides a very useful insight into what goes on during these rehabilitation sessions.

Situated in northern Utah alongside Hill AFB and its resident fighter squadrons, the OOALC and its 19,500 staff not only handle aircraft processing, including several F-4 weapons systems, but also provide many of the spare parts needed by front-line operating units. This umbilical extends as far afield as the Pacific, 12,000 miles away. Without the OOALC's continued back-up, front-line F-4s would quickly become unserviceable.

Far left, top: A Hahn AB-assigned F-4E on finals. The 5th TFW pioneered COMO under the USAFE acronym TAMS and proved the concept under simulated battle conditions during Exercise 'Salty Rooster' in 1978. (MAP)

Above: Phantoms undergoing PDM at Ogden. At its peak, in 1968, the OOALC was refurbishing 40 F-4s a month; the demands of the Vietnam War were the major factor. (USAF via Lt. Col. J. Winsett)

Below: A 67th TFS Wild Weasel F-4C receiving attention at Air Asia's Tainan facility in Taiwan. PACAF F-4/RF-4 PDM was conducted by Air Asia through to 1979, when the US 'de-recognized' the Republic of Taiwan and all work ceased. PACAF PDM is now carried out at Kim Hae, South Korea. (Ken Mackintosh)

The bulk of the PDM work is conducted in the repair hangars, where newly arrived F-4s are given a parking place within the shops and secured, disarmed and drained of fluids. More than thirty Phantoms can sit partially dismantled, propped up on jacks and looking much as they did when under construction in St. Louis. It usually takes over 10,000 man-hours of work spread out over five months before an F-4 departs, refreshed and ready for another tour of duty.

Many of the removable units, such as ejection seats, pylons and drop tanks, and especially those containing pyrotechnics, are taken away for a more detailed examination and overhaul in the repair shops, while the F-4 airframe is washed and scrubbed, ready for structural inspection; but the non-LRU technology characteristic of the Phantom means that by far the bulk of the overhaul must be conducted in, on or around the airframe itself, which is dismantled into large but manageable sections. Work can be painstaking and tedious: most of the electrical systems are put through a DITMCO circuit analyzer, which is able to detect wiring insulation breaks as well as faulty circuitry, but there are still several hundred essential 'end-to-end' wire checks and connections to be made as the electrical innards are ripped out and then installed afresh, suitably repaired or modified.

Other duties include the check-out of the undercarriage – the vital landing legs which have probably taken 500 or more heavy poundings since the last major overhaul – together with hydraulic and pneu-matic systems, to seal up leaking plumbing and hissing valves. Further time is consumed by the unentertaining job of checking and replacing sheet metal and rubber sealings. Spares needed on the repair lines are called up through an automated storage and retrieval system, but careful planning must be maintained, so that the storage facilities can respond to urgent requests for spares from the front-line units which take priority, most of which are handled by Ogden and sent on via MAC transports to the desired locations. Units temporarily assigned to foreign soils, on the other hand, usually take their own squadron spares with them, including a 3,000-part War Readiness Spares Kit (WRSK). In the event of hostilities, however, even they would lean heavily on the OOALC, especially as the co-located Ogden Arsenal is also a major source for conventional munitions. Computerized records covering the F-4 inventory (each Phantom has its own 'cyber' record) also help in aircraft processing. These files must be correlated with base Phased Maintenance Inspections (PMIs) to check on whether or not a given modification has been accomplished. The files act as a

Right: Facets of the PDM system: F-4 structural modifications are shown in the upper diagram and the structure protecting plan in the lower. (McDonnell Douglas)

Below: An F-4D about to be reunited with its wing assembly. The inboard flaps and BLC piping have yet to be installed. (Ken Mackintosh)

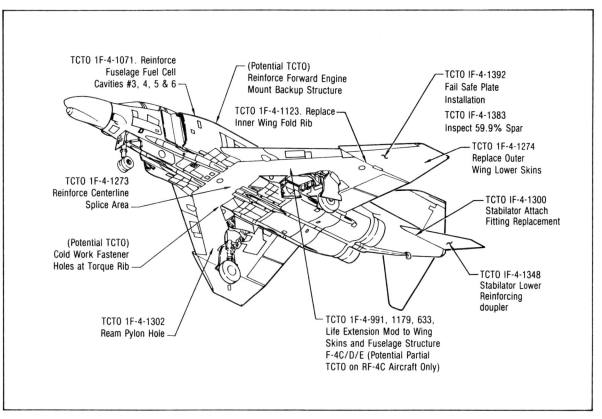

TCTO 1F-4-1071. Reinforce Fuselage Fuel Cell Cavities #3, 4, 5 & 6

(Potential TCTO) Reinforce Forward Engine Mount Backup Structure

TCTO 1F-4-1123. Replace Inner Wing Fold Rib

TCTO IF-4-1392 Fail Safe Plate Installation

TCTO IF-4-1383 Inspect 59.9% Spar

TCTO 1F-4-1274 Replace Outer Wing Lower Skins

TCTO 1F-4-1273 Reinforce Centerline Splice Area

TCTO IF-4-1300 Stabilator Attach Fitting Replacement

(Potential TCTO) Cold Work Fastener Holes at Torque Rib

TCTO IF-4-1348 Stabilator Lower Reinforcing doupler

TCTO 1F-4-1302 Ream Pylon Hole

TCTO 1F-4-991, 1179, 633, Life Extension Mod to Wing Skins and Fuselage Structure F-4C/D/E (Potential Partial TCTO on RF-4C Aircraft Only)

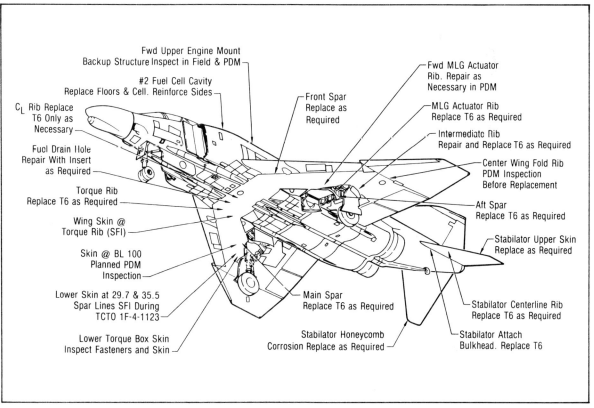

Fwd Upper Engine Mount Backup Structure Inspect in Field & PDM

#2 Fuel Cell Cavity Replace Floors & Cell. Reinforce Sides

Front Spar Replace as Required

Fwd MLG Actuator Rib. Repair as Necessary in PDM

MLG Actuator Rib Replace T6 as Required

C_L Rib Replace T6 Only as Necessary

Intermediate Rib Repair and Replace T6 as Required

Fuel Drain Hole Repair With Insert as Required

Center Wing Fold Rib PDM Inspection Before Replacement

Torque Rib Replace T6 as Required

Aft Spar Replace T6 as Required

Wing Skin @ Torque Rib (SFI)

Stabilator Upper Skin Replace as Required

Skin @ BL 100 Planned PDM Inspection

Lower Skin at 29.7 & 35.5 Spar Lines SFI During TCTO 1F-4-1123

Main Spar Replace T6 as Required

Stabilator Centerline Rib Replace T6 as Required

Lower Torque Box Skin Inspect Fasteners and Skin

Stabilator Honeycomb Corrosion Replace as Required

Stabilator Attach Bulkhead. Replace T6

Left, top: This is what happens to the F-4E when its nose gear fails. Radar and other equipment has been removed to facilitate work on the airframe. (Ken Mackintosh)

Left, bottom: Coated in primer and wearing a freshly repainted radome, an F-4D undergoes final reassembly before being towed to the paintshop. (Ken Mackintosh)

Above: Respraying in action, with only the dark green left to be applied. (Ken Mackintosh)

check-list, so that everything taken off gets put back on!

Perhaps the most time-consuming depot work is crash or battle-damage repair. Much experience was gained in this field during the first ten years of the OOALC's work with the Phantom, when the type was committed in its hundreds to the Vietnam War: patched up in Thailand or South Vietnam, the aircraft were shipped back to Ogden to undergo repair. Today, the task is complicated by the fact that some F-4s are composite machines, built up from several crashed or otherwise damaged F-4s by the battle-damage Rapid Aircraft Maintenance (RAM) teams who worked so hard in South-East Asia. Some of these oddities still fly happily with the reservists, while several bits and pieces from USAF Phantoms have also found their way on to seafaring Phantoms – there are several flak-peppered or salt-corroded Marine Corps F-4s with Air Force rudders, flaps and other components.

Routine structural repairs following visual, ultra-sonic and dye-penetrant inspections often necessitate the addition of unsightly plates or strips riveted on to the airframe to bolster its strength – the mark of a well-used jet. These are added on the basis of individual aircraft requirements, or for the whole fleet, subsequent to recommendations put forward following experience or fatigue testing. Reinforcing plates, added to F-4 all-moving tails, are a classic example.

Recent structural 'beef-ups' have included the Aircraft Structural Integrity Programme (ASIP), extending the life of all USAF F-4s via the careful addition of a centre wing-box fail-safe splice plate, new sheet metal, ribs, spars and attachment bulkheads to over 6,000 hours apiece. This safety margin in airframe fatigue life has given the Phantoms another valuable 1,500 hours of life, taking most long-nosed aircraft right through to the twenty-first century.

Retrofits concerned with upgrading the F-4s capabilities usually involve the installation of new avionics or weapons-wire bundles. Among recent examples are the AN/ARN-101 DMAS upgrade and the conversion of over one hundred F-4E fighters to F-4G 'Advanced Wild Weasel V' status, the latter undertaking having been described by one USAF officer as nothing less than 'a major sex change'. Minor technical orders, such as the recent ones requiring F-4s to be fitted with secure radio modifications and new fuel tank attachment points, number thousands in all, and cannot be detailed here for the sake of sanity!

Paintwork

As in private industry, the OOALC is increasingly adopting modern manufacturing techniques. Most notable, aside from the automated spares storage and retrieval system, is the introduction of automated processing equipment. At the present time this has only been applied to stripping and recoating the F-4's outboard wing sections, but by the mid 1990s it should be possible to push a Phantom into a robot-run shop and watch it emerge at the other end completely stripped down and repainted. This is all part of a broader project designed to reduce 'middle-aged spread' on the Phantoms as they accumulate more and more heavy coats of paint. Incoming processing requires all aircraft to be thoroughly inspected; unless the paintwork is seriously flawed the aircraft are simply given an overall coat of zinc chromate primer and a new camouflage topcoat – chemical stripping takes 140 manhours of tiresome effort. In 1984 Ogden introduced a new dry-stripping process which flings tiny plastic pellets at high speed, taking the Phantom down to its birthday suit in as little as 40 hours. Further studies in this field include a soot-free, semi-automatic, pulsed-laser paint-removing process. The new procedures will ensure that all F-4s are stripped right down during the PDM cycle, thus minimizing weight increases and allowing for a cleaner finish after

repainting – a process carried out after airframe and systems maintenance, prior to engine installation, which costs well in excess of $5,000 per aircraft.

Camouflage has gone through some radical changes over the past two decades. F-4s were originally delivered in a glossy Navy gull-grey and white scheme, but during the early days of American involvement in the Vietnam conflict it became evident that some form of cover was desirable to mask aircraft operating over jungle and rocky terrain. The OOALC was put to work, repainting all F-4s and two hundred or so Voodoos in a scheme comprising a disruptive two-tone green and tan-brown upperside camouflage pattern with pale grey undersides. Popularly known as 'Asian' or 'Vietnam' camouflage, this scheme was held in use on strike Phantoms until 1980, after which time the camouflage was extended to the undersides in place of the pale grey – known as 'wraparound' – to fall in line with the terrain-hugging tactics adopted by the USAF in the post-Vietnam war era. From 1983 the tan was replaced by charcoal grey, part of the 'European One' camouflage initiative, 'integrated over a period of time in order to use up the stock of the old colours', say the OOALC. Many air defence Phantoms, on the other hand, grew steadily more colourful. Completely stripped, from 1979 they were repainted in a glossy pale bluish-grey scheme and daubed with

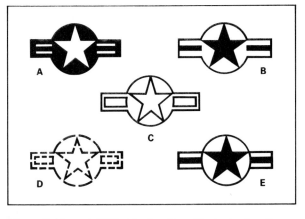

Above: F-4 low-visibility black national insignia stencils. Type A: More commonly associated with the Republic A-10A Thunderbolt II, this version has been used on a number of F-4Ds; 474th TFW (NA) jets, from Nellis AFB, Nevada, were a typical example. Type B: Used by the 363rd TRW on their RF-4C Phantoms when the aircraft were finished in Vietnam 'wrap-around'. Type C: Standard on F-4s wearing the 'European One' green/grey decor. It has also been painted on some Vietnam 'wrap-around' jets. Type D: Another widely used type, this 'broken-up' outline design was commonly applied to F-4s painted in the Vietnam 'wrap-around' finish. Type E: A variation on Type B, used for a time by 37th TFW F-4G Weasels sporting Vietnam 'wrap-around' camouflage finishes.

Left: An F-4D is fitted with General Electric J79-GE-15 turbojets after repainting; engine run-up checks and the pre-delivery test 'hops' come next. Most aircraft require about two sorties to cure all the glitches. (Ken Mackintosh)

F-4 COLOUR SCHEMES		
Federal Standard	**Colour**	**Application**
Navy-style, early 1960s and some Japanese F-4EJs		
FS 2/36440	Light Gull Gray	Upper surfaces
FS 17875	Gloss White	Undersurfaces and control surfaces
*Vietnam-era camouflage**		
FS 34079	Forest Green	Upper surfaces
FS 34102	Medium Green	
FS 30219	Tan Brown	
FS 36622	Very Pale Gray	Undersurfaces
Israeli camouflage†		
FS 34227	Green	Upper surfaces
FS 30219	Tan Brown	
FS 33531	Sand	
FS 35622	Pale Blue	Undersurfaces
Iranian camouflage		
FS 34079	Dark Green	Upper surfaces
FS 30140	Brown Earth	
FS 20400	Sand	
FS 36622	Very pale grey	
West German camouflage‡		
FS 24064	Olive Green	Upper surfaces
FS 26152	Basalt Gray	
FS 17178	Aluminium-grey	Undersurfaces
Korean Compass Gray camouflage		
FS 36320	Dark Gray	Mottled overall
FS 36375	Light Gray	
European 1		
FS 34079	Dark Green	Overall. Same pattern as Vietnam wraparound, with the grey colour following the old tan and the two greens remaining the same as before. A-10s use 34092 dark green. F-4s do not.
FS 34102	Medium Green	
FS 36081	Dark Gray	
Hill Gray I		
FS 36118	Dark Gray	Upper surfaces of wings and fuselage.
FS 36270	Medium Gray	Remainder of upper surfaces and tail.
FS 36375	Light Gray	Undersurfaces and sometimes the nose radome.
Hill Gray II		
FS 2/36118	Dark Gray	Upper surfaces and majority of undersurfaces.
FS 2/36270	Medium Gray	Forward fuselage flanks, tail and outboard wings.
ADC Gray		
FS 16473	Gloss Gray	Overall

*Vietnam 'wraparound' merely deleted the pale grey and extended the upper three colours to the undersurfaces.
†Some early Israeli Phantoms featured Vietnam-style 36622 pale grey and, in some cases, 34102 instead of 34227 green. These non-conformist schemes were a result of the emergency resupply effort in October 1973.
‡Luftwaffe Phantom camouflage colours are approximate FS numbers.

flamboyant unit markings and bold USAF logos to bring them in line with other interceptor aircraft.

In recent months, however, Ogden and the other centres have made a sudden switch to a three-tone ('Hill Gray I') or two-tone ('Hill Gray II') monochrome finish, destined to become standard on all USAF Phantoms in time. The new greys offer much improved visual protection in the murky skies that dominate north-west Europe or monsoon-ridden Asia. In line with this visibility reduction, black and grey paint has been used for national insignia, stencils and unit tail-codes (officially known as Distinctive Unit Identities, or DUIs) – a sharp contrast to the mid-1970s when prominent white stencil data gave USAF F-4s the appearance of flying billboards!

The camouflage changes were taken up following studies conducted by the Air Force Systems Command into signature reduction techniques, part of USAF's bigger 'Have Blue' effort. The Air Force Avionics Laboratory specially reconfigured an F-4D with radar absorbent paint, coated the black radome so that it was only transparent to its own fire-control frequencies, and flash-coated the canopy hoods, the twinkle of sunlight off regularly polished cockpit transparencies being a major giveaway with modern fighters. The test results showed a remarkable ten-fold reduction in the F-4's frontal radar signature, whilst just by removing the white access panel stencils, DUIs and the colourful decals, the visual, infra-red and radar signatures were reduced by as much as 50 per cent. The latter of these reduction techniques have now become standard, but despite the less 'jazzy' appearance of the USAF's venerable Phantoms their aesthetic appeal has not been diminished.

Wild Weasels

The Wild Weasel mission is much younger than the Phantom, dating back to the mid 1960s when the United States was embroiled in the Vietnam War. North Vietnam's Sino-Soviet supplied anti-air defences rapidly grew into a highly co-ordinated mix of AAA, MiGs and SAMs, all of which were controlled through communications arrays and radars. On 24 July 1965 the North Vietnamese shot down one F-4C and severely damaged three others with SAMs, all from the same flight and all in a matter of seconds. While the US aircraft were far from being clay pigeons or 'SAM magnets', losses to radar-guided or controlled anti-aircraft defences in the weeks that followed ran as high as 14 per cent on occasion – a totally unacceptable situation.

As an immediate counter, the Directorate of Defense Research and Engineering (DDR&E) drew funds for the rapid development of electronic warfare aids for tactical fighters under various Quick Reaction Capability (QRC) contracts. The systems that emerged were the origins of the modern self-defence package, first

simple noise-jammers plus some early-model threat warning systems, which were subsequently upgraded over the years. These were not enough on their own, however: something was required which could bite back. Brig. Gen. K. C. Dempster, then Director of Operational Requirements and Development Plans at USAF HQ in Washington, was set to work under a Blue Ribbon task force. This group convened for a seminar in August 1965 and came out with a unanimous verdict: create a force which would be able to destroy enemy radars – the common denominator of the enemy anti-aircraft network.

The first such teams were a stop-gap measure, flying

Below: A brace of F-4Cs from the 67th TFS, 18th TFW, approaching Kadena AB, Okinawa, in the twilight hours of 8 December 1971. The F-4C Weasel nearest the camera features an F-4D-type, Bendix APS-107-format radome. The 67th TFS flew around 450 combat sorties in SEA in 1972, lobbing Shrikes in a stand-off mode. (Via Ben Knowles)

seven twin-seat North American/Rockwell F-100F Super Sabres modified with Applied Technology Vector IV detection equipment and employing rockets, cannon and bombs to destroy enemy radars and SAM/AAA installations. These pioneers were followed in 1966 by the more sophisticated and faster F-105F Thunderchiefs (nicknamed the 'Thud'), better suited to the war over the North and equipped with AGM-45 Shrike anti-radar missiles (ARMs) and more modern RHAW equipment. With trained and skilled use by the 'back-seat ears' or 'Bears', radar type, status and relative bearing could be deduced for missile and bomb attack. As the electronic war intensified, around sixty of these F-105F 'SAM slayers' were brought up to F-105G status, complete with more comprehensive radar-detection equipment interfaced with a long-range AGM-78 ARM capability.

Despite the perilous nature of their mission, trying to outgun something designed specifically to shoot them down, the 'Thud' crews successfully and re-peatedly savaged the enemy's defences, safeguarding the main strike waves from attack by SAMs and flak, while supportive, radar-jamming EB-66s played tennis with electrons. Gaining a reputation for being first in and last out, providing covering fire for entire strike packages, the defence suppression crews came to be known by the mission name of 'Wild Weasel', adopted with some affection from that small carnivore which is so adept at sniffing out and destroying vermin. The name stuck.

At the close of hostilities in Vietnam, it was esti-mated that USAF losses over the North and Laos without Weasel or onboard self-protection systems would have been at least five times higher than those actually sustained. Towards the end of the war these were running at less than 2 per cent, despite the increased sophistication and unimaginable ferocity of the enemy defences. What was originally criticized as drawing valuable aircraft away from the main strike force became the most widely respected tactical mis-sion in the Air Force.

However, by 1975, after returning to George AFB to regroup, the veteran F-105G Weasel fleet had dwindled to a mere 44 available aircraft. These 'Weasel-Thuds' were battle-weary and were showing their age, while potential reinforcements were avail-able only in very limited numbers from twin-seat training stocks (by 1973 only seventeen F-105Fs remained in service). A replacement was urgent, yet there existed only two other aircraft on the inventory that might fit the bill – sufficiently large to house the necessary avionics, having the all-essential two-man crew of pilot and navigator to cope with the workload, and offering a newer, more reliable airframe: the F-4 and the F-111. The F-111 'Aardvark', however, was also the only aircraft in the Air Force able to conduct all-weather precision interdiction at this time, with the few surplus machines available for conversion already earmarked for the Pave Strike-derived EF-111A dedi-cated radar-jamming role (now whimsically called the 'Spark Vark'); besides, it was too cumbersome for the job. Possessing faster reflexes, and ideal for 'weasel-ing', was the ubiquitous F-4 Phantom II.

F-4C Weasels

In fact, a number of F-4Cs were already proving that they could 'weasel' effectively, albeit after a protracted development programme. Under the Wild Weasel IV project, initiated in 1966, some 36 early-model F-4Cs from FY63–64 Blocks 16–24 had been modified to the task to bolster F-105 numbers. The original IV-A package interfaced regular F-4C APR-25 and -26 threat-warning and missile-launch receivers with the special, long-range IR-133. But problems existed with this kit. The F-4C's voltage potential, supposedly ground potential, varied from spot to spot so that the various antennae could not be 'tied' together properly to produce reliable data on enemy radar activity. It took several years to cure the hiccups completely, with many changes of equipment in the meantime, most concerned with sorting out the rather muddled F-4 electronics – a recurring problem with the Phantom. The first operational Wild Weasel IVs entered service in 1969, equipped with the APR-25 and -26 plus the new ER-142 receiver to hunt down the enemy at long range. Blooded in combat in South-East Asia in 1972, flying operations over North Vietnam in support of the big 'Linebacker' aerial offensives, the 67th TFS 'Super Cocks' forward-located at Korat mounted just under 500 sorties without direct loss to enemy fire and put dozens of SAM sites out of commission. The primary weapon was Shrike; the much bigger and better AGM-78 Standard ARM, unfortunately, interfered with the F-4C's inboard flaps and so was not 'wired in'. Specialist training was provided by the 'Willie Weasel' college at Nellis AFB, Nevada, within the province of the 66th FWS.

Soon after the close of hostilities in South-East Asia the F-4C Weasel establishment was shifted to George AFB along with the 'Weasel-Thuds', and the aircraft were upgraded with the highly effective digital ALR-46 and -53 radar receivers and their associated, easy-to-digest alphanumeric displays. In this format the F-4Cs would act as the Air Force's first-line defence-suppression force in Europe and the Pacific for much of the 1970s. Twenty-six aircraft were split between the 67th TFS at Kadena, Okinawa, and the 81st TFS at Spangdahlem, West Germany; the balance was retained at George, for training with the 39th TFTS.

Like all previous Weasels, and Weasels today, the job of the 'back-seat Bear' (officially termed the Electronic Warfare Officer, or EWO), was to locate and identify hostile radars, using a combination of the radar-warning displays and sounds received on the headphones. In this capacity, the ALR-46 was used to identify immediately radar azimuth, on to which the 'Bear' would vector the pilot; the ALR-53 then helped to provide more precise long-range information on radar status for the purpose of attack. Stand-off attack, provided the F-4C had not come too close, or even overflown the site, could then be initiated using the Texas Instruments AGM-45 Shrike. Close in, cluster bombs would be used to finish the enemy off. 'Bear' *extraordinaire* Maj. Jerry Stiles, USAF Ret., who flew several Weasels (including the F-105F during the Vietnam War and the F-4C at Spangdahlem) and who is now in business as a defence-suppression consultant, takes up the story, comparing the aircraft and their different mission approaches:

I met up with the F-4C Weasel in 1977 at George AFB, California, in the Mojave Desert. There appeared to be little comparison between the F-4C and the F-105F other than they had the same type of mission and flew in the same skies. The F-4C was noisy, poorly air-conditioned (a real consideration in desert combat), apparently had no human engineering inputs when the Weasel cockpit equipment was installed, and was not terribly stable in the air. The F-105 on the other hand was a real 'Cadillac' and was a nice aircraft to fly.

The F-4C did have several distinct advantages over the F-105 'Thud', however: it had two versus one engine and, with both stoked up to maximum, had more than ample thrust – though no fighter pilot is ever satisfied with the amount of engine power available, so the latter statement will always be challenged! In some regards, the F-4C had slightly better visibility from the rear cockpit, which provided a better view of the combat environment – a definite 'plus'.

The Phantom had one distinct, though subtle advantage

Above: 81st TFS, 'Spang'-based F-4C Weasels clutching a mixture of fuel tanks, ALQ-119 ECM pods, inert Shrike training rounds and bulk chaff dispensing pods. (MAP)

over the F-105 in that it had never been built in a single-seat configuration. While such may not sound terribly important, to the Weasel mission it was, because it meant the F-4 crews were wedded to a team concept. The F-105 had a predominant number of single-seat airframes which led many of the pilots to develop habits and tendencies moulded towards single-seat proficiencies.

Ironically, one very distinct disadvantage that the F-4C had as compared with the F-105 was that it was a capable air-to-air machine. The F-105, being often compared to a 'lead sled', had little air-to-air acumen other than in the fact that it had a permanently installed 20mm gun and had gotten a few MiG kills. The mission of the 'Weasel-Thud' was thus dedicated to defence-suppression – little efforts were spent in honing skills in the air-to-air arena, even though such efforts are fun! The tactic to be used with the 'Thud' was that if someone was stupid enough to fly in front of its cannon, they would likely be shot down. Other than this, the air-to-air tactic which we espoused if engaged against a capable aircraft was to go like hell – no one could touch you in this mode. The F-4C devoted a lot of time training in the air-to-air role and this in my opinion tended to dilute the quality of the Weasels. There is only so much time that can be allotted to the mission at hand – every air-to-air training mission detracted from a dedicated Weasel training mission, even though the F-4 air-to-air advocates decried that such was an integral part of Weaseling. Those misdirected 'MiG-killers' who happened to stumble into the F-4C Weasel programme saw infinitely more MiGs ahead than SAMs, and hence real Weasel training suffered.

I should point out here that there are basically two types of Weasel missions and that each of these types, for a period of time at least, were practised almost mutually exclusively by each aircraft. In SEA, the F-105 would precede the attack forces into the target area, attack those SAMs that came on the air, and help cover the exit of the strike forces. The F-4C Weasel was used to a great extent to provide stand-off support with ARMs. This is not to say that both types didn't carry ARMs and that both occasionally didn't go in close and 'mix it up' directly, but primarily, to my recollection, the 'Thuds' often went in with the attack force whereas the Phantom Weasels stood off and lobbed in Shrikes.

When I thus entered F-4C Weasel training in 1977 I was surprised to find a number of changes from that which I knew in the F-105 eight years earlier. A good percentage of my time was now directed to the offence/defence against air-to-air threats, a good percentage was spent attempting to launch ARMs, and to a lesser degree, time was spent learning to find, identify and sort out the various kinds of 'enemy' radars, which I considered to be the real job of the Weasel back-seater. Mutual support within a two-aircraft element (against air threats, of course) was now the byword, and an inordinate amount of time was spent trying to manoeuvre into position to create or maintain this support. In the 'Thud', we had often operated independently with only minor consideration being given to these tactics.

The initial F-4C training I had was particularly challenging in that I had a hard time hearing and understanding what was going on! This may sound rather ridiculous, but I challenge anyone to fight a war, or do anything else equally fast-moving and demanding, when one of their senses is partially nullified. My problem stemmed from several factors. First, I had a new helmet which never quite fitted right, especially at the earphones, and it admitted a lot of cockpit and slipstream noises which in the best of circumstances are loud. Secondly, these F-4Cs were equipped with a certain type of external rear view mirror (which was subsequently discarded for the very problem I'm describing) which had been added to help provide defence in the air-to-air mode. (Am I at it again?!)

Another – albeit valid – noise factor was introduced in my initial F-4C Weasel training – noise jamming on the radio. Most of our missions out of George AFB were conducted on the Nellis AFB practice ranges which had a lot of simulated radars and radar signals. Whenever we operated on this range we had to be in radio contact with the ground, and by prearranged agreement the ground provided noise jamming. Well, jamming may hardly be the word, because it consisted of someone holding open a microphone on the frequency we were working and whistling, humming, singing or doing something equally irritating! It was crude, but it worked – we had to learn how to work around or avoid this distraction.

I departed George after this training and proceeded to Spangdahlem, Germany, where I was to 'unlearn' even more of what I thought were good Weasel traits. The primary reason for this was that in the European theatre there weren't any good ranges to practise on which contained a good assortment of 'enemy' radars. In fact, one of our best ranges was in Merry Olde on the Spadeadam

complex on the border of Scotland. It was disadvantageous in that each and every one of these emitted from the same small piece of real estate, much unlike the real world. After about your second or third time on the range you knew exactly where the radars were and the challenge of finding the target diminished rapidly. In the real world, one would hardly expect the foe to concentrate his radar systems at one spot and then put a big white radome on them!

It was in Spangdahlem where I, and the rest of us, met with the variety of rear-seat configurations into which the F-4C Weasel had been adapted. While in Stateside training, with only a few aircraft available in the training squadron, we had only barely been faced with such a wide variety of configurations. I can't remember now the exact differences, but on some aircraft, for instance, the airspeed indicator would be in one location on the panel and in a different location on others. Many of the switches and controls would be moved about and on some aircraft some were missing entirely. Nothing is quite as disconcerting as to reach for a control, especially in a time-compressed environment, only to find that it was not in the expected location. In the F-105F I had developed my kinesic capabilities in 'switch handling' to almost an orchestrated perfection because of the standardization which existed and, as a result, usually didn't have to duck into the cockpit to find that which I wanted – my hands did it all. Such certainly wasn't the case in the F-4C Weasel.

I do remember, though, that we did have a fine capability of locating the azimuth of any number of radar types which permitted us to, as a bare minimum, turn towards the signal and eventually overfly it. Overflight, in a number of circumstances, is definitely not the recommended practice of finding a threat, but one could do so if desired. One of the principal reasons we would turn towards a radar site was that such permitted the missile we carried, the Shrike, to acquire the desired target, thus

Below: An 81st TFS, 52nd TFW F-4C-20-MC Wild Weasel, 63-7607, on approach after a 1½hr training sortie. (Alec J. Molton via Knowles)

permitting possible destruction had we employed it. Another reason for turning towards the signal was to take advantage of an improved antenna configuration on the nose of the aircraft which permitted a reasonably accurate visual location of the target. Once found, we could then employ bombs, assuming they were carried on that particular mission.

The F-4Cs soldiered on in this capacity until 1979, when the last of the 30 survivors were withdrawn from active use and handed over, along with some other early-build F-4Cs, to the two fighter squadrons of the Indiana Air National Guard (ANG) at Terre Haute and Fort Wayne. The F-105Gs left George AFB soon afterwards, some going to the Davis-Monthan AFB 'boneyard' and others to the Dobbins, Georgia ANG.

Advanced Wild Weasel

The withdrawal of these two 'grey-whiskered' Weasels had been made possible by the arrival of the very long-awaited replacement – the Advanced Wild Weasel V, first recommended in 1968 and formally approved in the summer of 1970. Two Block 30 F-4Ds were initially converted for trials, 66-7635 and 66-7647.

The Wild Weasel V programme was centred around the AN/APR-38A Homing and Warning Computer (HAWC). This not only has the capability to analyse a substantially increased number of radar threats over its Weasel predecessors, but it can also furnish range and precise operating-frequency information alongside enemy radar azimuth, type and status. Integrating the hardware and writing the computer software programmes was a mammoth task in itself, but there were some setbacks also. A project officer from the USAF's electronic warfare office outlined some of the early development obstacles faced by the Air Force Systems Command (AFSC):

I was stationed for a tour in the Washington area within the AFSC, the developing Command for the USAF. Virtually everything which is developed for the Air Force, from shoestrings to bombers, is accomplished by AFSC. Because of the long gestation period of a weapon and because of the modestly short tour in the Command (four years), we often stated that we usually helped sire a project but rarely got to participate in the birth of the bastard! In my case, I didn't get to directly witness the birth, but I certainly participated during the breeding process and also participated in the offspring's upbringing.

I was put to work on the then F-4D Advanced Wild Weasel. Management of the overall task was assigned to McDonnell Douglas who served as the prime equipment integrator. Under them on subcontracts were IBM, who built the complex receiver equipment; Texas Instruments, who built the 'brains' of the configuration, the HAWC; Loral, who built the state-of-the-art displays and controls; and General Electric, who modified the existing lead computing gunsight.

The programme manager for this effort was located in the Aeronautical Systems Division at Wright-Patterson AFB, Ohio, the real focal point for all these undertakings. We at the HQ near Washington were more in the administrative and political undertakings associated with the effort. The programme manager when I initially joined on board was Col. Bob Hayden, who stayed with the project

for approximately one year and was followed by Col. Ross Rogers, who essentially completed the effort. A flight test organization for the Advanced Wild Weasel programme was established at Edwards AFB, California. Lt. Col. Frank O'Donnell was the test project officer and performed a super job in this role.

The programme seemed to evolve from one crisis to another. When I initially signed on, the big effort underway was to conduct, essentially, a 'smoke test' on the newly developed configuration. It was called a 'smoke test' because for all practical purposes, in order to conform with a DoD-mandated schedule, we had to initially test-fly the configuration by a certain date. Our goal was thus to cram the equipment into the F-4D, get it airborne, and hope that nothing caught fire – no smoke. We did, and it didn't, so we called the test successful and declared the milestone was met!

Fortunately, a more orderly progression of events followed which proved that it was possible to mate the APR-38 with the F-4D. As progress was made, rumblings developed on behalf of one of the subcontractors. We continued along in the effort hoping that their moan would go away, but it didn't and soon they were claiming that they would either have to have more money, back out of the programme, or go bankrupt. After a great gnashing of teeth we managed to find the dollars and everyone seemed placated.

This didn't last for long, however, in that one of the smaller sub-subcontractors wasn't able to come up with a reliable enough power supply for one of the black boxes. This really caused a problem because we had placed most of our eggs in relatively few baskets, and if any of them broke it would delay the whole programme – and delay it did.

The company at fault now admitted that it couldn't do the task as advertised, so one of the major subcontractors decided to do this relatively simple power supply effort themselves. The only catch was that it would take them an additional year to do so, thus delaying the effort by at least that amount.

Another development took place during approximately the same time period which also cast a shadow on the Advanced Wild Weasel. The central computer, the HAWC, a 32,000-word memory, became filled to the brim with '1s' and '0s' and couldn't digest any more. But we still had more to add, and now we couldn't do so without a larger computer – one with 64,000 words (the current capacity).

Thus, by this time in late 1973, early 1974, the programme faced several severe obstacles. We had a power supply that didn't work, a computer deficient in memory and, as might be expected, costs which were escalating. We had a non-performing product, an obliterated schedule and lots of costs – the programme was in trouble.

Fortunately for the Wild Weasel V project, the germ of electronic warfare again budded for us, this time in a Middle East war version. The Israelis and Egyptians were having a go at it, but the Egyptians were playing rough with some new SAMs, something we hadn't seen exported from the USSR before. It is well known that their newly acquired SA-6 batteries, along with some of their other radar-directed threats (such as the ZSU-23/4 AAA) really put a serious hurt on the Sons of Hebrew. The result for us was that increased impetus was gained for a new Weasel – if it could happen to them, it could happen to us.

Thus, as can often happen, a far-off war saved our skins. The big bosses in charge of the monies decided that the Weasel was a must regardless of cost and schedules – we

helped them reach this decision – and thus the pro-gramme was restructured to take care of the deficiencies and newly found needs.

It was concurrent with this new salvation that I came up with an idea which is still with the Weasel today – as long as we were going to spend time and money, why not put the advanced equipment in a newer airframe, namely the F-4E? The F-4D was certainly capable, but it hadn't been produced for some time, had seen a lot of combat service in SEA and had a few other problems.

One of these problems was that the F-4D lacked adequate internal space in which to put the Weasel gear – within reason that is. One of the space problems which had been a plague to the F-4D was that some of the black boxes had had to be tucked away into almost inaccessible dead space between the engines. Needless to say, this hot-spot required that we air-condition the sensitive electrical equipment – so special ducting had to be created – again through almost inaccessible territory. The lack of space was a real problem. Imagine what it would have been like in the field without the availability of the special factory jigs which would have been used to emplace the equipment!

Thus at my suggestion we began to investigate the possi-bility of adapting the F-4E into the Weasel configuration. One aspect immediately became evident, one which still causes my name to be raised in vain upon the lips of certain Weasel pilots – we'd have to remove the 20mm gun in order to accommodate the APR-38A.

We had studied the problem in depth and there was no other viable solution. The sensitive Weasel antennae had to be mounted in an assembly on or near the nose of the aircraft. No other place would do. Some suggested the wing tips, but vibrations there caused inaccuracies in the system. Some suggested under the fuselage area, but this limited signal reception to below the aircraft. We looked into placing the antenna configuration in a bump below the gun lip, but the instantaneous vibrations from firing the guns was in the order of 100 Gs. We even looked into placing the antenna complex above the nose radome, but this caused problems for the pilot in seeing ahead. We had to either remove the gun or remove the radar (and place the Weasel antenna behind this radome), but no one wanted to do the latter – it would limit the Weasel to visual conditions only. The gun had to go.

The programme schedule now proceeded at a more leisurely pace. The F-4D test flying continued, patched up as it was with a deficient power supply and limited

Above: F-4D-30-MC 66-7635, the original Advanced Wild Weasel test-bed. Note the bulge under the forward Sparrow missile well and the substantially enlarged radome blister. (USAF via Lou Sharp)

computer memory, and more was learned about the system. The emphasis for fast movement was lacking because the real effort awaited equipments yet to be perfected. Why push hard when we might have to do it all over again?

We had to come up with an official designation for the new Weasel. The differences between the Advanced Wild Weasel version and the 'vanilla' F-4E version were just too great to continue to use the same designation to be reasonably efficient. So a new designation was sought. My recommendation, which was not adopted, was to call the new Weasel the F-4W, in recognition of its role. The powers that be, however, rejected this idea in preference to the F-4G designation; the F-4W designation would be too high on the alphabet – the Navy's F-4S modification was still in its infancy – and, besides, the F-4G designation was more coincident with the designation of the F-105G Weasel 'Thud'. I stuck to my guns for a short while, however, especially when my research showed that the USN had already had a modification which they called the F-4G (the Navy F-4Gs, twelve of which were modified from regular Fleet F-4Bs, were used in the mid-sixties for automatic carrier landing trials). Although this USN designation was now defunct, I half-jokingly suggested that some day, some giant computer with a long memory would try and land the Wild Weasel on an aircraft carrier – I lost the argument, but still suspect that some day . . . !

With the F-4E airframe now nominated for the Advanced Wild Weasel mission, F-4D 66-7635 was stripped of its APR-38 and went on to serve with General Dynamics as a radar test-bed; the second F-4D was similarly decommissioned in 1975, and returned to front-line duty. In the meantime, McDonnell Douglas began the lengthy task of convert-ing the first F-4E Weasel, 69-7254, requisitioned from the 57th FWW. The job at St. Louis was a pro-tracted affair, as the preliminary installation had to be restructured to take account of the slightly different, newly perfected, pre-production black-box technology that was only just emerging from the subcontractors. A

Above: F-4G test-bed 69-7254 in flight in 1975. The machine sports a petite centreline test instrumentation pod. (McDonnell Douglas)

year later, in the autumn of 1975, and resplendent in a fresh coat of fiery orange paint on its fin and wing tips, the jet arrived at Edwards AFFTC to begin test work.

The initial tests, held from December 1975, covered the flight characteristics of the new F-4G configuration and basic avionics trials. Acting as a test-bed for new weaponry, the F-4G was routed from time to time over the nearby Navy-administered China Lake weapons range in California. This closely guarded complex includes the high-security Echo range which has simulated full-scale 'ships' – giant sandcastles shaped into frigates and bristling with 'Soviet fleet systems'.

Echo was used for F-4G integration flights with the Navy-funded AGM-88A High-speed Anti-Radiation Missile (HARM), a powerful new claw for the Weasel designed to supersede Shrike and Standard ARM.

As confidence in the project grew, so did the boldness of the F-4G's test markings – a proud Weasel was added to the intake ducts, complete with sunglasses, desert hat and serape. Sun protection was also provided for the rear-seat 'Bear' in the form of a white sunshade, which also served to hide the cockpit installation from prowling eyes.

West Coast tests continued through to 1977, after which time the two production-validation F-4G Weasels, the St. Louis-converted 69-7263 and the number one Ogden-reworked 69-7290, joined the test force. At this juncture in the development process tests

proceeded to the Follow-on Operational Test and Evaluation (FOT&E) phase at the land-orientated ranges offered at the Nellis AFB TFWC, where the aircraft could operate over the newly established electronic warfare range at Tonopah. These continued until mid-1978, concentrating on computer software refinements, together with some design-change recommendations that were passed on to the assembly lines at Ogden OOALC. All were minor. Ogden started work on the first production machines in late 1977. Individual aircraft put up for conversion were selected from F-4E production Blocks 42–45, based on their fatigue index.

New equipment and training

The story now moves to 28 April 1978, when the first production F-4G thundered into George AFB to a ceremonial welcome, piloted by Col. Dudley J. Foster, 35th TFW CO, and EWO Capt. Dennis B. Haney. This aircraft, 69-0239, went on to the 39th TFTS for crew transition training, followed by further F-4Gs at a steady flow of around three aircraft per month from the OOALC.

USAFE underwent transition from the F-4C to the F-4G Weasel soon afterwards. The first to cross the Atlantic, piloted by Lt. Col. Duke Green, Commander of the 81st TFS, and EWO Capt. Mike Freeman, touched down to a welcoming reception on 28 March 1979. The Spangdahlem ceremony is worthy of note because on that day there were no fewer than five different USAF strike-Phantom models parked on the base flight lines: the F-4C Weasel, F-4D, F-4D with 'towel bar' Loran, regular F-4E, and newly arrived F-4Gs! The last F-4G assigned to USAFE arrived on 3 November 1980, bringing the 81st TFS 'Panthers' Wild Weasel V establishment up to a full squadron complement of 24 aircraft. In the meantime, the Philippines-based 3rd TFW had also started to re-equip with a dozen Weasels, operated alongside the F-4Es of the 90th TFS 'Pair-O-Dice'; the first batch of shark-mouthed F-4Gs to complete the Pacific flight arrived in September 1979.

By the time the 116th and last F-4G was delivered in the summer of 1981, George AFB had had to undergo some organizational changes, necessary because of the 120-plus Phantoms all operated under the 35th TFW, creating a colossal administrative burden for the officers at the top and placing excessive support demands upon the ground specialists. Accordingly, on 30 March 1981, the 37th TFW 'Defender of the Crossroads' was reactivated to assume command over the Weasel force. The Wing comprises the 562nd TFTS, dedicated to training Weasel newcomers, and two operational squadrons, the 561st and 563rd TFSs.

New arrivals assigned to the 562nd TFTS transition are usually fairly experienced F-4 flyers, with around 500 hours on fighters, though there are some LIFT graduates assigned for a tour on the F-4G, and this trend is on the increase. The basic course takes some 62 training days, of which 56 are assigned to flying, beginning with the F-4E and then progressing to the F-4G under Phase Two. Weasels demand that newcomers know the F-4 inside and out before they are let loose on the expensive F-4Gs.

'Jerry' Stiles, who returned to George in 1979 for a tour in the F-4G, now takes us through the background to a training flight, not untypical of other Phantoms:

> The Mojave Desert hadn't changed much from my short visit there a few years prior and neither had the radar

Left: Advanced Wild Weasel V nose. The new glassfibre chin-pod replaced the old gun fairing. (McDonnell Douglas)

WEASEL TRAINING (562nd TFTS 'WEASELS')

F4G00WW basic conversion course

Ground training	310hrs, including 20 in simulator and 21.5 on APR-38 and 'part task' training mission planning and the F-4.
F-4E Phase One	Pilots 10 sorties/13hrs; EWOs 7 sorties/ 8.4hrs. Includes 2.6hrs low-level flying.
F-4G Phase Two	Pilots and EWOs 22 sorties/28.3hrs. Includes at least one night sortie.

Type Conversion Course

F-4D/E to F-4G	Pilots and EWOs 20 sorties/26.5hrs.

IF4G00WW Instructor Course

Ground training	69.7hrs, including 19.5 in simulator.
F-4E	Pilots 6 sorties/10.6hrs; 'Bears' 4 sorties/ 5.3hrs.
F-4G	Pilots and 'Bears' 9 sorties/12hrs.

Note: Hrs/sorties are averages, based on recent training.

---

environment against which we trained. Our typical training mission still consisted of taking off from George AFB, head north by north-east for approximately 180 miles (to Nellis) and then engage the various simulated radar threats which were scattered over the massive range complex in northern Nevada. I never knew how many simulated radars there were on this complex, commonly called Tonopah after the nearby town, but there were a lot.

A typical mission would normally consume around six hours of your time even though the flight would normally last less than an hour and a half. We were required to show up for the mission briefing at least two hours prior to take-off, but because of the planning often necessary we often arrived long prior to that – a real grind when take-off was scheduled for 6.00 a.m.!

The mission briefing would be conducted by the crew leading the flight and would encompass all parts of the mission, including any emergency procedures. The lead crew would normally draw the mission routing on a chalkboard, describe each sequence which would occur along each leg, further draw tactical formations on the board and explain how we would all interact in the simulated combat area, explain specific target attack tactics and techniques, and in general cover how the whole operation would be conducted. While it looked good on the board, it rarely happened as planned because of the many, many factors which would change – but, such is

similar to that in combat so perhaps the training was near the real thing.

An hour prior to take-off the air crew, all fitted out in parachute harnesses, anti-G suits, helmets, maps and all sorts of other paraphernalia would 'step' to the aircraft, which was usually located within 200 yards of the squadron building. After arriving at the aircraft the crew would scan the maintenance forms and learn the status of that particular jet and would note which discrepancies still existed (I never saw an aircraft without some type of maintenance still remaining due – almost all were very minor). The crew would then divide up tasks and start the 'walkaround' of the aircraft; the pilot would ensure the flying portions were working, and the back-seater would check all of the weapons, pods and external stores in general, to ensure that they were adequately installed. The crew would then climb into their respective cockpits and run further checklists in the seat, getting the aircraft ready for engine start. Electrical power for this function was provided by a turbine-driven electrical power cart which had been pulled into position near the jet. This same cart provided the compressed air with which the engines were placed into initial motion during engine start.

Below: A production validation Weasel, 69-7263, in flight over the Nevada Desert and armed with a TGM-65B Maverick missile, June 1978. (USAF photo by SSgt. Joe Smith)

Above: In the F-4G, a bulbous APR-38A nose fairing replaced the F-4E's gun; the F-4G's nose pitot is marginally longer than the F-4E's probe too. (Author)

At a predetermined time, normally such that we would taxi out of the starting slot 20 minutes prior to take-off, the flight leader would check his flight in over the radio and would signal us to start engines. With engines started we could activate all of the onboard equipment because the engines themselves provided cooling air to them. It was at this time we would determine the final status of all our equipment. For a time period, when our monies for spare components were scarce, it would be at this stage that the mission was stopped because we'd find that particular equipment was 'on the blink' and it wouldn't be worthwhile continuing. [Under the Carter Administration, 1977–80, in an effort to appease the 'hawks' in Washington, money was made available for continued procurement of new weapons systems at the expense of spare parts, creating appalling availability rates. The logistics shortfall in spares has since been remedied. Author.] We would taxi out for final pre-take-off checks, taxi on to the runway, do a final engine run-up and then proceed on our way.

Over Nellis, the traffic controllers provide a corridor for entry over Tonopah, the big electronic warfare range. The flight of two or four Weasels then engage the simulated radar threats, with the senior 'Bear' ('Papa Bear') calling most of the shots; the decisions as

to whether the Weasels press home their attacks, what ARMs are employed and which targets are to be 'struck' rests in his hands. Emphasis is placed upon demonstrating the use of the APR-38 to the 'Baby Bears', and in honing the pilots' terrain-hugging flying abilities.

After an airborne period of approximately an hour and a half, we'd be on final approach back for the field, having invested in a concentrated training effort. We would next stop the jet at its parking pad, disembark from the aircraft and walk into maintenance debriefing to tell the maintenance men what was wrong with the jet and to fill in the forms. When things were particularly wrong with the jet, these meetings could consume around an hour and could result in some 'lively' conversations wherein the air crew would claim a particular malfunction, only to be countered by the maintenance men stating that the malfunction couldn't be duplicated and that the air crew had malfunctioned rather than the equipment!

The crews would next assemble in the flight briefing room from which they had commenced and, depending upon the complexity of the mission, would conduct a debriefing which would last from a few minutes to several hours. During these debriefings there would be a candid exchange of lessons learned and mistakes made because such direct interface, it had been learned, tended to save lives in the real combat environment.

Comparing the cockpits of the F-4C and F-4G Weasels, Stiles went on to say:

Above: A 563rd TFS, 37th TFW F-4G Weasel on approach. The three MiG kills belong to the squadron, not to the Phantom. (MAP)

Back to the F-4G cockpit layout it can be said that, effectively, they are all standard. About the only deviation I can remember is that occasionally two adjacent, similar control panels (when the wiring attached to them permitted) would be reversed in position. Additionally, the rear cockpit fuel gauge, an innovation on the F-4G, would occasionally be missing – its electrical connections, somehow, sometimes caused variations in the front cockpit fuel readings, not an ideal situation!

I rate the cockpit layout of the F-4G on the same order as the F-105 – very good. The F-4C Weasel came about rather hectically during the war period and suffered many changes before it finally worked. Apparently, the people in charge at the time decided, after the numerous delays with the F-4C Weasel, to 'take what they had' after the bugs were worked out, with the result that many cockpit variations existed. The F-4G effort was a well thought out modification which resulted in a good cockpit.

The heart of this cockpit instrumentation is the displays of the radar-receiving AN/APR-38A computer. Having identified type, azimuth, range and status, the HAWC then displays this information in both cockpits. The pilot has a small display similar to the routine F-4E RWR indicator, but the 'Bear' plays with a much larger, more comprehensive set of displays – three in all. The main display is a large Plan Position Indicator (PPI) just to the left of and above his regular F-4 radarscope. This primary presentation enables the 'Bear' to maintain a high degree of control over the proceedings. This is important because, unlike the miniature radar warning systems used by other strike Phantoms, which employ inputs from the threat warning system to assist with jamming operations, the F-4G's WRCS, LCOSS and missile armaments all rely on priority threat information dispatched from the HAWC. The computer will automatically flash up the priority threats it is receiving (up to 5, 10 or 15, depending on the setting; range sensitivity is also pre-selected by the 'Bear'), the greatest of which is indicated by a triangular surround. This assessment is based on pre-programmed data in the HAWC,

which is periodically readjusted to take account of the evolving nature of potential enemy threats. Alternatively, the 'Bear' can override the triangled threat by placing a diamond cursor over another he considers more dangerous, effected by the use of the right console slew control. Once positioned in place, the computer will then automatically adopt that choice in lieu of its own.

To the right of the main presentation there are two other luminescent-green, TV-type displays – the 'panoramic' and 'homing' indicators. These allow the 'Bear' to examine in greater detail the actual frequencies being used by hostile emitters, their proximity to the aircraft and their proximity to one another; on the basis of this information the 'Bear' may decide to override the automatic HAWC choice. Warning sounds on the headphones assist this process, and an experienced 'Bear' intuitively knows whether there is something wrong – the HAWC is far from infallible, and only provides half the solution.

Having been selected by the 'Bear' or HAWC, the priority radar-threat data is then fed into the attack systems. The computer 'remembers' where the target emitter is located by freezing its position into its memory. This enables the pilot to pop the Weasel back down behind cover while the 'Bear' sets up the weapons. Once the F-4G has been put on course for the target, an emitter-marking reticle will slide into view on the pilot's gunsight to assist in line-up for rocket, bomb or missile attack. For missile attack, the priority information is also fed directly to an AGM-78 Standard ARM or an AGM-88A HARM via a digital Navigation Coupler Unit (NCU) interface; if the anti-radar weapon is sequenced for launch, and if the enemy radar is within the missile's firing parameters (its 'launch footprint'), it may be let loose for the kill.

Weasel teeth

One of the disadvantages of the earlier Shrike AGM-45 is that it cannot be fed such priority threat information by the HAWC. Shrikes are pre-set to home on to specific frequencies and are thus usually launched as a deterrent: the enemy on the ground does not know whether it is tuned to his radar operating

Above: A 'Spang'-based Wild Weasel comes in to land, with leading-edge slats very much in evidence. (USAFE)

Above right: F-4G-44-MC 69-7300 roars down the runway with afterburners ablaze. (Kurt Thomsen via Knowles)

band(s), and so shuts down to avoid being hit. This 'downright intimidation', as one 'Bear' termed it, may force radars to shut down even if a Weasel is merely 'sharpening his claws' nearby. But when ready to bite, one of a pair of Weasels will turn on the radar and pull up in an exhilarating loft launch manoeuvre, firing its Shrike skyward for maximum aerodynamic and ballistic reach. The break while the radar shuts down in response to the ARM is often sufficient for a second Weasel to sneak in and drop conventional 'iron' or cluster munitions, taking the enemy by surprise. This missile and bomb duet is still frequently practised by the Weasels, as evidenced by the regular use of a combination of inert Shrikes and MER bomb racks over the Nellis ranges.

In the bombing mode, F-4Gs have retained the full F-4D/E capabilities, enhanced by what is described as a 'pseudo blind bombing capability'. This is catered for by the red reticle on the modified gunsight, which shows the position of the priority threat selected by the HAWC or 'Bear'. With this, the pilot does not require an external visual reference for attack. Instead, by lining the reticle up with a green cross in the centre of the gunsight (the cross is slaved to the caged radar boresight in a 'dive–toss' attack), and pickling the bomb load, the pilots can nose the Weasel through cloud, bad weather or darkness and put bombs right on the target. The cluster munitions which are generally used scatter several hundred tennis-ball-sized explosives, any one of which will render a radar inoperable.

Production of both Shrike and Standard ARM has now ceased, but reasonably large quantities of both missiles remain in stock, and will continue to be used

for a few more years. Development of the HARM started well over a decade ago, and the Weasels achieved IOC with the type in 1984. The principal advantage offered by HARM over the earlier Standard ARM is its high speed, as indicated by the 'H' prefix. This should enable a Weasel to knock out a radar before the anti-aircraft system can inflict any injury. With the dish out of action, either the SAMs will have lost their mid-course guidance information or the Weasel will no longer be illuminated, and so even if a SAM has already been fired it will have difficulty finding its target.

The HARM goes beyond the HAWC tie-up of the Standard ARM in that it can be used in a 'point and shoot' mode – either against targets of opportunity or in self-defence – the missile's own AWG-25 radar-receiving processors assessing the operating frequencies of a hostile radar, then locking on to it and homing in. Alternatively, in the 'pre-brief' mode, the HARM may be launched in a more random manner, after which time it will zoom up to high altitude to look for radars of specific frequencies, as pre-programmed into it before or during the mission. In this capacity, salvos of HARMs could be launched against front-tier Soviet-built anti-aircraft systems, such as the 'Pat Hand' and 'Straight Flush' radars of the SA-4 and SA-6, enabling friendly strike forces to penetrate walls of front-line SAMs, which remain groundborne and impotent. The feed-in from the HAWC is used for striking specific targets at long range, with an off-axis launch capability from treetop height up to 40,000ft. Otherwise, at longer ranges, the HARM might well decide on its own initiative to lock on to a much lower priority threat in a heavily radar-saturated environment.

The Weasels have recently been fitted with another new weapon in the form of the Hughes AGM-65D I^2R model of the Maverick, with night and limited adverse-weather capabilities. As on the F-4E, lock-on with both the TV (A/B) and I^2R (D) versions is accom-

plished by using pre-launch seeker pictures on the radarscopes for target line-up and lock-on. The APR-38A will also cue the Maverick seekers on to the priority threat without assistance from a sensor pod such as Pave Tack (which the Weasels do not use), but the greatest advantage the AGM-65D gives the Weasels is that they are now able to identify a radar which is not transmitting at the time. This counteracts a favourite tactic employed by radar operators to foil Weasels and their ARMs – transmitting just long enough to get adequate information for attack, by using several radars tied together to provide a complete picture. However, even when they stop transmitting, the imaging infra-red seeker can pick up the heat from such sites, which show up on the F-4G radarscopes as white patches, distinct from the surrounding terrain. Readiness with the new weapon is currently well under way with both the Weasels and the ARN-101 F-4E squadrons. A new, combined TV and

ARM seeker is being developed for the Maverick by Hughes Missiles. If the target radar shuts down the missile switches over to TV guidance automatically, permitting visual lock-on via data-link. In one recent test the trials target switched off but got successfully 'zapped' by the dual-mode test weapon.

Tactics and future developments

Over the next decade, Weasel mission planners will be exploiting prior knowledge of hostile radar locations to an increasing degree. These positions can be made available by radar-listening TEREC-equipped RF-4C Phantoms, or EF-111A Ravens, mapping the enemy's electronic order of battle (EOB), or through another concept that has also been some years in the making, the PLSS or Precision Location Strike System. Fitted into Lockheed TR-1As, PLSS can calculate the bearing, location and classification of enemy radars along a whole front at extreme stand-off ranges. Two or more TR-1As compare, between them, the incoming Time Difference of Arrival (TDOA) of enemy radar signals; this enables their companion ground-based PLSS computers, to which they are radio-linked, to pinpoint enemy radar sites and electronic C^3I installations using a form of 'inverse Loran' (as the US DoD has euphemistically described the technique) in a fraction of a second. The processed data is then transmitted, in turn, to friendly attack aircraft carrying HARMs or DME-equipped GBU-15 glide bombs for stand-off strike well out of LOS to the targets. F-4Gs can thus fly into a hostile zone with missiles or glide bombs cocked ready for rapid launch. Having cleaned

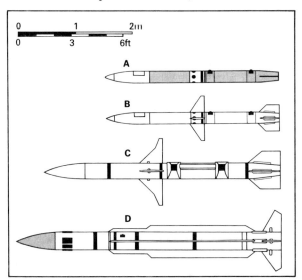

Left: Anti-radar missiles: A. Texas Instruments AGM-45 Shrike training round, without fins and painted blue and white. Used by F-4C Weasel and F-4E/G Phantoms. B. Texas Instruments AGM-45 Shrike proper – the live round. C. Texas Instruments AGM-88A HARM, the new high-speed ARM for the Weasels. Used by F-4Gs and Navy jets. D. General Dynamics Pomona AGM-78 Standard ARM as used by F-4Gs and Navy A-6E Intruders.

Above: A 3rd TFS 'Peugeots' hunter-killer F-4E lets loose a deadly, live GBU-15 cruciform-winged glide bomb. The Phantom carries an AXQ-14 data-link pod for stand-off communication with the weapon. (Rockwell International)

Left: One of Col. Bill Hillman's 'Warhawks', in flight with Sparrow and Shrike missiles plus centreline Fletcher tank and Westinghouse ALQ-131 ECM pod. Spangdahlem's hunter-killer F-4Es are being replaced by General Dynamics F-16C/Ds, which will operate alongside the F-4Gs. (USAF)

Below: 563rd TFS 'Aces' F-4Gs parked in a string at George AFB in November 1981. (Mil-Slides)

out an unfriendly sector – or at least eliminated the more dangerous points – the Weasels will then be able to break out and create a reasonably safe corridor to the primary target for allied strike traffic, either by using weapons left over from the initial confrontation or by frightening the enemy into 'closing down shop'.

The introduction of these new weapons systems and related guidance aids has already had an even greater benefit for the Weasels than originally envisaged. Because the ARN-101 F-4E can use the DME GBU-15 and is also due to be wired up for HARM carriage, it can act as a potent support machine, easing the workload off the Weasels which are now being allocated an

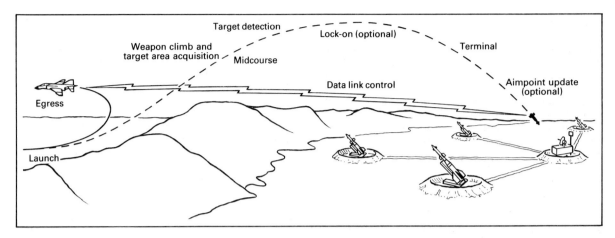

increasing number of counter-C^{3}I tasks in addition to their traditional pure defence-suppression work. Clark Field's 'Pair-O-Dice' pioneered such joint tactics, using their F-4Es as Shrike ARM bearers in support of their limited number of F-4Gs, the success of their combined hunter-killer efforts leading to the 52nd TFW in USAFE in 1984 redistributing all available F-4Gs and ARN-101 F-4Es equally among the 23rd TFS 'Hawks', 81st TFS 'Panthers' and 480th TFS 'War-hawks', turning the unit into an entire Weasel Wing or, as the Spangdahlem-based professionals call themselves, 'SAM-busters' – though the F-4Es are now in

the process of being phased out in favour of F-16C/Ds, with the E-models going to George's 37th TFW. This streamlining has effectively doubled the Weasel force! To provide equal performance envelopes, all F-4s are receiving the F-15-type 600 US gallon centreline tank (T.O. 1F4-1308), allowing 6g manoeuvres with full fuel loads; back-up hunter-killer F-16s can cope with manoeuvres of up to 9g.

Clark crews perfect their skills over the nearby Crow Valley range, and participate in the regular PACAF 'Cope Thunder' joint exercises when detachments fly over the South Korean- or Okinawa-based Air Combat

Maneuvering Instrumented (ACMI) ranges near Osan and Kadena ABs, respectively, homes of additional Pacific-based Phantoms. USAFE F-4Gs, deprived of a realistic range for many years, will soon be able to enjoy the brand new Polygone electronic warfare facility. Polygone straddles France and West Germany with a multitude of sophisticated multiple threat emitter simulators (known as 'Mutes'), providing enough elbow room for aggressive 'Weaseling'. Weasels also pitch their skills against US Army SAM-Hawk missile batteries, which at the same time teaches the Army some rudimentary counter SAM-suppression tactics (on the basis that the Soviet Union has fielded a 'Wild Sable' counterpart).

Other co-operative tactics being developed by the Weasels include liaison with the EF-111A Raven jamming aircraft. Should certain areas become too densely saturated with enemy anti-air defences, the EF-111As could be sent in to clear a swath through enemy radars. Current operators, the 390th Electronic Combat Squadron (ECS) at Mountain Home, Idaho, and the 42nd ECS at Upper Heyford, England, use one of three support modes: stand-off jamming outside enemy territory, where they can loiter for up to four hours; interdiction support, flying alongside friendly aircraft deep into enemy territory; or CAS, providing front-line jamming along the FEBA for close air support aircraft or rescue teams.

Considering the power available to the EF-111As and their extraordinary jamming abilities (pilots refuse to fly near one of these aircraft because of the microwave radiation hazards), the Weasels have to learn to work with the Ravens without having their own APR equipment blotted out by friendly disruption – this forms an important element within the 'Green Flag' electronic warfare manoeuvres. Using spot-noise or deception modes, however, the two aircraft can co-operate quite well. The EF-111As, by jamming systems operating in different frequencies from those the F-4G crews are seeking out, will allow the Weasels to carry on 'sniffing' for other radars without having their nostrils blocked. In a passive mode the EF-111As can also help to flush out enemy sites for further Weasel investigation. The actual tactics employed are strictly classified at the present time, but much joint training goes on, as exemplified in USAFE with the formation of the 65th AD. Established in 1985, the 65th consolidates 66th ECW Ravens, Compass Call EC-130Hs and 52nd TFW F-4 aircraft into one electronic warfare battle organization, dedicated to foiling enemy anti-air defences.

Detachment 5

Detachment 5 of the Air Force Tactical Air Warfare Center (TAWC) is conveniently located at George AFB, where it performs trials of new Weasel-related technology, vitally important to such a mission but modestly described by one Det. 5 Officer as 'nothing

Left, top: F-4 mission profile for low-altitude indirect attack with GBU-15(V)1/B (TV data link).

Left: F-4G 69-251, the 37th TFW Commander's Wild Weasel, complete with multicoloured fin pod. The blue denotes the 562nd TFTS 'Weasels', the golden yellow the 561st TFS 'Black Knights', and the red the 563rd TFS 'Aces'. The machine wears the new semi-gloss 'Hill Gray II' scheme; F-4Gs started to appear in these subdued colours in August 1987, and by mid-October that year nearly twenty 37th TFW F-4Gs had been resprayed. (SSgt. M. Dugre)

Below: The Wild Weasel bristles with antennae: at far right is the SST-181X Combat Skyspot aerial, at centre the APR-38A omni antenna, and at left the nav/comm antennae. (Author)

cosmic'. The closeness of George, in flying time, to the Nellis TFWC and China Lake range obviated any requirements for permanent detachments at those centres; because of the limited number of spare F-4Gs, and the fact that they require special maintenance, it was also considered more expedient to base the test force at George. A trio of aircraft wearing TAWC badges and 'OT' tail codes have been specially set aside.

One of Det. 5's achievements has been a breakthrough in Weasel training techniques. When new crews are first assigned to George for training, the Nellis Tonopah ranges present them with a challenge. They are introduced to these with more experienced crews. Unfortunately the simulated radar sites, with all their realism, are designed to train non-Weasel crews as well, so the simulated radar sites are large and fixed, sticking out obtrusively in the pale desert. F-4G crews, after the initial 'Nellis Shock', typically get to know exactly where the radars are after a dozen sorties.

For this reason, in 1981, one ingenious Det. 5 Officer came up with the SPS-66 Nitnoi (Thai for 'little one'). Adapted off-the-shelf from a Raytheon marine radar, the Nitnoi is used as an expendable, easily relocated target against which Weasels can practise live bomb and ARM attack. It is also, as its name implies, rather petite, putting more emphasis back on the APR-38 scopes in the cockpit and less emphasis on external visual identification. This is important because Soviet radars would be extremely well camouflaged and difficult to spot. Strike crews overflying Tonopah had been developing a tendency to look for the radar dishes and vans and not the source of the radar energy. Nitnois can be dismantled for carriage in a regular F-4 baggage pod, enabling the Weasels to take their 'friendly enemies' with them elsewhere for training.

F-4G equipment trials being carried out at the present time include a vast memory growth for the HAWC – from 64 to 250k. The chief reason for this expansion is to integrate a more comprehensive software programme, so that the APR-38A is able to identify radars on the basis of much weaker or shorter

Above: A brace of F-4Gs painted in 'Hill Gray II' Ghost Grays and assigned to Det. 5 of the TAWC at George AFB. The aircraft were previously assigned to the 562nd TFTS, but in July 1987 they received new 'OT' tail codes. Fin-caps are chequered blue atop the background FS 36270 medium grey camouflage paint. (USAF photo by SSgt. M. Dugre)

exposure to radar signals. Current terrain-masking tactics call for two or more F-4Gs to pop up alternatively in 'pogo' style, so that the radars can be monitored but the enemy does not get a chance to lock missiles or guns on to an individual Weasel. But it is still a very dangerous game – Weasels may have to work over open country where there is little available cover. The HAWC upgrade lessens the danger by reducing the 'pop-up' time required for radar-analysis from several seconds down to a very quick sniff, thereby mitigating the hazards associated with intimidatory tactics, or allowing the crews to carry out more surprise attacks. This is all part of the F-4G's Performance Upgrade Program (PUP), to be incorporated under two phases: the first, known as the Weasel Attack Signal Processor (WASP) update, now in progress, and the second, known by the acronym DRG, by around 1988, at which time the improved HAWC will become known as the AN/APR-45, optimized for use with the HARM AGM-88A.

After nearly five years of successful operations with the Lear-Siegler AN/ARN-101 DMAS, it was decided to try the package out on the F-4G. Tests commenced in March 1983, and F-4Gs are being fitted with the system as they undergo PDM at Ogden (T.O. 1F4G-504). This provides an 'uncanned' true all-weather defence suppression capability unrivalled anywhere in the world. The only external difference between the F-4E and F-4G ARN-101 make-up is that the F-4G does not use the Loran module, and hence lacks the distinguishing dorsal spine antennae feature which would have turned the already bristling Weasel into a spiky porcupine. There was simply no space in the fuselage spine in which to put the new navigation aid, but this is of little importance as Weasels are hunters, using their radar receivers to find their prey.

3. IN FLUX

Testing

In addition to the Weasels flown under Detachment 5 at George AFB, a large assortment of Phantoms is scattered throughout the United States at various initial and follow-on test centres. While not always involved with F-4 developments *per se*, these Phantoms are used in Air Force, Joint Service and contractor trials for various ancillary tasks that usually affect the day-to-day operations of F-4s sooner or later – whether connected with weapons, pods, avionics, mission tactics, or even something as mundane but essential as a runway to come home to!

Because of its long and successful career the robust Phantom has been involved in no small number of tests – more than any other aircraft in Air Force history, in fact. To a great extent, its widespread use as a trials platform has been a direct result of its adaptability, durability and two-man crew (the pilot to fly the aircraft within a carefully prescribed test profile and the back-seater to monitor and control test equipment), but the sheer quantity of Phantoms available has also been a deciding factor, with the result that, over the past 29 years, the F-4 has percolated into even the most remote test efforts.

Apart from the 'big-league' bases dealing with such development work, a number of F-4s are used by small test organizations. These include a selection of bril-
liant dayglo-red and white models that operate from Ogden OOALC – F-4C, RF-4C, F-4D and F-4E marks – as check-flight pilot proficiency aircraft and back-up test machines, operating over the Wendover-Dugway test range in Utah; and a handful of other camouflaged examples, which are used from time to time by various defence corporations on loan as equipment trials and chase aircraft. McDonnell Douglas, of course, have operated many Phantom variants over the years. A number of other F-4s, usually patched-up crash-damaged machines, deprived of engines and ignominiously stacked on fixed jigs, have been used for electromagnetic related signature test work under the auspices of the Electronic Systems Division at Rome Air Development Center, New York. Additional redundant Phantoms act as technical training bodies on which new ground crews can learn some elementary skills, tearing them apart and putting them back together again week after week. More than twenty grounded 'GF-4' Phantoms are used in this capacity by

Below: An F-4D from Kirtland's test-force over the New Mexico desert in the early 1970s. The machine carries some Maverick test rounds. The centreline pod is painted glossy white with a cream-coloured nose and red bands; the tail stripe is white with orange triangles. (Hughes)

the primary Technical Training Centers at Sheppard, Texas, and Chanute, Illinois – the F-4 ground-crew schools – while numerous retired F-4Cs are now corroding on the sides of front-line airfields as dummies upon which battle damage repair teams can realistically practise their vital metal-bending skills.

Bygone F-4 test units

Before the 1976 AFSC reshuffle, several test units operated the Phantom. The biggest of these now semi-defunct operators was the Kirtland Air Force Special Weapons Center, located in New Mexico adjacent to the Texas border, which had command over the 6585th Test Group. The aircraft were split up, as required, between Kirtland and the nearby Holloman AFB and White Sands missile test range, where advantage could be taken of the maintenance and support resources offered by the co-located 49th TFW, at the time flying over 75 F-4Ds. The 22-aircraft test force included five F-4Ds and an RF-4C, their duties concentrating primarily around Joint-Service projects such as HIT-VAL, a lesser-known combat evaluation that pitched special ECM-equipped Phantoms through simulated barrages of SAM, AAA and other automatic weapons fire in an attempt to judge the counter-ECM or ECCM effectiveness of the Army's SAM-Hawk batteries and guns.*

Due to the rapid attrition of Fleet F-4B/Js (the equivalent of a full USAF Wing was lost under night and instrument conditions alone between 1970 and early 1973), and the consequent lack of spare jets for test work, the F-4Ds assigned to the 6585th TG were also regularly employed by the Navy for various 'proof of concept' trials. One rather extraordinary series of tests flown in conjunction with the Navy at this time involved a novel approach to shooting down enemy aircraft, developed under the Pave Arm project. Known as 'Brazo' (Spanish for ARM), this weapon was modified from a Sparrow air-to-air missile to home on to enemy aircraft radars. In a series of tests, live Brazos were fired against transmitting BQM-34 target drones, all achieving 'kills', as· planned, and providing much promise for the programme. Intended as a passive means of stealthily knocking down enemy fighters and radar-toting command posts, the whole project fell under the budgetary axe and was terminated in 1977, along with many other third-generation Joint-Service missiles under development at the time, including the equally successful Agile, Claw and Seekbat, weapons that would have given the F-4 the killing power of the advanced F-14 Tomcat. These rash missile cuts are the underlying factors which compel the Phantom, after some twenty years of periodic upgrades, to continue to use Sparrow and Sidewinder as its primary air-to-air armament.

Today, two major USAF test centres employ the F-4 as a test-bed. One of these performs pure development and evaluation work under the guidance of the AFSC, while the other conducts trials of new equipment for both TAC and AFSC, paving the way for successful front-line deployment.

Edwards Air Force Flight Test Center

Renamed in honour of Glen Edwards, who was tragically killed in June 1948 flying the YB-49 'flying wing', Edwards AFFTC and its 300,000-acre test range in southern California has been acquainted with the F-4 ever since the type entered USAF service. Indeed, even before that time, some preliminary work was carried out at Edwards with Navy and Marine Corps F-4As and Bs leading up to the record-breaking flights, including Top Flight, Skyburner and several other newsworthy efforts, such as the fly-offs against the Convair F-106 which ultimately pressed the Air Force into adopting the Phantom. At this time the AFFTC was at its peak, as popularized in Tom Wolfe's book and the spin-off film *The Right Stuff*, and its aircraft flew some 36,000hrs annually.

The primary responsibility of the AFFTC is to perform initial and follow-on flight tests of new aircraft in the developmental stage. These include basic flight clearance, formulating the tables on the maximum and minimum limits of an aircraft's performance, weapons separation trials with dummy or inert ordnance, and avionics refinements. Typically, since the F-5E and F-15 programmes, aircraft will undergo 'Joint Test Force' or 'Combined Test Force' work, flown and maintained by a mixture of both primary manufacturing contractor and USAF personnel. With regard to the 23 F-4s flown from Edwards, these are all managed by the 6512th Test Operations Squadron, AFSC. Today, basic flight work with the F-4 itself has long since finished, but the Phantoms still perform a number of important support tasks.

The five RF-4Cs are used primarily by the USAF Test Pilot School. Curriculum missions in the RF-4C are designed to show pilots how to push aircraft to their limits to ascertain their performance and general flying qualities, and also to demonstrate dissimilar-aircraft chase techniques, developing skills for photographic and remote control work with other aircraft, missiles or remotely piloted vehicles. The nine F-4C/D models are mainly used for towing TDU target darts for weapons trials, so that new fighters under test can shake off a few rounds and have any related quirks resolved. They, too, are also used for pilot-proficiency rides and chase work. One F-4C, 63-7654, was recently used to test the Standardized Central Air Data Computer (SCADC) that will eventually be used by nearly all USAF aircraft. The SCADC is being refined to work in conjunction with a number of other subsystems, ranging from the autopilot to CARA, a brand new combined radar altimeter that calls out verbal warnings over the intercom if the aircraft is too low or the pilot is performing something the computer considers a bit tricky and out of bounds. As modern fighters fly lower and faster than ever before, there is an increasing demand for safety aids.

The eight F-4Es are rather different from those

---

*Better known are the air combat and air intercept evaluations ACEVAL and AIMVAL, carried out at Nellis TFWC in the late 1970s to help formulate new air-to-air weapons requirements.

Above: Built as an F-4D-28-MC, 65-0713 later served as a YF-4E prototype alongside 62-12200. It is depicted with a cluster of Hughes Maverick missiles, recording cameras, and a test boron-composite rudder. Note the black and white test boom. (USAF via Lucille Zaccardi)

Overleaf: Major (now Brig. Gen.) Tom Swalm's 'Thunderbirds' Phantoms, photographed in 1971. The display team flew F-4Es from 1969 to 1973. (McDonnell Douglas)

operated elsewhere within the USAF, and have been specially modified solely for chase tests. These are all 'hard wing' models, with no leading-edge slats, and can be readily distinguished by their unusual paint scheme. Originally, these F-4s were flown sporting overall white but, during the last few years, some have acquired the odd mixture of operational 'wrap-around' fuselage colours together with glossy white wings. The compromise has its roots with the 'Thunderbirds' Aerial Demonstration Squadron who from 1969 thrilled thousands of spectators with these aircraft during their dare-devil precision formation flying displays – an awesome repertoire of four Phantoms and eight J79 turbojets. In 1973, with the advent of the 'energy crisis' precipitated by oil shortages following the Arab-Israeli war, the team opted to convert to the more economy-conscious T-38A Talon trainer (though an equally strong motive may have been concern for safety factors following some display accidents).* Retaining their dazzling white, the jets were duly relinquished to the AFFTC, where they were destined to serve out the remainder of their fatigue lives as trials platforms. Their assignment to Edwards was not based purely on the fact that they could retain the major part of their pristine decor: as display aircraft, these particular F-4Es had virtually no operational avionics installed on board, lacking rear-seat attack and self-defence controls, weapons computers and gunsights, and so could only be effectively used for pure research work. In the place of mission equipment has come a series of purpose-built black boxes.

One such package, taking up the radar space in four jets, is a telemetry device designed to monitor and report on the status of cruise missiles. These have been in use since 1979, the normal procedure being to follow and film the terrain-skimming missiles while maintaining a standby posture in case the test articles need redirecting or must be self-destructed for safety purposes.

One of two YF-4Es that has seen service at Edwards, 62-12200, underwent so many changes throughout its career that some mention must be made of this extraordinary beast. This Phantom started life on the production lines as a Navy F-4B, number 266 out from St. Louis, but it subsequently found itself in USAF hands where it served as the YRF-4C reconnaissance test-bed. After 1966 the YRF-4C adopted a gun for YF-4E tests and then, from June 1969, undertook the slatted-wing Agile Eagle programme. In April 1972 yet another metamorphosis occurred when the Phantom took to the air with a totally reworked fly-by-wire (FBW) or 'electric jet' flight-control system. This was proving technology which was later applied to the F-16. The 'Electric Phantom' differed from its peers in using a FBW computer to convert pilot control inputs

*Interestingly, the counterpart Navy/Marines 'Blue Angels' display team downgraded their F-4Js from thrusty J79-GE-10s (the naval equivalent of the F-4E's GE-17) to GE-8s, as used in their F-4B/N and RF-4B models (the naval equivalent of the F-4C/D and RF-4C's GE-15s). Throttle procedures were adjusted accordingly, with pilots requesting 'more go' advised to select afterburner at 89 per cent of military thrust.

into electrical commands for the control surface actuators, without making use of the traditional direct hydraulic and electrohydraulic linkages. On 29 April another modification was evident as the aircraft took off from Lambert Field with forty square feet of canards added to the intake sides. These were married to the FBW system for advanced Control Configured Vehicle (CCV) tests, and were never intended for application on to operational F-4s. Flown as a technology demonstrator at Edwards, the CCV Phantom was later partially dismantled and has since been retired, pensioned off in 1979 to the Air Force Museum where it can still be seen today.

Recent tests involving F-4s that have been completed at Edwards include KC-10A Extender aerial refuelling compatibility sorties, soft-soil take-off and landing tests, a new mobile aircraft-arresting system, and 'Have Bounce' – fibreglass-reinforced aluminium runway repair matting.

The new F-4 arrester systems are based on standard F-4 recovery equipment technology that was first introduced over a decade ago. Although routine Phantom landings are assisted by the air brakes, wheel brakes, engine run-down and a neat 'pop-out' drag 'chute, operational squadrons can call on back-up arresting systems (either the BAK-12 or -13) to halt an aircraft suffering an engine or hydraulic emergency. The BAKs, which comprise a single carrier-deck type of wire or emergency net, drawn out of two mechanical friction-braking devices on either side of the runway, can halt a 40,000lb, 140kt Phantom in less than 300yds.

The two new systems that recently completed their tests – Gulf & Western's Portarrest and the All American Engineering Company's Mobile Arresting Gear (MAG) – are mobile equivalents of the BAK-12 and -13, which can be transported by MAC aircraft to damaged bases and set up quickly by the ground support crews to recover friendly fighters on battle-shortened or dangerously wet or icy runways. Successive tests have demonstrated that either system is

Above: The CCV, canard and fly-by-wire configured YRF-4C in action in August 1974. The trim is medium blue on a glossy white airframe. (McDonnell Douglas)

Right, top: All American Engineering's mobile arrester gear halts AFFTC RF-4C-18-MC 63-7744 during tests at Edwards. (USAF photo by 1st Lt. William Bridges, via Kevin Mulligan, AAE)

Right, bottom: Gulf & Western's Portarrest aircraft recovery system set up at Edwards in October 1983. The package successfully performed twenty F-4C recoveries in the space of an hour. (Gulf & Western)

capable of handling twenty Phantoms an hour, and the devices have since moved to operational bases for full trials.

The other damaged-runway aircraft-recovery aid that recently completed preliminary testwork at the AFFTC is 'Have Bounce' matting – about 1½in thick and designed to be placed over hastily-filled runway potholes. There were fears to begin with that as the F-4 hit the lip of the mat the bounce in Have Bounce might be excessive – the Phantom is notorious for flipping on its wing tips during tyre blow-outs or hard sit-downs. With the F-4s retaining their structural integrity, this matting has since moved on to Eglin for further tests, and will soon find its way on to operational bases.*

All this peripheral work contrasts sharply with the 1970s, when the F-4s were front-line fighters. At that time, the Center operated several slatted F-4Es. Most of these were loaned by the Nellis-based 57th FWW and used for air combat evaluations, flying against the new YF-16 and YF-17 lightweight fighters, which at the time were undergoing competitive flight-testing at the AFFTC. Today, as the F-4 retreats from front-line service, so the numbers at Edwards are destined to shrink. According to the 6512th TS, feasibility studies

---

*The USAF operates special 'Prime Beef' and 'Red Horse' civil engineering teams for runway repair and airfield defence work. These squads train at nearby Tyndall and so can be called in to help with the tests at Eglin.

are in fact being conducted into possible replacements, but the two-man crew of the sturdy F-4 means that it remains a valuable test asset for a number of operations and will remain in service there for many more years. Also earmarked to use the F-4 into the 1990s are Eglin's Armament Development Test and Tactical Air Warfare units.

Armament Development Test Center

Situated in north-west Florida on the Gulf of Mexico, this AFSC unit concentrates its efforts on armaments and related sybsystems. Everything that has found its way on to the F-4's pylons had undergone tests here, including laser designators, FLIRs, electronic warfare aids, Sidewinder missiles, and the usual ever-evolving flow of both 'dumb' and 'smart' munitions.

The actual numbers and types flown by the 3246th Test Wing fluctuate a great deal, with F-4s often undergoing conversion and reassignment to the base following rework at Ogden, or subsequent to a squadron disbandment, as the unit must keep very much up to date with the latest cockpit, wiring and other operational configurations. Normally there are over a dozen Phantoms assigned, and out of these there is usually a resident 'hard core' of seven or eight F-4Cs and Ds at all times. Most of these machines have been with the ADTC since the late 1960s, but the two F-4Es on strength possess both slats and the ARN-101 DMAS (a third F-4E was written off recently). RF-4Cs come and go for special tasks. Test work on weapons and other equipment is conducted on two levels. First there is the 'white shirt' contractor testing under which the equipment manufacturers can fine-tune their devices; this is followed by 'blue shirt' USAF operational trials, which put the systems through simulated base and combat conditions.

Because of Eglin's location, most active ECM work is performed only at night between 1.00 and 6.00 a.m.

to avoid blotting out the local TV and radio networks, though the ADTC makes maximum use of secure, anechoic chambers. The flight test crews must also exercise great care because of unwanted listeners cruising back and forth in the Gulf, looking more like pirate radio stations than fishing trawlers! Other points that must be carefully kept in check include the obvious hazards associated with experimental munitions: in the late 1960s, during tests of tablet-sized percussion-activated explosives designed to pick up movement along the Ho Chi Minh Trail, an F-4 accidentally dispensed several thousand of the 'pills' on a popular Florida beach. Very embarrassing!

The fashionable image of the ADTC is one of air crews hell-bent on destruction and technocrats with computers monitoring the ability of 'smart' weapons to knock out targets with increasing precision. In reality, the evaluators are equally concerned with the mundane. Does the new cluster bomb 'scatter' in the required pattern? Does the new mine bury itself in the earth sufficiently to conceal its deadly presence? It is just as much a matter of peering into 'holes' as toying with figures. Air crews, too, must be fully aware of the parameters in which they are confined in order that

USAF F-4 TEST UNITS

Unit	Base	Command	Tail-code	Tail markings
3246th Test Wing	Eglin ADTC, Florida	AFSC	AD	White fin band with red diamonds superimposed
6512th Test Operations Squadron	Edwards AFFTC, California	AFSC	ED	Dark blue fin band with white 'Xs' superimposed
6585th Test Group	Kirtland AFB, New Mexico*	AFSC	–	White fin band with orange triangles superimposed
OOALC Ogden Logistics Center	Hill AFB, Utah	AFLC	–	Red and white fin, sometimes with 'Hill AFB' logo
57th Fighter Weapons Wing	Nellis TFWC, Nevada†	TAC	WA	Black and yellow chequered fin band
4485th Fighter Weapons Squadron	Eglin ADTC, Florida	TAC	OT	Black and white chequered fin band

*Disbanded 1976. †Disbanded 1985.

Above: A beautiful in-flight shot of ADTC F-4D-31-MC 66-7716, showing off a Westinghouse AN/ASQ-153 Pave Spike designator/ranging pod. The aircraft is painted in glossy FS 16473 grey but carries standard Vietnam-type dark green and pale grey outboard wing tanks, while the centreline pod is glossy white with a red band. (Westinghouse)

Left: An Eglin-based 3246th TW F-4E brandishes a short-chord winged GBU-15 glide bomb. The white store is an AXQ-14 data-link pod. (Rockwell International)

they produce accurate test results: although deviations from the intended delivery path can be compensated for by computation, officers have budgets to observe, and good test air crews are those who can do the job near first time, accurately, safely and within costs. Air time is at a premium, and prototype munitions are invariably scarce.

From 1970, Eglin undertook the massive 'Pave Strike' development effort, which embraced the second- and third-generation 'smart' and ARN nav-strike technology discussed elsewhere in the book. A considerable amount of money was invested in improving the F-4's air-to-ground capability. At the present time, Eglin is busy at work on fourth-generation guided weapons, designed to reduce the USAF's dependency on laser and TV guidance by substituting more advanced, self-contained, autonomous target-searching technology. Development has just started on Paveway IV, a new 'lob and forget' precision-guidance kit for Mk. 84 2,000lb bombs. Infra-red and radar signatures of a specific target (for example, a T-72 tank) are fed into the seeker before take-off. After weapons release, infra-red homing and high-frequency, millimetre-wave sensors will compare potential targets with the pre-programmed data, lock on

totally autonomously, then guide themselves to the target. Just recently developed is the CBU-87 'spin-up' cluster bomb, which can be lobbed from low altitude on to SAM sites and other lucrative (but heavily defended) targets in a stand-off manner, to minimize exposure to enemy defences. Area weapons like the CBUs are very useful in that they do not require absolutely pin-point deliveries, and work on improving existing stock is always in progress. Regular 'iron' bombs, for example, have a tendency nowadays to ricochet off modern hardened targets, so Project 'Have Void' is aimed at providing the weapons with stronger cases for extra penetrative power.

Also fresh from Eglin – and contrasting sharply with the recent efforts at Edwards – are several devices optimized for counter-air, airfield strike work. The BLU-107/B Durandal, designed by the French weapons specialists Matra, is one such weapon. This short, torpedo-shaped bomb is used to destroy enemy runways. The real advantage offered by this neat cylindrical package is that the assailant needs use nothing more complex than a simple bomb ejection rack. After release, Durandal fires a rocket motor and charges into the runway. Having burrowed its way through the concrete top surface, a large warhead (which may have a delayed fuse to hamper runway repair efforts), blossoms and tears up the paving, leaving a crater over 15ft wide and up to 7ft deep. Following some improvements incorporated into the basic design after tests at Eglin, the USAF has negotiated a production contract with Matra, and the F-4E is scheduled to carry up to twelve at a time as a runway destroyer.

Complementing and ultimately due to replace Durandal is the more versatile Brunswick Defense Low Altitude Dispenser (LAD). Built as a technology

demonstrator, LAD is basically a large flying box packed with one of a variety of submunitions; some fifteen different area-denial types have been tested as compatible to date. An F-4 travelling at 500kts can deliver LAD at stand-off ranges of up to 5nm, or up to 12nm if the dispenser is assisted by a rocket motor. After release, LAD uses pre-programmed autopilot or inertial mid-course guidance. This hauls it up to cruise and dispense altitude, then steers it on course for the target so it can perform its bomb-sprinkling mission while the attacker has long since departed. Using guided submunitions, the dispensed bomblets can autonomously seek out radars or tanks, or unguided munitions can be dispatched to cut a series of slices through a runway. The stand-off capability of LAD turns counter-air and defence suppression into much more palatable missions for strike crews. Tests will be continuing for a few more years.

Advanced ECM

Although new countermeasures under trial at Eglin are strictly classified, it is known that a number of weird and wonderful advanced ECM devices were test-flown during the 1970s. Two of these were designed specifically for use by Phantoms, developed under the Compass Ghost effort, a project which aimed at filling in the blind spot of the Weasels – defence against electro-optical anti-aircraft weaponry.

Left: An F-4D out over the Gulf of Mexico equipped with Matra BLU-107/B Durandal anti-runway rocket-assisted bombs. (Matra)

Below: An F-4D from the Eglin test force taxies on the runway, armed with live test rounds of the AIM-9J Sidewinder missile (painted orange). Note the lowered leading-edge flaps and the yellow claw painted on the splitter plate. (Ford Aerospace)

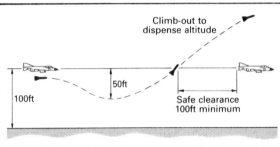

To foil heat-seeking missiles, the USN and USAF worked on a joint venture called Multibrick. Several ECM devices were test-flown, the principal system meeting with the greatest success being the Sanders AN/ALQ-140, a small 25lb installation fitted into the drag 'chute door of F-4B/C Phantoms. This infra-red countermeasures (IRCM) fitting used a Cesium Lamp, developed by Northrop, which blew out carefully controlled blasts of infra-red energy from the rear via a mechanism resembling an extractor fan, so that it caused premature detonation or unlocked heat-seeking missiles fired into the defender's rear quarters. Northrop fielded their own series of wing-mounted AN/AAQ-8 pods based on their Cesium Lamp module, about 50 of which remain in stock for use by RF-4C Photo-Phantoms and MC-130E/H Combat Talon/Hercules. Further advanced work in this field is being carried out by Northrop under QRC82-03.

A related but fundamentally different development was called the Airborne Optical Countermeasures (AOCM) system. Many ground-based anti-aircraft weapons, ranging in complexity from ringsight-aided

Top: F-4D-31-MC 66-7741 out over the Gulf armed with a Brunswick LAD demonstrator. Note the recording cameras located under the port intake duct. (Brunswick)

Above: Brunswick LAD flight profile. Release is as low as 100ft at ranges of up to six miles.

Below: An F-4C at Eglin equipped with the rare '5-band' AN/ALQ-131 jamming pod. Note the turbine on the nose of the pod to provide the extra power necessary for this stretched model. (Westinghouse)

guns through to wire-guided missiles, rely on eyesight to point or steer the weapons – either directly or through a telescopic device of one variety or another. The AOCM used several 'flash detectors' bolted on to an F-4C test-bed, which looked at the quadrants below the jet to pick up gun flashes. The flash detectors in turn cued two lasers: the first provided range information to concentrate the optics of the other, and the second was set to give out very high-power pulses in the green part of the spectrum in which the human eye is most sensitive. The effect of a short burst of this, even through sighting systems, was to 'blind AAA crews', and render gunfire at least temporarily inoperative. While the AOCM itself evolved into something so large as to require dedicated AAA-suppressors, simpler derivatives may be on the hangar shelf somewhere for quick strap-on in the event of hostilities. The fact that the US Army recently invited contracts to develop protective eye gear for its anti-aircraft crews, as a counter-countermeasure, is evidence of the existence of this sort of device. Training with the Pave Spike and Tack designators is restricted to secure training ranges for the same reasons, though any comment on an ECM application would be speculative.

Refinements – Fighter Weapons Squadrons

After basic 'blue shirt' IOT&E has been accomplished at Eglin, and all looks well, with a production contract looming and the USAF happy, the new weaponry or other devices then move on to Nellis TFWC, Nevada, for FOT&E before entering operational service. These tests are quite simply combat procedure rehearsals.

Until very recently the Nellis establishment included a special F-4E wargames force, the 422nd Test & Evaluation Squadron (TES). With the shutdown of the F-4E TES and 414th FWIC in 1985, these trials are conducted by visiting units, or special detachments such as George's Det. 5. Normally, a special part of the range is set aside for their use, at the southern end of the Nellis complex near Dogbone Lake. There they can fly their Phantoms virtually unrestricted, putting men and machines through their full paces, spearheading a new book of tactics. ECM equipment can be put into operation during a full 'Green Flag' electronic wargame, while more secret developments can be thrown in against the vast array of simulated and real Soviet radar equipment scattered over the exhaustive Northern Tonopah part of the ranges. The USAF operates a dozen or so MiG-21 'Fishbeds' and some three surviving MiG-23 'Flogger' Soviet fighter-bombers which, alongside a number of Warsaw Pact radars, were swapped for Phantoms with Egypt under the Camp David agreement or captured over the years by the Americans and their allies.*

Further along the development chain, and based back at Eglin AFB, is the 'Combat Echo' 4485th FWS, equipped with three RF-4Cs and ten F-4Es. As their organizational name suggests, this team concentrates its efforts on correcting weapons and sensors quirks in a follow-on mode in support of combat-ready squad-rons, an evolving series of evaluations and revaluations that occur throughout a system's operational life cycle. Gone are the days when a weapon or sensor always performed as advertised, regardless of who used it or wherever it was employed. Modern military 'strap-ons' are so sophisticated that changes to tactics or minor alterations in production models may cause unexpected malfunctions, degrading accuracy or performance below an acceptable minimum level, so the Combat Echo group rewrites operating procedures, re-programmes software or re-tailors hardware in order to solve any such hiccups. This includes teaching new tactics on the use of modified weapons and sensors to selected emissaries from operational combat squad-rons – which is the main reason why the Echo unit is permitted to use such large quantities of live ammunition.

Combat Echo air-to-ground trials are performed under the auspices of the Eglin TAWC Director, while air-to-air support trials are conducted at the nearby Tyndall Air Defense Weapons Center, where the participating crews can take advantage of the huge air combat range out over the Gulf of Mexico, the preparatory hunting ground for all new air defence pilots.

*In much the same way, it is highly probable that the Soviets have assembled at least one Phantom from all the components retrieved from downed aircraft in South-East Asia and the Middle East. Sensitive aircraft like the F-4G carry extensive self-destruct equipment to burn up the electronic gear. (A Hawaii Guard F-4C carried big red stars for a short while, during the filming of an episode of the TV detective series *Magnum*, in which a Soviet pilot 'defected' to Hickam AFB.)

Below: The strange, fan-like device protruding from the F-4B's drag 'chute door is the Sanders AN/ALQ-140 Multibrick infra-red countermeasures system, a highly classified device. Interest in IRCM has been renewed in the light of recent combat experience in the Lebanon and Libya. (Sanders)

Transition

It was a cool but emotional day at Torrejon AB, twenty miles east of Madrid, Spain. The ceremonial colours were posted and both the Spanish and American National Anthems were played. Maj. Jim Shope, narrator for the resident USAFE's 401st TFW, greeted the dignitaries over the public address system, then guided the assembled crowd through the ensuing events of the salute:

> If you will look to your right you will see a flight of four F-4Ds from the 613th Tactical Fighter Squadron, commanded by Lt. Col. Jim Evans, entering the flight pattern. The 613th will be the last squadron to convert to the F-16 and will hold down the Wing's operational mission until the last possible time before converting. Here at Torrejon for almost thirteen years . . . as the F-4s pass by us in fingertip formation and depart to the east, we are watching the passing of a proud era at Torrejon AB.
>
> If you will look to your right again, you will see a flight of four F-16 Fighting Falcons from the 612th Tactical Fighter Squadron commanded by Lt. Col. Chuck Coleman entering the flight pattern. The 612th is the first squadron to convert, followed by the 614th, presently in training.

After more than a decade of flying the F-4, on 5 February 1983, the 401st formally waved goodbye to its Phantoms.

A similar, end-of-an-era ceremony was held at Luke AFB, under the Arizona sun, three days earlier. Another long-time F-4 Wing, the 58th TFTW took on the job of Phantom crew training in 1971, and, by 1975, there were no fewer than 85 F-4Cs assigned to the base, all brightly decorated with 'high-viz' training stripes. By the time the programme had ended in November 1982, with the last F-4C departing to serve with the California ANG at March AFB, Luke had qualified more than 3,200 pilots and WSOs. The first F-16s, newly coded 'LF', arrived on 6 December, paving the way for a new aircraft and mission for the 58th in the 1980s. These two formal switch-overs represented just the tip of a melting iceberg: throughout the second half of the 1970s, front-line F-4 strength ran down rapidly, as Phantoms were passed on to the ANG and AFRES.

Attrition
Combat losses and peacetime attrition also contributed to the front-line reductions. Four hundred and fifty-one USAF Phantoms were lost to hostile fire in South-East Asia between 1965 and 1973,* while losses

---

*Figure based on DoD OASD (Comptroller) of 17 October 1973.

Right: 401st TFW F-4D-31-MC 66-7735, based at Torrejon AB, Spain, was one of seventy Phantoms relinquished in favour of F-16s in 1983. (USAFE)

Below: One of the biggest F-4 units in the 1970s was Luke's 58th TFTW, which had some 85 C models on strength. This example, from the 310th TFTS, has a dark green fin cap and carries an inert AIM-9J Sidewinder training round. F-4C 63-7420, the fifteenth to be built, started its Air Force career in 1964 with the MacDill-based 4453rd Combat Crew Training Wing in Florida and ended it with the Texas Guard, at Ellington ANGB, which is giving up its F-4Cs in favour of newer fighters. (USAF photo by Ken Hackman)

USAF F-4/RF-4 LOSSES TO HOSTILE FIRE, SOUTH-EAST ASIA, 1965–73

Location	1965	1966	1967	1968	1969	1970	1971	1972	1973
S. Vietnam	2	5	15	24	19	6	3	11	–
N. Vietnam	10	38	77	43	1	3	–	56	–
Laos	–	6	9	13	45	26	22	9	1
Cambodia	–	–	–	–	–	–	2	–	3
Thailand	–	–	–	–	–	–	1	1	–
Totals	12	49	101	80	65	35	28	77	4

Note: Grand total of 451 includes aircraft lost to rocket and mortar attacks on bases but excludes 67 lost in operational accidents.

to accidents, averaging out at a dozen aircraft a year, began to eat into stocks after the production of new aircraft had ceased in 1976. This was accelerated by the disposal of USAF assets overseas: Spain received 44 surplus Phantoms in the early 1970s; South Korea, in addition to 36 ex-USAF F-4Ds which they purchased over a decade ago, have recently received 30 more as attrition replacements; Egypt received 36 F-4Es in 1979 under Operation 'Peace Pharaoh', part of President Carter's pledge to Egypt within the Camp David settlement; and Turkey, who were originally scheduled to receive some of Egypt's Phantoms (no longer up for resale), have, subject to Congressional approval, been allocated fifteen USAF F-4Es to fill the gap. Another 80 F-4Es are currently on offer to Greece and Turkey to bolster NATO's southern flank. Follow-up transactions are certain to be approved over the next few years, and several countries are already weighing up the prospect of obtaining surplus American machines.

To date, over 300 F-4s have been given, exchanged

Below: F-4D-28-MC 65-0710 makes for the runway at its 'home drome', Bentwaters, England, in 1977. The aircraft later served with the 401st TFW in Spain. (MAP)

or sold to foreign countries directly from USAF stocks. Taking attrition, foreign disposals and Vietnam combat losses as a whole, USAF numbers have been reduced by over 1,000 machines, to leave just 500 in front-line, active service. USAFE exemplifies this trend most clearly. In 1975, at peak F-4 strength, all but one Wing flew the Phantom – nine Wings and an additional squadron. By comparison, USAFE strength today adds up to a mere four squadrons, with more on their way out. PACAF was an all-F-4 force until 1979, flying ten squadrons; today, only five squadrons remain. TAC, home-based in the Continental United States, has experienced a drastic reduction in full-time numbers: since 1976, there has been a net loss of over a dozen squadrons.

Ready Team

Of course, every front-line air force needs to modernize at regular intervals. In the case of the USAF, this re-equipment programme, known as Ready Tactical Enhancement and Modernization (Ready Team), has been the driving philosophy behind the massive F-4 reductions. Three aircraft types have been principally responsible for ousting the Phantom from active duty service: McDonnell's successor to the F-4, the versatile F-15 Eagle air superiority fighter, first delivered in November 1974; General Dynamics' nimble and lightweight swing-role 'electric jet' companion, the F-16 Fighting Falcon, joining operational units in November 1978; and Fairchild Republic's tank-busting A-10A Thunderbolt II, affectionately referred to as the 'Warthog' and delivered between 1976 and 1984. While production of the A-10A has now ceased, with over 630 remaining on the inventory, F-15s and F-16s are emerging from the assembly factories in Missouri and Texas in increased numbers. Just under two thousand of these fighters are operational, and production will

Above: An ex-479th TFW, George-based F-4E languishes in the Rosamund, California, scrap-yard in 1972 after being written off in a training accident. (MAP)

continue through to at least 1992, by which time the USAF should have taken delivery of a staggering 3,000 Eagles and Fighting Falcons. As more of these jets become available, Phantom numbers will dwindle further. More significantly, the year 1988 will see the F-16 eclipse the F-4 numerically.

A similar procedure has cut US Navy and Marine Corps strength from a delivery total of 1,313 Phantoms to, by August 1985, a mere 248 aircraft, with complete phase-out scheduled well ahead of the USAF. In common with Spain, who was never totally happy with its WRCS-less F-4Cs, the Navy forces are upgrading to McDonnell Douglas/Northrop F/A-18 Hornets. The F-4 has had to suffer the indignity of an advertisement campaign whose copy states 'Move over Phantom!' The F-4 community at McDonnell Douglas, though mindful of the enormous value behind F-15 and F/A-18 sales, has managed to shed the odd tear. Their catch-phrase of the 1970s, 'Phabulous Phantoms Phorever', has been revised, with their 'phamous phigure' peering through a telescope into the distance and adding 'Well, almost phorever'.

As Maj. Jim Shope made clear in his narrative, USAF's Ready Team machinery has a dual purpose – not just to modernize the Air Force with new fighters, but to do so without any serious repercussions on operational availability rates during the actual changeovers; after all, TAC's motto proclaims 'Readiness is our profession'. This is achieved by inflating a Wing undergoing conversion. By moving in extra ground crew and other support personnel to keep the base up

to strength, whole squadrons, one at a time, are freed to rotate back to the USA to undergo retraining. This way, gradually working through the entire Wing, the second F-4 squadron disbands for retraining when the first achieves 85 per cent (C1) combat-ready status with their new aircraft, and so on, so that the Wing is always able to call on at least two mission-ready squadrons. On average, about 40 per cent of the F-4 air crews transition to the Wing's new fighter, while the remainder of the crews are made up from instructors (usually without a previous fighter tour), pilots from other postings and LIFT graduates. Re-forming as cohesive units at the conversion base, squadrons often return with their new mounts in rapid, successive waves, so that 20–30 F-4s are displaced from the Wing in a matter of hours! Before Ready Team, whole Wings were declared C4 (non-deployable and less than 55 per cent ready), as they gradually worked up to C1

WELL ALMOST PHOREVER

Phabulous Phantoms Phorever

status with their new aircraft over a period of time, often leaving a gaping hole in front-line strength that lasted as long as a year.

There has had to be a bit of crew 'juggling'. The front-line fighters replacing the strictly two-man F-4s are all single-seaters – the twin-seat 'tubs' found at operational F-15 and F-16 bases are used for Stan/Eval and visitor-orientation flights, while only one twin-seat A-10 was ever built. From the active Air Force point of view, this has been a positive bonus. The surplus of back-seat WSOs has created an inordinately high level of rear-seat maturity in those few remaining active F-4 squadrons, providing these largely specialist units with a high level of expertise and professionalism. Looked at from the other angle, the Guard and AFRES did not have enough air crew on hand to fill the seats of the hand-me-down Phantoms – they were converting from a predominant number of single-seat F-100D Super Sabres, F-102A Delta Daggers, F-105B/D Thunderchiefs and F-106A Delta Darts.* To fill the slots, massive liaison with the active service had to be maintained, while the ANG undertook its own increase in air crew recruitment. This included canvassing ex-active Air Force crews, several of whom were eager to resume flying jet fighters after a lull of several years. Promising new candidates up to the age of 30 were also given the opportunity to train as navigator/WSOs.

While there are always enough volunteers to fill the spaces, the time delays incurred in training sufficient people has created some friction in the cogs, so that the reservists cannot wholeheartedly adopt the Ready Team procedure. The situation is further complicated because, with one or two exceptions, the part-timers cannot be deployed as a collective squadron for retraining. Annual 'Summer Camp' training periods are far too short for newcomers to cram in all the skills required to fly or maintain an aircraft as complex as the F-4. However, rather than reverting to the old method of declaring a unit non-deployable, disbanding their equipment, and getting them gradually to work up to C1 status with new aircraft over an eighteen-month cycle, the units stay operational on a number of their old types, while small groups of personnel undergo complete, conversion, or requalification training at dedicated reservist F-4 training centres. Today, these bases include McConnell in Kansas, Kingsley Field in Oregon and Boise in Idaho. Here, trainees are put on temporary duty (TDY) full-time assignment, as if they were mobilized for action, providing the necessary time in which to adapt to their new mission and aircraft. This involves carefully agreed arrangements with employers, and is aided by the fact that several air crews have active-duty experience with the same model Phantoms – sometimes the same aircraft! Type-to-type F-4 conversion is conducted in a similar fashion and, as several Guard crews commented, the process may initially involve 'downgrading'. Many officers flying F-4Cs or F-4Ds have combat experience in the F-4E. Lt. Michael Braun from the Texas ANG similarly noted that because so

many of the Guard crews do have prior active-duty experience, upgrading as more F-4Es become available 'would come very smoothly' – though the 'would' as opposed to 'will' hints that he, like many other part-timers, have set their sights and hopes on newer F-15s and F-16s.

Once the initial batches of air crews have gone through their re-training programmes, they in turn act as instructors for the remainder of their unit, helping to wean them off 'Century Series' jets and four-engined 'heavies' and introducing them to the more functional F-4s as they return from the basic conversion centres. Typically, each reserve squadron or Group manages 20–26 mission-ready F-4s. Ground crew re-train with four F-4s pre-positioned for this purpose and, like the air crew, convert to the Phantom in larger numbers as more aircraft become available.

The time lost in reserve transition has been reduced from over a year and a half down to a double-aircraft overlap cycle of between six months and a year. The actual time taken depends on the condition of the aircraft at the time of hand-over. Many F-4s undergo extensive preparatory work before their reassignment by spending upwards of $100,000 on each aircraft to get them primed for immediate use. This includes either a PDM overhaul, or a PMI checkout at the former operating base, subject to whether any technical modifications are due, and the number of hours clocked up since the last major 'medical'. The remainder of the forces take their aircraft as they come. Some are signed for in very poor condition, in several cases 'hangar queens' which have been merely patched up for despatch to the Guard. The often tatty paintwork after a couple of years' hard front-line flying just adds to the crew chiefs' anguish! But sheer devotion enables the ground crews to bring the F-4s methodically up to operational status within 3–5 months.

The Phantom has done much to boost Guard and AFRES fighting power, but the aircraft does have its critics. TSgt. Leland H. Weppler from the California Guard noted that 'the F-4D is not a popular aircraft at the Fresno ANGB. We had hoped to convert to a newer-generation fighter, and the noisy F-4 has severely compounded our community relations efforts; aside from some Weapons Systems Officers, favourable comments are hard to come by'. The novelty of the Phantom wore off fast at many bases, whose crews dream of old days with the F-105 'Thud', F-101 'One O-Wonder' or sleek F-106 'Dart', or who relish the possibility of acquiring new or recently built bubble-canopied 'Teenagers', as the F-15 and F-16 have become popularly known. Ironically, many of the Guard units that received F-4s only did so because their ground and air crewman skills were so great that higher authority deemed that they were best qualified to cope with the irksome beast, freeing units with less good maintenance records to upgrade to easy-to-

*The exception to the rule was the McDonnell F-101B/F Voodoo, a twin-seat interceptor. All ex-F-101B/F operators went on to fly F-4s in the air defence mission, though the Minnesota Guard had a brief affair with RF-4Cs.

ervice F-16s. There is a certain degree of bitterness involved. As compensation top F-4 units such as those at Georgia, Hawaii and Louisiana are receiving F-15s. Nevertheless most experienced crews, well-versed in the harsh realities of the climate in Europe and the mugginess of the Orient, have fostered a deep respect for the F-4's trusty all-weather performance, and the eventual departure of the Phantom will cause more than few tears to trickle down the cheeks of the weathered faces of the Air Force's veteran crew chiefs.

Future changes

As the 1980s roll on, more and more Phantoms will be displaced as 'Teenager' production picks up under multi-year procurement. Accordingly, the last three quadrons of F-4Cs will be phased out by FY90, with the few remaining F-4Ds following soon after. Active units will maintain their hunter-killer F-4Es as long as the ARN-101 F-4Es hold their important edge over the F-16; but several new factors are coming into play, upon which TAC HQ has placed high hopes, designed to bolster the F-16's capability.

First there is the Hughes AIM-120 Advanced Medium Range Air-to-Air Missile (AMRAAM). This is the NATO-wide replacement for the faithful Sparrow, with one supreme advantage over its predecessor: whereas Sparrow relies on target 'painting' by the launch aircraft's radar, AMRAAM, after being set on course by the launch aircraft, uses its own inertial mid-course guidance and independent active radar seeker to provide a 'fire and forget' target-tracking and homing capability. Furthermore, unlike salvoed Sparrows, which all glide to the same target, ripple-fired AMRAAMs can be despatched for a multiple kill, with each one earmarked for a different target. Before AMRAAM, there was a lot of concern over the replacement of front-line F-4Es in PACAF and USAFE with F-16s because the Fighting Falcons were unable to engage enemy aircraft at stand-off ranges using Sparrow – their radar simply did not have the facility

to 'paint' the targets. AMRAAM changes the balance (boosting F-16 air combat capability by a factor of six, claim Hughes), and Block 25 AMRAAM-4 F-16s, with their magnificent manoeuvrability and improved track-while-scan APG-68 radars, will be able to provide a highly capable replacement. Additionally, some 400 Block 15 APG-66 radar-equipped F-16 'Plus' models currently in service are AMRAAM compatible. The only catch is that AMRAAM IOC has already been put back to 1989, three years late, and may be delayed further.

The second factor is the Martin Marietta Low Altitude Navigation Targeting Infra-Red for Night (LANTIRN) system, an automated, dual-pod package designed as a quick 'strap-on' for the F-15 and F-16 to give them the same night-time attack capabilities as the DMAS/Pave Tack F-4s. By combining a target-searching FLIR, laser rangefinder, laser marker and terrain-following radar with Marconi's advanced head-up display (HUD), LANTIRN makes the one-man fighter a creditable night-fighting machine. Critics argue that the automation does not adequately reduce the pilot's workload to a safe level, and that only the twin-seat variants should be used for the LANTIRN mission. In any event, the USAF intends to buy enough sets to equip some 700 jets, including the sophisticated twin-seat F-15E Strike Eagle – a worthy successor to the ARN-101 F-4. The final boost for the little Falcon is Shrike ARM capability, with QRC tests underway at China Lake in an effort to re-equip the F-16 as a fully-fledged team-mate for the F-4G-led hunter-killer Wings. LANTIRN- and Shrike-equipped Falcons will start displacing ARN-101 F-4Es on a one-for-one basis from 1987.

The replacement of the reconnaissance RF-4C and

USAF F-4 UNIT CHANGES

CONVERSIONS

Unit	Base	Command	From	To	Date	Tail-code
8th TFW	Kunsan AB, South Korea	PACAF	F-4D	F-16	1981	WP
18th TFW	Kadena AB, Okinawa	PACAF	F-4C/D	F-15	1980	ZZ
21st TFW	Elmendorf/Eielson, Alaska	AAF	F-4E	F-15, A-10	1982	FC/AK
31st TTW	Homestead AFB, Florida	TAC	F-4D	F-16	1986	ZF
32nd TFS	Soesterberg, Holland	USAFE	F-4E	F-15	1978	CR
33rd TFW	Eglin AFB, Florida	TAC	F-4E	F-15	1979	EG
36th TFW	Bitburg, AB, West Germany	USAFE	F-4E	F-15	1977	BT
48th TFW	Lakenheath, UK	USAFE	F-4D	F-111F	1977	LN
49th TFW	Holloman AFB, New Mexico	TAC	F-4D	F-15	1977	HO
50th TFW	Hahn AB, West Germany	USAFE	F-4E	F-16	1981	HR
56th TFW	MacDill AFB, Florida	TAC	F-4D	F-16	1979	MC
57th FIS	Keflavik AB, Iceland	ADTAC	F-4E	F-15	1986	–/IS
58th TTW	Luke AFB, Arizona	TAC	F-4C	F-16	1983	LA/LF
81st TFW	Bentwaters/Woodbridge, UK	USAFE	F-4D	A-10	1980	WR
86th TFW	Ramstein AB, West Germany	USAFE	F-4E	F-16	1986	RS
363rd TRW	Shaw AFB, South Carolina	TAC	RF-4C	F-16	1982	JO/SW
388th TFW	Hill AFB, Utah	TAC	F-4D	F-16	1978	HL
401st TFW	Torrejon AB, Spain	USAFE	F-4D	F-16	1983	TJ
474th TFW	Nellis AFB, Nevada	TAC	F-4D	F-16	1980	NA

REDUCTIONS

Unit	Base	Command	Aircraft	Sqns. lost	Date	Tail-code
10th TRW	Alconbury, UK	USAFE	RF-4C	30th TRS, 32nd TRS,	1976	AR
				1st TRS	1987	
26th TRW	Zweibrucken AB, West Germany	USAFE	RF-4C	17th TRS	1978	ZR
35th TTW	George AFB, California	TAC	F-4E	39th TFS	1984	GA
57th FWW	Nellis AFB, Nevada	TAC	F-4E	414th FWIC, 422nd TES	1985	WA

GAINS

Unit	Base	Command	Aircraft	Sqns. gained	Date	Tail-code
37th TFW	George AFB, California	TAC	F-4G	561st TFS, 562nd TFTS, 563rd TFS	1981	WW
67th TRW	Bergstrom AFB, Texas	TAC	RF-4C	45th TRTS, 62nd TRTS	1982	BA
347th TFW	Moody AFB, Georgia	TAC	F-4E	68th TFS, 70th TFS, 339th TFS	1976	MY

Note: The 18th TFW and newly redesignated 363rd TFW continue to operate a squadron of RF-4Cs each. Moody's 339th TFS has been redesignated the 69th TFS.

Wild Weasel F-4G is an entirely different matter. These two aircraft are in a class of their own and, at present, there is no available substitute which can compete with them in terms of mission gear and performance. Plans are afoot to upgrade several RF-4C squadrons to special Block 25 RF-16D twin-seat 'Foto Falcons', which will carry a reconnaissance cupola containing advanced CAI optical cameras, Loral synthetic aperture radar and Texas Instruments passive infra-red sensing technology. TAC envisages buying enough cupolas to fit up to 400 Foto Falcons, though the bulk of the RF-4C force will remain on the active list well into the 1990s, on special assignments.

Replacing the F-4G is also unlikely to take place until at least 1995, and plans to convert another eighteen F-4Es to F-4G standard have already been put into full swing. The first new delivery from Ogden, F-4G 69-0305, was handed over to George's 'SAM-busters' on 12 June 1987, providing a further lease of life for this 'King of Phantoms'. Several alternatives are being studied as possible long-term replacements: the F-16 was favoured at one time, but the most likely candidate appears to be a derivative of the twin-seat F-15E Strike Eagle. Corporate-sponsored tests have been carried out in St. Louis using an F-15B with a chin fairing, ideal for housing the APR-45 or its successor, though funding restrictions are likely to delay replacement until the turn of the century.

But plans are often fickle, subject·to changes in budget, and some recent ones have caused considerable anxiety among the reserve forces. Originally, pending the introduction of the updated models of the 'Teenagers', F-4 strength was destined to remain relatively static as production aircraft were to be fed into newly formed Wings so that the USAF could expand and achieve its goal of 27 active and thirteen reserve fighter Wings by the early 1990s. Budget cuts have delayed expansion. Instead, the USAF now aims to phase early model F-16s into the reserves to replace F-4s at a faster pace than scheduled originally – at a rate of about 150 aircraft annually – leaving just the special F-4 teams in forward locations, and a modest number of 'long-nosed' variants with the Guard and AFRES. The balance (the F-4Ds in particular) are destined to travel one way to the Davis-Monthan open air military storage and reclamation depot in Arizona, where they will lie wastefully derelict until broken up for scrap metal, butchered from time to time to provide cheap spares for foreign operators. Yet the whole course of events may take another very different turn: the 'Rhino' has a way of charging through obstacles, adapting to new technology and requirements.

Reserve Strike

America's independence was founded upon her militia, so it comes as no surprise that today, 200 years later, the USAF auxiliaries, the Air National Guard and Air Force Reserve, are maintained as two of the strongest links in the nation's defence. No fewer than 32 such squadrons operate Phantoms, sixteen of which are dedicated to ground attack – a sizeable force by international standards, overshadowing most major foreign air arms, and one which provides a vital sixth of TAC's CAS and interdiction muscle.

Although quasi-independent in peacetime, and partly funded by their home state (to which they owe considerable allegiance – though one shudders to think of the potential applications of a supersonic fighter-bomber to local emergencies!), the ANG forces are subordinate to TAC, their 'gaining Command'. Within 48hrs of alert notice, Maj. Gen. John B. Conaway's Guardsmen would drop pens and other professional paraphernalia, strap into their aircraft, and be deployed from their home bases according to TAC's 9th or 12th Air Force plans. The AFRES, too, used to fall within this procedure, but on 1 May 1983 the organization changed from such a Direct Reporting Unit (DRU) to a Separate Operating Agency (SOA); accordingly, in the event of a crisis, TAC HQ would field Gen. John Taylor's own 10th AF (AFRES) F-4s alongside the full-time Air Forces.

This constant state of readiness in both the ANG and AFRES is a reflection of the 'Total Force' concept, due recognition that the reservists are far more than 'weekend warriors'. A significant proportion of them have previous experience in the active forces – 30 per cent of the air crews flew combat missions in South-East Asia – with the result that some have as much as four times the number of hours on the F-4 than their less experienced active colleagues. Coupled to this high experience level, the Guard and AFRES effervesce with unit identity. The comparatively small size of their outfits makes them highly cohesive, close-knit fighting units. Despite their civilian commitments, the reservists nearly always far exceed the minimum number of flight hours required, and further compensate by concentrating their efforts on just one or two major tasks. Active air crews may perform ground attack, air defence and maritime operations, together with a whole host of mundane administrative jobs essential to an operational base, so that it is not uncommon for a Guard or AFRES crew actually to clock more time in a specific strike mission. USAF exercises and competitions often see the so-called 'part-timers' thrash their full-time *confrères* and fly away from the meets with the cup.

Below: A cluster of F-4Cs gathers around a KC-135A Stratotanker for 'jet-juice'. All the aircraft are from the Arkansas Guard, the F-4Cs from the 188th TFG. (ANG)

AIR NATIONAL GUARD AND AFRES F-4 STRIKE UNITS

Unit	Wing/ Group	Base	Configuration	Capability (see key)	Tail markings
113th TFS	181st TFG	Terra Haute, Indiana	F-4C	V	HF
184th TFS	188th TFG	Fort Smith, Arkansas	F-4C	V	Arkansas
196th TFS	163rd TFG	March AFB, California	F-4C	V	California
89th TFS	906th TFG	Wright-Patterson AFB, Ohio	F-4D	M	DO*
93rd TFS	482nd TFW	Homestead AFB, Florida	F-4D	M	FM*
121st TFS	113th TFW	Andrews AFB, Maryland	F-4D	P	DC
127th TFS 177th TFTS	184th TFG	McConnell AFB, Kansas	F-4D	V, P	'Jayhawks'
160th TFS	187th TFG	Montgomery, Alabama	F-4D	P	AL
170th TFS	183rd TFG	Springfield, Illinois	F-4D	M	SI
457th TFS	301st TFW	Carswell AFB, Texas	F-4D	L	TH†
465th TFS	507th TFG	Tinker AFB, Oklahoma	F-4D	M	SH†
704th TFS	924th TFG	Bergstrom AFB, Texas	F-4D	L	TX†
110th TFS	131st TFW	Saint Louis, Missouri	F-4E	P	SL
141st TFS	108th TFW	McGuire AFB, New Jersey	F-4E	P	NJ
163rd TFS	122nd TFW	Fort Wayne, Indiana	F-4E	P	FW

Key: M = Maverick only; P = Pave Spike and Maverick capable; L = Loran D Pave Phantoms, with Pave Spike and Maverick capability; V = 'Vanilla', with no special capability.
*To F-16 FY88. †To ARN-101 F-4E FY89.

'Jayhawks'

The first of the ANG strike units to convert to Phantoms was the 170th TFS, 183rd TFG, at Springfield, Illinois, which began its transition from ancient Republic F-84F Thunderstreaks to F-4Cs on 31 January 1972, drawing aircraft from active stocks at George AFB. Since then, the Guard's strike-Phantom contingent has expanded to eleven squadrons, three of whom are at the moment getting to grips with the gun-equipped F-4E, breaking the active force's monopoly on the type after some eighteen years of uninterrupted front-line service.*

The AFRES commenced its transition to Phantoms six and a half years later, starting on 1 October 1978 with the 93rd TFS 'Makos' (more commonly known as 'The Humping Boys from Homestead', with reference to its base thirty miles south of Miami on the tip of Florida). Commanded by Lt. Col. D. M. McDowell, the 93rd's lengthy transition from majestic EC-121s to F-4Cs was finally completed in 1981. Four more AFRES Phantom units followed suit over the next two years, all equipping with F-4Ds, including a brand new Group in Ohio, the 906th TFG 'Buckeye Phantoms', which worked up to mission-ready status with its new mounts at Wright-Patterson AFB during the course of 1983. To complete the transition, that summer the 'Makos' traded in its F-4Cs for WRCS-equipped aircraft, standardizing the AFRES Phantom force around the superior F-4D.

To keep the reserves fully crewed, complete courses are provided by the 18th TFG, Kansas ANG.† Located at McConnell AFB just outside Wichita, the 184th 'Jayhawks' have the distinction of being one of the largest Phantom units, with some 57 F-4Ds present at the base. Camouflage schemes chequer the base in carnival fashion: given the dramatic changes to decor in recent years, the flight lines are dotted with Vietnam wrap-around, 'European 1', Hill Gray I and II, and even glossy ADC grey machines! The 'Jayhawks' run two, quite different squadrons which pool these Phantoms, the 127th TFS and 177th TFTS, both of which are assuming greater importance as the auxiliaries become the focus for Phantom operations.

Below: A 184th TFG 'Jayhawks' F-4D, nicknamed 'Lips III', on the ramp at McConnell AFB, Kansas. The aircraft is F-4D-30-MC 66-7553. (Kansas ANG photo by TSgt. Genelle Clifton)

Prior to 1984 the 184th's only squadron was the 127th TFS, the largest fighter squadron in the Western world with over forty F-4Ds. Handling the conversion of all new Guard strike air crews while maintaining a deployable force on standby, the unit grew in size until it was split into the two components. According to Maj. Mike 'Crash' Cassidy, Instructor Weapons Systems Operator (IWSO) with the 'Jayhawks', the unit eventually decided to use the new squadron designation 177 for the TFTS because 'it has no history and we felt it apropos that we create the history ourselves!' Looking to the future, the 184th TFG

Below: A close-up photograph of F-4D number 553's nose-gear door artwork. (Kansas ANG photo by TSgt. Genelle Clifton)

Above: A 170th TFS, 183rd TFG Illinois Guard F-4D-31-MC (66-7725), a Maverick-capable Phantom. The aircraft is painted in 'Hill Gray II' decor with matching grey 'SI', serial number and state logo on the fin. (MAP)

exudes self-confidence. A recent USAF inspection team rates the 'Jayhawks' as best Replacement Training Unit (RTU) school in TAC.‡

The 177th TFTS's complete 'BG' training course for new lieutenants lasts some six months, putting pilots through an average of 63 sorties, WSOs through a testing 57 sorties, and both through 250hrs of academics plus 45hrs on part-task trainers and simulators. The 177th TFTS turns out top-quality F-4C/E crews as well as flyers for the sizeable F-4D community, the returning novices going through 'slat' and related training after returning to their home unit. It also provides 'CG' 'requal' and 'IG' instructor courses, as needed: 'The CG course is generally for a guy who already has fighter experience and is getting "qualed" in the F-4 for the first time or used to fly the F-4 but has been out of the cockpit for a while'. 'Standard' transition training puts pilots through seventeen sorties and WSOs through twelve, while the refresher 'transition only' course requires an average of six sorties. The actual hours flown vary considerably with crew skill,

---

*By 1984, fifteen F-4C/D squadrons had formed, but four have since left the Phantom fraternity and moved on to 'Teenagers' – Georgia, Louisiana, Vermont and San Antonio, Texas.
†Complete courses were also supplied by TAC: Luke's 58th TFTW handled F-4C crews, and Homestead's 31st TTW F-4D training. Both Wings have since re-equipped with F-16s.
‡A new RTU, the 161st TFS, is due to form with F-16s shortly, and will operate alongside the Phantoms.

Top: 'Naughty Lady', the nose-gear artwork of Kansas F-4D-31-MC 66-7772, assigned to pilot Capt. Ed McIlhenny and IWSO Maj. 'Crash' Cassidy. The crew chief is Bill Hayden: 'A good jet and a good crew chief!' reports Maj. Cassidy. (Kansas ANG photo by TSgt. Genelle Clifton)

Above: More Kansas nose-gear door artwork, this time belonging to 65-0798 and reading 'Kansas Crop Duster – KANG Pest Control'! (Kansas ANG photo by TSgt. Genelle Clifton)

Below: A glossy grey Kansas F-4D nicknamed 'Dragon Lady', a name more commonly associated with the U-2/TR-1. (Kansas ANG photo by TSgt. Genelle Clifton)

and the programmes are flexible enough to cope with differing abilities. The bulk of the 'Jayhawks' Phantoms are 'vanilla' F-4Ds, and these ably meet the basic course requirements. Objectives include handling, operating procedures, instruments, tacan navigation and ILS approaches to the field, radar, formation-flying (including two-ship take-offs and landings), aerial refuelling, and low-altitude target ingress, with the emphasis on standard air-to-air and air-to-surface doctrines – air intercepts, air combat training, and ground attacks in 'pop-up' and 'curvilinear' attack profiles, using Sparrow and Sidewinder air-to-air missile simulators (inert rounds with active seekers) and BDU training bombs.

Experienced instructor crews are highly skilled in their art and over the years have developed many of their own special tactics. WSOs, in particular, have developed integrated modes of attack to exploit fully the Phantom's true potential. In Kansas the 'Jayhawks' centre ground attack modes around a handful of flexible options: 'dive–toss', offset, dive-bombing, loft-bombing, and low-altitude bombing and strafe. Integrating 'special' equipment with the basic WRCS permits flexibility, and choice during the attack phase – the 'Wizzo's capability in furnishing the attack computers with accurate co-ordinates, target elevation and cursor alignment preparatory to a visual attack being crucial. Failing this, pilots became adept at 'popping-up' just in time to gain good target acquisition, initial designation and drift-assisted sight realignment with minimum exposure. Undergraduates at McConnell have teamwork moulded into them at a very early stage, with IWSOs instructing a significant portion of pilot as well as WSO academics, part-task and simulator training, as well as keeping an eye on things during the flying phases from the back seat. Instructor Pilots (IPs) teach their apprentices how to be potential 'MiG-killers', working hard on aggressive, tactical air combat while demonstrating how not to get into trouble with some of the F-4's idiosyncratic handling characteristics. A limited amount of 'Wizzo' aircraft handling, moreover, is a useful if unofficial part of the training which the more experienced and wiser F-4 pilots encourage: should the pilot become incapacitated, there is a set of controls in the back, and it is the navigator who is going to have to get the aircraft home!

The total student flow is quite large, with a new class of 10–15 junior officers showing up approximately every six weeks. What this means is that, in the period just prior to one class graduating, the IPs and IWSOs have to cope with four RTU classes simultaneously. Because of these demands, and because of the complexity of the Phantom, the 'Jayhawks', in stark contradiction to the Guard's tradition, are composed almost entirely of full-timers, including no fewer than 55 of the 63 IPs and 25 of the 27 IWSOs.

The mission of the 127th TFS is arguably even more important. With the shut-down of the active-duty, Nellis-based 414th F-4 Fighter Weapons Instructor Course (FWIC) in 1985, the Kansas Guard assumed

'JAYHAWKS' TRAINING COURSES

Type	Duration	Pilots Academic (hrs)	Training devices (hrs)	Flying (sorties/hrs)	WSOs Academic (hrs)	Training devices (hrs)	Flying (sorties/hrs)
F4000BG: Complete training for new lieutenants	11 ground training + 109 flying training days	249.3	45.8	63/80.8	250.3	44.5	57/73.4
F4000CG: 'Requal' for ex-F-4 pilots	Transition only: 7 ground training + 10 flying training days	50.2	16.8	6/9.9	–	–	–
F4000CG: Conversion training for fighter crews	Standard course: 7 ground training + 28 flying training days	113.8	26.8	17/22.5	117.8	25.5	12/14.1
F400FWS: – FWIC, the 'F-4 doctorate'	102 calendar days/78 training days	280	2	54/57.6	280	2	54/57.6
F4000WT: Tactical Leadership Programme	12 calendar days	51	1.5	6/7.2	51	1.5	6/7.2

the responsibility of advanced training for both active-duty and reserve officers – all carefully selected candidates with a minimum of two years on fighters, 300hrs on the F-4 and IP- or IWSO-rated. As Maj. Cassidy pointed out, 'The 127th's extremely demanding three month training programme effectively grants its graduates a PhD in tactically employing the F-4'. The 'Phantom doctorate' flying opens up with the air-to-air phase (*à la* 'Top Gun') embracing 27 sorties or 24.5hrs on basic fighter manoeuvres, intercepts and dissimilar air combat training (DACT), then progresses on to the second phase, air-to-surface tactics. Another 27 sorties or 32.2hrs are generated, during which time all aspects of the F-4's delivery systems are aired at the Smoky Hills range and in the Mid-West skies. The 127th TFS makes full use of the Group's limited number of 'smart'-capable F-4Ds. Stores carried vary according to whether the sortie is part of the air-to-air or air-to-ground phases, but during the course of 102 calendar days students are permitted to expend 2,000 chaff and 1,120 flare cartridges, 1,200 rounds of 20mm 'Gatling' gun ammunition, 114 BDU-33 training bombs, 72 high- and low-drag Mk. 82s, 24 live Mk. 82s, four CBU-58 cluster bombs and two inert and two live GBU-12 LGBs, not to mention both a Sparrow

Below: An SUU-23/A gunpod-toting F-4D-28-MC, 65-0710, leads an element of 'Jayhawkers' to the take-off runway at McConnell AFB. (Kansas ANG photo by TSgt. Genelle Clifton)

and Sidewinder air-to-air missile launch – a staggering amount of pyrotechnics!

FWIC undergraduates are continually assessed and must attain at least 80 per cent at written examinations as part of 280hrs' academic training. The grading of observed tests ranges from 'Dangerous'(!) – a fail – up to Grade 4 ('Performance reflects an unusually high degree of ability'). The wash-out rate is negligible, though F-4E pilots have a tougher time in that they must first undergo a 'de-slat' course before embarking on the FWIC, to avoid getting into trouble in the 'Jayhawks' 'hard-wing' Phantoms. Much theoretical combined-team training is included in the syllabus – liaison with EF-111A Ravens, F-4G Wild Weasels, EC-130 Comfy Levi and Compass Call posts, and E-3 AWACS – while air crews must be familiar with systems they may not encounter at an operational level, such as the GBU-15 glide bomb. The philosophy of the course is to expose crews to increasing levels of responsibility so that they eventually develop into skilled tacticians. It works in a 'building-block' manner: 'Crews initially observe briefings and fly the less demanding positions in the flight, but will eventually be expected to lead the most demanding of tactical scenarios'. FWIC graduates go back to their home units to perform duties as weapons and tactics officers, with a specially thought-out instruction plan tailored to the unit's mission, to advance the unit's skills, coach crews in preparation for new systems about to be

Above: F-4D-32-MCs 66-8727 and -8758 utilize Pave Spike laser pods and the Loran D nav-attack package, with its distinctive 'towel bar' atop the dorsal spine. Wing tanks and centreline SUU-23/A 20mm gun pods are also carried. (Texas AFRES photo by TSgt. Melanie A. Kasick)

Right: A Pave Spike-equipped Loran D-mod 'towel bar' Phantom F-4D looking neat and functional, 1981. (Author)

fielded, and sort out problems that may arise with weapons or tactics. The Guard are far better qualified to handle the F-4 FWIC than the active forces. As Maj. Cassidy points out with some pride, 'The 184th TFG is one of the true repositories of F-4 experience and expertise. When I left the active forces in 1979 the WSO's average time on the F-4 was about 860hrs – we considered that quite high. Here at McConnell the average IWSO has over 1,500hrs, with many of us having 2,000hrs on the F-4 alone. I don't know how familiar people are with flying time in jet fighters, but anyone who has 2,000hrs in fighters is *very* experienced, a real "old head".' In April 1985 Lt. Col. Wayne Yarolem from the Indiana Guard established a new milestone by completing 5,000hrs in the Phantom!

The annual itinerary
The actual tasks assigned to the strike components of the Guard and AFRES revolve around CAS ('looking for trouble'), counter-air (denying the enemy his air power), and battlefield area interdiction (BAI), along

and just behind the FEBA, though most squadrons have a secondary air superiority role – 'MiG-hassling', not interception duties – while others perform limited maritime support (TASMO) anti-shipping duties.

Training activities for the Guard and AFRES are identical, and can be classed in three categories, intermittent flying training, Unit Training Assemblies (UTAs), and 'Summer Camp'. General flying training ensures that each crew clocks up the minimum standard of 40 sorties a year. Ground technical specialists and civil service employees, 30 per cent of whom work full-time, help to keep the bases running smoothly to facilitate these random training sorties, usually flown from Tuesdays through to Saturdays. The number of hours flown each month varies from crew to crew, depending on their civilian schedules, the unit schedules and the general unit deployment plans, but just about all air crews are well ahead of the minimum number of hours required.

Team co-ordinated operations are held on one weekend each month, when all crews don uniforms for the UTA and train as an integrated Group, flying to nearby ranges in their home or an adjacent state at a strenuous 300–500ft at 425–500kts, to perfect their basic bombing, rocketry and gunnery skills and to develop tactics with 'smart' weapons. To provide further zest to the UTAs, TAC may spring an Operational Readiness Inspection (ORI), in which chemical and biological warfare protection drill may be practised, forcing crews to dress up in heavy protective clothing and to scrub Phantoms clean after each

mission, adding a difficult but essential factor to the training programme.

To ensure success, the Guard and AFRES ply their trade with precision munitions. All Guard F-4Es are Pave Strike and Maverick capable, while no fewer than 213 F-4Ds are 'smart' – all of these being compatible with Maverick and 88 of them being able to integrate ASQ-153 Pave Spike laser-ranging into their ballistics computer for 'iron' bomb delivery, or to guide LGBs to target. Moreover, 39 of the 'Spike' jets are 'towel bar' Pave Phantoms, which now operate over Texas cattle country. The Loran D updated machines were reassigned to the AFRES in 1981 because of the valuable experience the Texans had already gained in troubleshooting and maintaining the 'T-Stick II/Thud' – a similarly equipped, ARN-92-assisted model of the F-105D which operated at Carswell AFB for much of the 1970s. Keeping the same people well versed with similar systems has paid off: the Texans enjoy high mission-capable rates with their 'towel bar' jets, providing a very useful all-weather bombing capability for the USAF.

The standard mission equipment for the Phantom is made up from a maximum of 13,500lb of assorted rockets, 'iron' and cluster bombs, including the General Electric six-barrelled SUU-16/A or -23/A Vulcan gun pods. Up to two Vulcans at a time can be attached, symmetrically, under the wings, but the big pods are more typically carried on the ventral fuselage centreline in lieu of a 600 US gallon drop tank. The SUU-16 is the earlier of the two models, introduced in

Above: An angry-looking SUU-23/A 20mm 'Gatling' gun pod installed on F-4D-29-MC 66-7466 when serving with the 479th TFW at George AFB. (A. Collishaw via P. Davies)

Below: Sectional drawing of the GPU-5/A gun pod (top) and cutaway view of the SUU-23/A pod (bottom), mounting the GAU-13/A and GAU-4 'Gatling' guns respectively. (General Electric)

Below right: A 131st TFW, Missouri ANG F-4E in the earlier Ghost Gray 'Hill Gray I' camouflage decor, with a red fin cap and an aggressive sharkmouth. Several Missouri Guard F-4E 'drivers' are ex-388th TFW pilots with combat experience in SEA in the 'hard-wing' Phantom. The two MiG kill stars on the splitter plate were gained in 1972 against 'Fishbeds', one of the kills being made by ace Capt. Jeff Feinstein, WSO, on 31 May. (McDonnell Douglas)

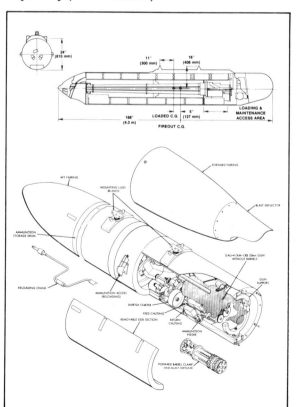

the mid-1960s in response to the pleas from 'MiG-killer jockeys' in South-East Asia (and which subsequently gave the 366th TFW their nickname of 'Gunfighters'), and uses a pop-out ram air turbine generator to provide electrical power for the internal M61A-1 20mm Gatling gun. This model was soon superseded by the SUU-23, which employs the later, more reliable, gas-powered GAU-4 20mm gun. Four of the seven gun barrels have small holes drilled in them, which pass a portion of the cartridge propellant gas back through a piston to drive the barrels. Gun start is effected by an electrical inertia system. A fifth of a second after the firing trigger is pressed, the barrels speed up to spew out 90 rounds a second, spinning up to fire 100 rounds a second as soon as the electrical starter has disengaged. The incredibly high rate of fire creates a loud noise akin to heavy fabric being ripped, but with much more lethal results! To provide added fire power, 20mm gun pods and LAU rocket pods are at present being supplemented by General Electric's GPU-5 GEPOD, a meaty four-barrel 30mm 'Gat' housing a 353-round drum. This model is based on the company's GAU-8A seven-barrelled Avenger gun which lends the A-10A Warthog its famous 'tanks for breakfast' image; their 30mm shells possess the ability to puncture tanks at ranges of up to 1.3nm, or shred 'soft' targets, such as radars or trucks, at distances of more than 2nm.

The combined effect of these rockets and guns when using the Phantom as high-speed airborne artillery pieces, laying down a barrage in support of friendly ground forces, is dramatic. Throwing the enemy into disarray, even momentarily, provides the necessary leeway for friendly ground or vulnerable heliborne forces to reconsolidate, counter-attack or move to more favourable ground. Helicopter gunships are a vital element in modern armies, but there are places where they dare not venture; so the Army and Air Force work together, evolving joint tactics which not only allow both forces to co-operate, but also have a 'force multiplying' effect. Helicopter gunships, with their 'nap-of-the-earth' flying and close-in kill capability can 'take out' the nearby deadly enemy AAA systems, while the Phantoms, with their radar-jamming equipment turned on full for mutual protection against the bigger SAM threats, roll in and pour their bombs, or salvo their rocket and guns, pulverizing the chief opposition with relative impunity. Joint-service CAS tactics take up a major part of the training for Phantom operators, who liaise with the all-essential Forward Air Control (FAC) target-markers.

Finally, there is 'Summer Camp', an annual fifteen-day concentrated training session under which air and ground crews are put on full-time TDY, as if mobilized for action. Summer Camp usually means shifting the fighter squadron and its support personnel to another base – sometimes a bare base in the middle of the American desert, or perhaps a foreign, overseas deployment. Under the Checkered Flag programme, each Guard and AFRES unit is required to deploy

overseas once every three years, to familiarize crews with the European or Pacific terrain and weather conditions and to get acquainted with the rigours of trans-oceanic crossings. Unit commanders visit their foreign co-located base every year to show their faces, familiarize themselves with the locale, and make any necessary preparations for a forthcoming deployment. Alternatively, the Phantom air crews might find themselves taking part in the Kansas Air Guard's Tactical Leadership Program (TLP); pitched against the 'enemy' in the middle of a 'Red' or 'Green Flag' mock battle; or competing at a 'Gunsmoke' ground attack meet.

The TLP is a two-week course modelled along the lines of the NATO six-week TLP held at Jever, West Germany. 'Essentially it's a mini-FWIC but with emphasis on combined, composite mission planning', and includes 51hrs' academics plus six sorties, with considerable input on NATO operating procedures. The Nellis 'Flag' manoeuvres, held in six-week blocks, with participants from the Guard and AFRES deploying for a fourteen-day segment, are designed to put air crews through simulated war, computerized combat training which is so lifelike that crews' nerves get rattled; yet they have the luxury of being able to learn from their mistakes. The basic idea is to get air crews over their all-essential first ten 'combat' mission hurdles in the survival learning game; after this time they refine their tactics, honing their skills, testing the effectiveness of new ideas and fine-tuning 'the three Ts – tactics, training and technology'. A typical 'Red Flag' training sortie is hair-raising for the uninitiated: a simple bombing mission may involve tangling with Northrop F-5E Tiger II 'Aggressors', providing valu-able air combat experience against dissimilar aircraft types, coping with the simulated AAA and SAMs 'illuminating the radar warning scopes like a Christmas tree', and demanding spontaneous decisive action, and then, to top it all, co-ordinating with friendly C^{3}I aircraft – a very busy affair.

Biennial Nellis 'Gunsmoke' meets are an entirely different ballgame. These two-week-long air-to-ground shooting matches evaluate the performance of competing teams, each of whom put carefully planned holes in the desert floor in an effort to gain top marks. The various legs of the meet call for 10-, 20- and 30-degree gun and dive-bomb attacks, low-level ingress followed by a Snakeye 'laydown' attack and, finally, a carefully timed (±5-second) navigation exercise culminating in a standard dive-bombing run. Marks awarded, out of a possible total of 10,000, have placed Phantoms down the league for the last three meets, but the small margin between the top and bottom scores is indicative of the high overall standard and does not reflect badly on the F-4 teams. No sour grapes – it would be more than interesting to see the placings of the F-4 units relative to the other contenders had the event taken place at night, using optical sensors, a Loran nav-aid and stand-off 'smart' weaponry, under which conditions the Phantom would outshine its competitors. Within its limits, however, 'Gunsmoke's' clean-air, 'OK Corral'-style venue still makes for a useful meet: there is a lot of bravado, and side contests such as 'weapons lodeos', where both air and ground crews can come together for an enlightening exchange of views, fight things out in good spirits, and get more time over the extensive Nellis ranges.

Electric armour

Because of the long and illustrious career behind the F-4Cs and Ds, their arduous involvement in South-East Asia and the fluid, ever-evolving nature of elec-

Below: An F-4D with early-format Bendix nose RHAWS and a Westinghouse multiple-band, 'long' AN/ALQ-101 ECM pod. (Westinghouse)

tronic warfare, the fleet has undergone many changes in the make-up of its self-defence equipment. Early F-4Cs were delivered 'nude', without any self-protection devices on board and relying purely on crew skill to dodge flak and kill, outrun or outmanoeuvre enemy fighters. At that time, in the early 1960s, self-defence packages were considered a luxury to be applied only to strategic bombers, but the initial heavy losses to SAMs over North Vietnam in the summer of 1965 rapidly changed that view. Applied Technology quickly arrived on the scene with RHAWS, designed to detect and alert the crew to enemy radar activity. The earliest RHAWS equipment was the Vector IV, which comprised the AN/APR-25, providing azimuth data on enemy SA-2 radars, and the companion APR-26, which provided SAM launch warning.* The devices were added to the nose cone and to the top of the fin trailing edge. Warnings were flashed up on the cockpit indicators and panels as azimuth strobe lines and launch warning lights, which took some effort and experience to decipher. But they played a vital part. On warning of a SAM launch, the crew would dive their Phantom down towards the ground, often heading right into the SAM. This enabled them to get below the minimum 500ft operating altitude of the early missiles and, with good crew judgement, pull hard turns in the terrifying game of SAM-dodging.

Changes and alterations since those early days have been extensive. In an attempt to break Applied Technology's monopoly as RHAWS supplier, the USAF decided that the F-4D should receive the Bendix AN/APS-107A. This alternative equipment, introduced on Block 30 machines and retrofitted to earlier examples, added a new bulge to the ventral radome blister and introduced a set of four triangular log periodic homing antennae screwed in around the nose barrel, since upgraded to APS-107E standard, resulting in the deletion of the nose barrel antennae and the addition of a blunt fin-cap receiver.

In the comparative calm of peacetime operations, the USAF has followed a highly organized, well thought out approach to upgrading F-4C/D RHAWS. Those aircraft assigned to the air defence mission, where threat warning equipment is of little value, continue to rely on the Vietnam-era systems (and in several squadrons the equipment and associated displays have actually been removed). Strike F-4Ds have been gradually upgraded with the easy-to-read alphanumeric AN/ALR-60 RWR series. Retrofitted since 1981 during PDM cycles, F-4Ds have been receiving a double-sized installation – a rather grotesque cluster of radar-warning 'frogeye' antennae on their nose radome blisters and drag 'chute doors. The package is superb, even if the new format does not score highly in terms of aesthetics: while the ALR-69 has broad frequency coverage, it is pre-programmed to 'sniff out' only a portion of the enemy radar network, namely those weapons tracking radars anticipated *en route* to the target and back. By combining the two sets of RWRs, these F-4Ds are able accurately to deduce enemy threats across a larger number of radar-operat-

Above: Close-up views of the recent F-4D AN/ALR-69 RWR retrofit. (Kansas ANG photo by TSgt. Genelle Clifton/Author)

ing bands, facilitating broad-band jamming when used in conjunction with a pair of Compass Tie-modified AN/ALQ-119s. With signal processor and software upgrades, this series will continue to provide the F-4D with threat-warning capability through to the type's eventual withdrawal.

Like their active counterparts, reserve forces can also call for help from a large assortment of jamming systems. These include not only the modern generation 'penaids' but also several Vietnam-era systems which remain in stock and which continue to play a valid role, albeit in low-threat areas or as 'threat simulators' in air defence battles. Back in the 1960s, F-4C/Ds employed two sorts of jamming pods, both of which were designed and supplied by Hughes under

*F-4Es introduced the upgraded APR-36 and -37 RHAWS before switching to the more advanced ALR-46, -69 and -74 RWRs.

QRC-160 for pure noise jamming: the AN/ALQ-71 was geared to confuse early model SA-2 'Fansong' radars; and the ALQ-72 was programmed to fox MiG-fighter fire-control radars. These were later supplemented by the Hallicrafters/General Electric AN/ALQ-87, available in a number of different configurations, each of which was designed to cope with a specific type of ground or airborne radar threat. Two pods with different settings were frequently carried on each Phantom during strikes on the more risky routes over North Vietnam, so that when working together the aircraft could cope with the multiplex operating frequencies of the enemy GCI, MiG and SA-2 radars. After 1967, Westinghouse entered the fray and soon became the primary supplier, its ranking boosted by its high-technology QRC-335 AN/ALQ-101 combination noise- and deception-jamming pod. This was gradually fattened and stretched in length as new modules were added for expanded coverage, eventually paving the way for the highly successful follow-on AN/ALQ-119 and -131, at present the mainstay jamming devices. Pods are carried on the inner wing pylons or under the forward Sparrow missile wells.

Protected by active ECM over North Vietnam, F-4D Phantoms assisted in the unenviable task of chaff carpet laying, using AN/ALE-2 or -38 bulk dispensing pods to provide a mattress of radar-blotting particles over which friendly strike forces could, with good timing, fly obscured from view. The use of these systems is extremely limited nowadays. Chaff-laying modes required the pilot to fly the F-4 on straight, level courses which made them optimum targets for MiG attack. The duty was later passed on to unmanned RPVs, much to the relief of all concerned! Instead, air crews today must be more self-reliant. Accordingly, F-4Ds now use Tracor's AN/ALE-40 chaff and flare 'Square Shooter' modules, but these have not been fitted to F-4Cs. The logic behind this is simply that a substantial number of F-4Cs were assigned to dedicated air defence squadrons, where the use of ECM is extremely limited: on the contrary, these aircraft must work against enemy ECM in order to find their targets, and onboard ECM, adding to the electronic mêlée, may only serve to hinder their task. If F-4Cs urgently require protection, or require chaff for Phantom

Below: A magnificent photograph of a March AFB-based 163rd TFG F-4C Phantom being readied for take-off. The California Guard logo on the fin is blue and white. (California ANG)

versus Phantom air combat training, they can rely on the old Vietnam 'one shot' method – release metal strips stuffed into their air brake compartments.

Back-up

As with their active colleagues, most maintenance on the reserve F-4s is carried out on the flight lines, weather permitting, with periodic Phased Maintenance Inspections in the hangars. F-4Ds are rotated through Ogden or Sacramento ALCs for PDM every 48 months, F-4Es through Ogden every 54 months, and F-4Cs through the Boeing Military Aircraft works in Kansas every 36 months, where they receive their vital deep servicing and TCTO/TO changes.

Reservists differ slightly from their active peers in having practised decentralized '*de facto* COMO' for some time. The small size of their units meant they never got entangled in the large, centrally organized machinery which so badly affected front-line F-4 serviceability up to the late 1970s. Their job is also eased by the fact that the aircraft are flown less often (but not less strenuously), easing the pressure on the ground crews. F-4Ds are limited to +8.5g and −3g, while, contrary to popular belief, speeds in excess of Mach 1.5 (let alone maximum speed) are rarely exercised by strike crews. Fuel economy and airframe conservation are the chief limiting factors, while even practice stores create considerable drag, though when the major overhauls are carried out each aircraft is put through its full paces in an exciting but back-breaking thirty-minute supersonic check-flight.

The large US reserve Phantom contingent permits a lot of useful spares exchange between units – a practice which tends to ensure a good supply of parts and WRSKs across the board. Several units are receiving spruced-up maintenance facilities, designed to create a better and safer working environment, for example hangars with improved insulation together with a new interior coat of white to take the strain off ground crews' eyes. Some 100 'hush houses' are also being installed at reserve air bases, enabling the maintenance staff to perform engine run-up checks without fear of generating nuisance lawsuits! The complex, 20-year-old F-4Cs and Ds are averaging routine 'home drome' mission-capable rates of over 64 per cent, which anyone who is familiar with the muddled innards of an F-4 will recognize as outstanding. Combat training deployments sharpen these figures.

The Phantom paintwork is carefully maintained by the Guard and AFRES. The ground crews are led by men and women from the old school who consider the aircraft the personal property of the respective crew chief (and who at times can be reluctant to let an inexperienced pilot manage his 'baby'!). Much effort goes into keeping the aircraft looking good, with the result that the part-timers' machines are undoubtedly some of the smartest in the Air Force. Individual ground crews and crew chiefs have gone to extreme lengths to add finishing touches to the otherwise drab 'European 1' or 'Hill Gray' camouflage schemes: ingenious but subtle additions include state names and flags, sharkmouths, colour trim on the canopy rails and – a very widespread Guard practice – restoring the metal gleam of intake lips and pylon tips and in some cases chrome-plating them! Vietnam MiG-kill stars are retained with pride, while many units have become so attached to their jets that each of their Phantoms has been specially christened or daubed with elaborate artwork. Names such as the Texas AFRES 'Jumbo Jet' or Kansas Air Guard's 'Naughty Lady' may be less exotic than the Hawaiian ANG birds of paradise ('Ewa Ewa' and 'Koloa' to name only two), but all show a mark of endearment.

4. SPECIAL MISSIONS

Interceptor

The USAF squadrons flying the F-4 in the dynamic role of air defence utilize onboard equipment that has changed little since its original service introduction. This reflects the fact that the F-4 was, from the outset, optimized for this mission – that was, after all, what McDonnell had intended when the foundations of the basic Navy design were laid down around the Aero 1 intercept avionics.

Although the F-4 ranked as one of the world's best interceptors in the fifteen years leading up to the introduction of the F-15 Eagle, it is somewhat ironic that the USAF only started to employ squadrons wholly honed to the air defence mission as newer, more capable aircraft were becoming available. The turning point came in April 1973 when the 57th FIS, based at Keflavik AB, Iceland, exchanged its aged Convair F-102A Delta Daggers for F-4Cs. Since that time the popular but weapons-limited 'Century Series' interceptors have been gradually phased out of use, to be replaced, one for one, by McDonnell F-4s or 'Teenagers'. The last F-102 had gone by 1978; August 1982 saw the final F-101 Voodoo sortie from Ellington ANGB, Texas, when the last of the breed flew to McClellan in California to become a static show piece; and the few remaining F-106 Delta Darts still flying are to be withdrawn from service shortly.

Over the last decade the air defence fleet has grown in size to nine F-4 squadrons; all of these are maintained ready by the Guard, under the direction of the 1st Air Force, TAC (formerly Air Defense, TAC) or PACAF. These units are tasked with the defence of the skies of the Continental United States (CONUS), protecting the homeland from airborne enemy intruders, as part of the big US-Canadian North American Air Defense (NORAD) chain. This mission requires each unit to maintain a minimum of two aircraft, fully armed and fuelled, and cocked in a constant state of vigil – 24 hours a day, 365 days a year – on quick-reaction duty (known as 'Zulu Alert' in NATO circles), both at the home base and at required detachment bases. This may even include an overseas TDY assignment such as the Guard 'Creek Claxon' standby force at Ramstein AB, West Germany, in 1986 – the first such deployment of its kind with NORAD F-4s.

Crews wait togged up in their flying gear, in nearby

Below: A Bicentennial chequertailed F-4C-20-MC, 63-7618, piloted by Lt. Gerstacker and WSO Capt. Fischer takes to the air in 1976. This aircraft is the subject of Detail & Scale decal sheet No. 01-48. (R. R. Leader via Peter E. Davies)

ready-rooms, where they break the tension with endless reading, TV and card playing. When a potentially hostile aircraft appears on the early-warning surveillance radarscopes, the units spring to life. Air and ground crews are scrambled and sprint to their aircraft. There is not time for a pre-flight walk-around to check weapons or control surfaces, or for the ritual kicking of the tyres – the crews jump straight into their aircraft, don helmets, pull their harnesses tight, and light the engines. Ground crew pull out safety pins and clear the aircraft to go. Within five minutes of alert notice a pair of Phantoms are screaming into the sky, clawing for height with fiery afterburners. Barring serious communications or radar malfunctions, they proceed on their way, vectored by the all-essential ground controllers on to the unidentified radar images for a closer look. Behind these aircraft, all units provide reinforcements in the form of two back-up Phantoms, which are ready to go within fifteen minutes.

Whether a Phantom crew will be required to shoot first and ask questions later or go in for a close examination of the UFO will depend upon NORAD's Defense Readiness Condition (DEFCON). DEFCON 5 is the usual, no-emergency condition; as things hot up, so the numbers count down. Assuming a more relaxed state of affairs, the Phantom crews will accelerate and move in close to the intruders, cutting off any aggressive penetration into the Air Defense Identification Zone (ADIZ). When the target has been acquired on the F-4's radarscope, by TISEO or radar, the crew will give the call-sign 'Judy'; ground control now takes a back seat and the game passes to the Phantom crews.

The UFO may be a harmless but irritating light aviation machine straying into sensitive military air-

Above: Chequer-tailed F-4Cs from the 'Black Knights' lined up at Tyndall for 'William Tell' 1976, the first such meet in which USAF Phantoms participated. (R. R. Leader via Knowles)

space, or a weather balloon that has drifted from its tether. Alternatively it may be a Soviet reconnaissance machine circling in international airspace; or even the ultimate article – a 'Backfire', 'Blinder' or 'Blackjack' bomber, zooming in over the horizon to make a surprise attack and wreak havoc with a belly full of nuclear-tipped weapons. If the intruder is identified as hostile, the crew will be instructed to do one of a number of things, again, depending on the general state of alert: establish radio or signal communication

Below: F-4C-19-MC 63-7589 chalked up its MiG-21 'kill' on 2 January 1967 during Operation 'Bolo', in the capable hands of 'Triple Nickel' 555th TFS 'jocks' Wetterhahn and Sharp. It is depicted here in the spring of 1978 at Keflavik AB, Iceland; it later served with the Combat Echo detachment at Tyndall ADWC, Florida. (MAP)

Above: 'Ace in the Hole' insignia is evident on the nose of this 147th FIG F-4C as the crew give a 'thumbs-up' signal to the cameraman. The Phantom is equipped with live AIM-7 Sparrow missiles. (Texas ANG)

Left: A shiny F-4C-19-MC, 63-7591, in an 'alert' hangarette at Ellington ANGB, Texas. The ADC grey paint tucks well into the white intake ducting. The bottom of the nose-gear door is painted red. (Texas ANG)

Below: F-4E-32-MC 66-0304 touches down at Keflavik AB, Iceland. The 57th FIS aircraft were some of the smartest-looking Phantoms the author has ever seen. The 57th FIS now operates F-15C/D Eagles. (MAP)

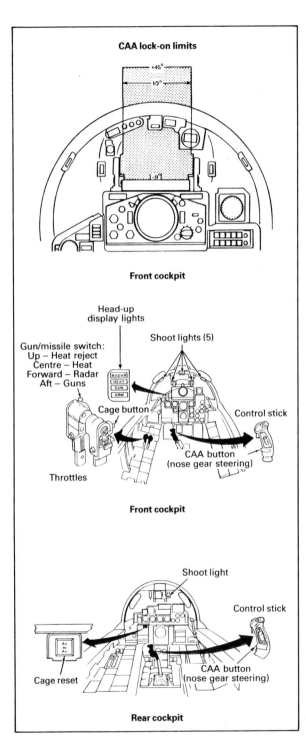

CAA lock-on limits

+45°

10°

-9°

Front cockpit

Head-up
display lights

Shoot lights (5)

Gun/missile switch:
Up – Heat reject
Centre – Heat
Forward – Radar
Aft – Guns

RADAR
HEAT
GUN
ARM

Cage button

Control stick

CAA button
(nose gear steering)

Throttles

Front cockpit

Shoot light

Control stick

Au
to
Au

CAA button
(nose gear steering)

Cage reset

Rear cockpit

Above: F-4E LRU-1 'Auto-Acquisition' mode. Lock-on limits (top) depict field of auto-acquisition in the 'ACM', close-in, visual mode; front cockpit (centre) shows 'valid firing opportunity' shoot light and radar/weapons systems select modes; and rear cockpit (bottom) depicts shoot light and auto-acquisition select. (Westinghouse via John J. Harty, McDonnell Douglas)

and escort the aircraft away or order it to the ground to be seized. Alternatively, the crew might be instructed to shoot it down.

Weaponry

If required to terminate the flight of the trespasser, the F-4 crews can call on a number of sidearms, each designed to operate within carefully prescribed attack parameters. As the Phantom closes in on the target, each of these options comes into play in sequence. First comes 'Fox 1' – the AIM-7 radar-guided Sparrow missile. From the outset the F-4 was tailor-made to work with Raytheon's Sparrows. Up to four of these may be carried at a time, semi-submerged under the F-4's fuselage, any one of which is capable of toppling an enemy from the sky at a mere $125,000 a shot.

At the start of pure air combat operations, USAF Phantoms employed the less reliable AIM-7D, later replaced by the marginally better AIM-7E. Today, the types used include the definitive Sparrow III AIM-7E Upgraded and -7F models, which offer increased reliability with the added bonus of both greater stand-off and shorter minimum range capabilities. These missiles rely on the Phantom's APQ fire-control radar and APA radar-set group to track a target with radar energy at ranges of up to 40nm – the Sparrow nose modules use their semi-active radar-homing (SARH) guidance to lock on and glide to the 'painted' target.

Painting a specific target with radar outside visual range in the 'heads down', long-range intercept, blind mode is conducted by the WSO, who will put his brow on the rubber radarscope hood and lock the radar on to the target. This slews the Sparrow SARH noses on to the enemy preparatory to launch and furnishes a 'command course' steering dot and angular steering error circle on the pilot's scope to help him line up on the target and get in the correct lead firing position. Once launched, the Sparrow will accelerate to Mach 4, while the pilot holds the Phantom on course for the enemy – this ensures that the radar continues to track the prey to assist in missile homing. Detonation of the Sparrow's 66lb warhead is then activated automatically by impact or proximity fusing, the missile's continuous rod charge erupting into a fireball containing two and a half thousand steel fragments.

As an alternative to the WSO acquiring the target, the pilot can use auto acquisition when the enemy is within visual range. With the click of two switches the radar is caged and its thin pencil beam points directly out of the front of the F-4's big plastic radome. The gunsight reticle points in sympathy with the radar boresight, so that when it is put right on the target lock-on follows automatically. The F-4E's new Westinghouse LRU-1 air combat digital 'mod', refitted to all F-4Es, takes this one stage further, and allows the pilot to use auto-acquisition in an off-axis 'super search' mode, to acquire and track targets off to the left or right for the lethal AIM-7F. The off-axis capability extends 45 degrees up, 5 degrees left and right and 9 degrees down – in effect, anywhere in the front windshield. Missile 'valid firing opportunities' are provided

by cockpit lamps, which light up on the canopy frame as a head-up cue to the pilot. These modes are especially useful in the time-compressed environment of close-in or low-level interception work, giving the pilot the freedom to haul the nose of the beast around the sky and take advantage of tactical air combat manoeuvres. After the target has been acquired, the radar will continue to track the enemy, and pre-selected Sparrows can be launched for the kill.

Above: 'Happy Hooligans' F-4D-25-MC 64-0945 lets loose an AIM-7 Sparrow missile in pursuit of a drone over the Gulf of Mexico. (Capt. Larry Harrington, North Dakota ANG)

Below: F-4D-24-MC 64-0930, the second production D-model Phantom, fires an AIM-9J Sidewinder heat-seeking missile during missile update tests in the late 1970s. Note the lit afterburners, indicative of the high rate of knots being achieved. (Ford Aerospace)

 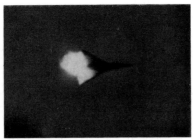 

Should the target come within the minimum effective range of Sparrow (at low altitude, as little as a few hundred yards on the latest models), the pilot will switch over to 'Fox 2' – the AIM-9 Sidewinder. Gaining its name from the deadly twisting rattlesnake that loves the heat of the desert, Sidewinder is so renowned for its potency that North Vietnamese and Arab pilots hitting the 'panic button' are known to have ejected from their aircraft prematurely just on the sight of a launch flash. Combat results with the modern versions show a kill rate exceeding 90 per cent in all weathers! Supplied in many variants since its early Naval Weapons Center design origins, the USAF Sidewinders are all heat-seeking, infra-red homing versions by either Ford Aerospace or Raytheon. Early models used by the USAF F-4s, such as the AIM-9D, required the pilot to manoeuvre into an enemy's six o'clock position so that the seeker could lock on to the target's hot jet pipes; the E and J models expanded the launch envelope to the rear hemisphere, while the latest all-aspect AIM-9N/P and L/M models can be launched against a target from any angle, even off-axis from the front quarters!*

To confirm target lock-on, the pilot will put the enemy aircraft in his gunsight; growls coming through the headset will tell him when the seeker has acquired the target and is ready to be fired. As a preparatory lock-on aid, auto-acquisition inputs from the radar are used to slew the missile seekers automatically on to the target. Once launched, often in pairs as an insurance policy, the Sidewinders will home on to the

target autonomously, their rear-fin gyro wheels twirling them through the sky until burn-out or detonation. Active optical fusing enables their 25lb warheads to detonate either on contact with the target or in close proximity. The effect of a direct hit is better left to the imagination, but the latter mode is still sufficiently punchy to blow the tail off an enemy fighter.

If the F-4 closes on to its target too fast for 'HEAT', the pilot can switch over to 'Fox 3', the 20mm Gatling gun. This is where the F-4D's and E's LCOSS gunsight comes into its own. The LCOSS uses inputs from the radar (for target range), Central Air Data Computer (to provide air density, F-4 AOA and air speed) and gunsight gyro lead computer (to input F-4 manoeuvres and acceleration) so that it can compute the position of the gunsight reticle aiming dot, thus providing the correct lead firing angle to the pilot; its position in the pilot's line of sight to target compensates for gun cartridge ballistics and the position, attitude and closure rate of the F-4 relative to its quarry. With his gunsight pipper 'intercepting' the target aircraft, the pilot squeezes the firing trigger, commanding an almost instantaneous 100 rounds a second to 'down' his target.

But using full LCOSS capability against a highly

---

*The AIM-9E is an upgraded B model, the J an upgraded B or E model which has been redesignated AIM-9N or in turn upgraded to AIM-9P standard. The AIM-9L/M versions are brand new. An imaging infra-red homing model called the AIM-9R is currently under development.

Left, top: An AIM-9P Sidewinder 'takes out' a PQM-102A Delta Dagger Pave Deuce drone in a head-on, look-down attack over the Gulf of Mexico. (Ford Aerospace)

Left, bottom: Painted in glossy grey with a spectrum-coloured rudder, New York's F-4C-19-MC 63-7541 claimed its MiG-21 'kill' on 5 November 1966 when flown by 'Gunfighters' pilots Tuck and Rabeni Jr. New York recently converted to F-4Ds, along with the Michigan Guard. (MAP)

Above: A pair of 526th TFS 'Black Knights' F-4Es from Ramstein AB, West Germany, on the return leg to the air base following a low-level air superiority mission in June 1983. The aircraft are 'armed to the teeth' with Sparrow and Sidewinder missiles. The 526th TFS was the last USAF Phantom squadron to perform dedicated air superiority. (USAF photo by MSgt. Don Sutherland)

Overleaf: F-4D-29-MC 66-7458 from Eglin's 4485th Combat Echo unit basks in the midday sun in Florida. In the foreground are live Sidewinders. (Ford Aerospace)

USAF F-4 AIR DEFENCE UNITS			
Group	Squadron	Base	Transitions
107th FIG	136th FIS	Niagara Falls, New York	F-101→F-4C→F-4D
119th FIG	178th FIS	Fargo, North Dakota	F-101→F-4D
142nd FIG	114th TFTS	Kingsley Field, Oregon	F-101→F-4C
	123rd FIS	Portland, Oregon	
144th FIW	194th FIS	Fresno, California	F-106→F-4D
147th FIG	111th FIS	Ellington ANGB, Texas	F-101→F-4C
148th FIG	179th FIS	Duluth, Minnesota	F-101→RF-4C→F-4D
154th CG	199th FIS	Hickam AFB, Hawaii	F-102→F-4C→F-15
191st FIG	171st FIS	Selfridge ANGB, Michigan	F-106→F-4C→F-4D

manoeuvrable foe weaving patterns across the sky in and out of radar may prove difficult: the pilot may find the pipper dancing around on his combining glass like a marionette! To avoid this distraction, auto-acquisition is disengaged and the LCOSS assumes a fixed, 1,000ft range. Provided he is properly distanced, with the pipper on the enemy, the cannon shells should pump into the target. If the enemy is playing really hard to get, 'Fox 4' (an unofficial joke) can be used as a last resort – with one hand on the stick and the other grasping the seat ejection ring, crash into the opponent!

Mission accomplished and armament or fuel expended, the Phantoms return to their home base and eagerly awaiting ground crews for re-arming and refuelling, and the possible addition of a pair of red stars sprayed on the splitter plate.

Infra-red eyes

Navy F-4Bs originally incorporated the Aero 1 ACF Electronic AAA-4 infra-red sensor to supplement radar in locating airborne targets, this device protruding prominently from beneath the nose radome with a glazed tip. Its job was simply to acquire the heat emissions of potential targets outside the range of Sidewinder, and then cue the AIM-9s to the same spot for rapid target acquisition. No USAF F-4 was delivered with the package, although the nose fairing was retained on the F-4C and later retrofitted to the F-4D to house RHAWS. But changes are afoot: the ANG is hoping to install the Hughes Infra Red Search and Track Sensor (IRSTS) aboard selected F-4Ds. Modified from redundant F-106 stock, IRSTS has, in the hands of the North Dakota ANG, successfully demonstrated its ability to search and track targets independently and in conjunction with radar. Maj. Ronald W. Saeger from the 'Hooligans' elaborates:

EXPLOSIVES B

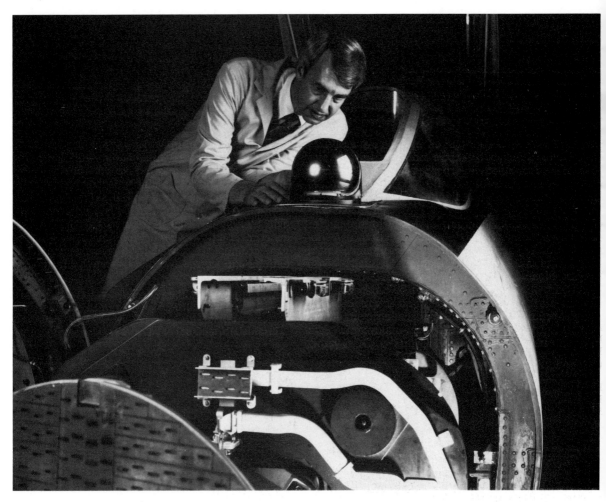

IRSTS was developed by Hughes Aircraft Company for use on F-101/102/106 interceptor aircraft. During a ten-year period, 2,000 were built. These systems served the Air Defense fighter community well for many years, and a proposal was made in the early 1980s to adapt the system to the F-4, which was assuming the Strategic Air Defense mission. If the proposal proved to be feasible, a total of about 180 F-4Ds would be retrofitted. The proposal was presented to the Ogden Air Logistics Center by the ANG/AFRES Fighter Weapons Office. In August 1984, Hughes was tasked by the OOALC to develop and test the integration of their improved IRSTS with the F-4D APQ-109 radar system.

The heart of the IRSTS was a cooled cross-array lead selenide detector. Prior to 1980, the cooling was provided by a bulky, closed-cycle liquid nitrogen (conventional refrigeration) system. Beginning that year, Hughes replaced the nitrogen system with a solid-state, four-stage 'Peltier Effect' type of thermocouple. This allowed a large weight and space saving in the aircraft. F-4D 64-0945 was selected for the flight test which was conducted by the 119th FIG, North Dakota ANG, at Fargo. The flight test period began on June 29th 1985, and ended 32 sorties later the following October.

The IRSTS was integrated with the APQ-109 radar system in a manner which allowed *independent* or *slaved* operation of the radar antenna and the IR seeker head.

Above: Van Nuys, California: an IRSTS mounted on F-4D-25-MC 64-0945. The IR detector moves on a gimballed mechanism to track a target. It can be slaved to radar or *vice versa*, or works independently, to furnish target position on the radarscope. Also just in view is the F-15-type Hughes APG-63 pulse-doppler radar, which would offer the F-4D a true clutter-free, look-down capability with clear, combined IRSTS and radar target symbology on the cockpit 'scopes. If the IRSTS retrofit goes ahead, the sensor will be located under the nose to reduce the slightly higher cockpit noise generated by the blister, and to enhance the IRSTS's FOV. (Hughes via North Dakota ANG)

This meant that for the first time the F-4D could track two targets simultaneously. Another advantage of the IR system is that it is passive – it does not radiate RF energy – and therefore cannot be detected by the target which it is tracking. The IRSTS is also immune to jamming by RF spectrum electronic countermeasures. The addition of a second system also meant that one could still be used to search for targets while the other was tracking a previously located aircraft.

The IRSTS was successful in that it proved that the 'off-the-shelf' seeker heads could be installed and integrated with the F-4D radar system [for under $140,000 per aircraft – cheaper than a modern air-to-air missile round.

Above: The pride of Adj. General Alexander P. MacDonald's outfit – one of 22 F-4Ds assigned to the North Dakota ANG, 'parabraking' at the close of a training sortie. (MAP)

Below: Crews make the 300yd run for their F-4Es during Profile 3 of 'William Tell' 1982. The aircraft are from the 57th FIS, which now operates F-15s. (Lt. Col. Jerry Hicks)

Author]. However, the IR system could be better adapted and employed with a newer-generation radar system. The primary limitation is that both systems are displayed on the same scope and cannot be observed simultaneously. Current synthetic systems used on F-14/15/18 aircraft would be ideal for allowing simultaneous radar and IR symbology display.

The Hughes IRSTS could be a cost-effective improvement to the capability of any airborne detection system. This seeker would be especially effective if integrated with a digital processor and display system. Hopefully, the North Dakota ANG F-4D flight test will not be the end of the road for a venerable and proven reliable search and track system.

The big Soviet-built bombers can draw on enormous power supplies for radar jamming, possibly providing stand-off cover for their air-launched cruise missiles, and so IRSTS may prove a crucial back-up. The project hangs in the balance.

Defunct weaponry

Just as the F-4 has used a mind-boggling array of air-to-ground stores over the years, so it has come to grips with an almost equally multifarious selection of air intercept weapons. In place of Sidewinder, the Block 26 F-4D introduced the Hughes AIM-4D ('D for Dogfighting') infra-red-homing Falcon missile. Falcon was cheaper and offered more punch, but it also had several drawbacks. First, although it, too, was carried on the inner wing pylons in pairs, the LAU-42 launch rails and their complex cryogenic seeker-cooling support equipment took up the entire pylon. Sidewinder rails are fitted to the sides of Phantoms' inner wing pylons and do not compromise air-to-ground or ECM stores carriage, other than by increasing the all-up weight of the aircraft by a nominal 170lb a missile, and USAF-model Sidewinders are completely self-contained, with seeker-cooling installed within the missile cases, making them easy to 'down-load' and change if a hitch occurs. Furthermore, the AIM-4D's disappointing performance in terms of MiG kills – only four in Vietnam – was due to the missile's reliance on contact fuses built into the rear fins, requiring a direct hit every time for a kill. The famous Ubon-based 8th TFW 'Wolfpack' went so far as to remove Falcon and substitute Sidewinder on their F-4Ds! Hughes' indignant reply came a year later in 1969 when they embarked on a project to add proximity fusing to Falcon (and the AIM-4D was to be re-dubbed the AIM-4H), but this was abandoned in 1971 after newer and even better models of the Sidewinder had emerged.

Another even shorter-lived weapon, which in fact never saw combat or operational service with the F-4 although it was a mainstay weapon of the F-101 Voodoo and F-106 Delta Dart, was the Douglas AIR-2A Genie. This package was evaluated on an F-4C at the AFFTC, one missile being carried on each inner wing pylon in the same fashion as a large bomb. Its use was fairly simple: the missile was armed and launched on an intercept course for an 'enemy bomber formation'. A rocket motor, 'pop-out' fins and a gyro would hold Genie on course, while the pilot hauled the F-4 out of the vicinity of the launch area as fast as possible, for crew safety. Once within lethal range of the enemy bombers, the missile's proximity fuses set it off, or the WSO would ignite the warhead by remote control, detonating a nuclear device capable of creating a 2,000ft-wide fireball. A B-model was also available, using a large conventional explosive, while the ATR-2, a live training round, exploded into a magnificent big white smokeball, an impressive sight that was regularly demonstrated over the Gulf of Mexico within eyeshot of Cuba and its Warsaw Pact guests.

Weapons which never got beyond the developmental stage included Brazo, discussed earlier, and Seekbat, a modified AGM-78 Standard ARM refitted with an infra-red seeker. Intercepts by both Japanese and Israeli Phantoms consistently failed to catch full-throttle MiG-25 Foxbats, so, with this in mind, General Dynamics Pomona proposed the AIM-97 as a

Foxbat-killer. In spite of active foreign interest, it never entered production.

In 1968, similar tests were carried out by the US Navy, which integrated the long-range Hughes AIM-54 Phoenix missile, carried semi-submerged in the F-4's ventral 600-gallon fuel tank. At this time, the USN were hovering between a cancelled F-111B and a 'paper' F-14A Tomcat – both of which were designed to carry the superb Phoenix, but neither of which was available for service – and so the Phantom was seen as a potential user for the weapon, despite the limitations of its onboard radar equipment for work of this sort. A special swing-wing F-4 with new avionics was envisaged as the operational Phoenix missile platform. For good reasons this time, the successful development of the Tomcat ultimately caused the USN to abandon the Phantom-Phoenix venture.

Air Combat Training

Periodic air combat training, for AFRES, Guard and active units, routes the aircraft to their respective ACMI ranges: Osan in South Korea; Nellis, Nevada, or Tyndall, Florida, in the USA; and Decimommanu in Sardinia, where European and USAFE air crews congregate each winter for mock combat. Swift F-5E 'Aggressors' from USAFE's 527th TFTAS, PACAF's 26th TFTAS or TAC's 57th FWW provide DACT opposition, simulating Soviet-built MiG fighters, with other allied aircraft types providing an alternative challenge. As a point interceptor possessing rapid acceleration, and packing a big offensive load of eight AIMs, a 20mm 'Gat' and two sets of eyes the F-4 is by and large unrivalled; as a dogfighter, though, it 'wades into a fight like a big dinosaur', as one F-4E pilot noted. DACT in the F-4 demands the best pilots *and* the best out of them, but, once experienced, Phantom pilots can outfly most opponents, using guile and aggression.

The Guard operates its own specialist interceptor training centre at Kingsley Field, Oregon; prior to 1984 the job was performed solely in Kansas by the 'Jayhawks', who had to integrate both strike and air defence crews into the same training routine ('Very honestly it was a pain in the butt to try and mesh the two syllabi!'). Under the direction of the 114th TFTS, formerly the 8123rd Fighter Interception Training Squadron, new crews who have undergone a gruelling down-to-earth officer, survival and basic flying train-

ing course gain confidence with the 'hard-wing' F-4C during a follow-on 33 pilot and 28 WSO training sorties spread out over seventeen weeks. Training flights for the fledgeling interceptor 'jocks' and 'radar heads' cover three basic operations: classical fighter manoeuvres, air combat manoeuvring and point interception. The first of these teaches supportive flight discipline – learning how to work with a flight leader for mutual offence or defence. Air combat manoeuvring 'head bangs' the crews against one another,

Below: An F-4D assigned to the California Guard's 144th FIW sits on the ramp at Fresno. 65-0763 served at Bentwaters/Woodbridge, England, and Homestead, Florida, before being reassigned to the Guard. (California ANG)

Phantom to Phantom, so that they learn how to juggle into a firing position against a dynamic foe. Point interception work is practised in conjunction with the essential ground controllers, who vector the F-4 crews on to targets being monitored by ground control intercept radar.

Phantom-to-Phantom training, although criticized long ago in the 'Red Baron' report as not providing a realistic Phantom *versus* MiG scenario (because of the Soviet fighters' comparative manoeuvrability and diminutive size), does, nevertheless, remain useful. This is because of the NORAD reliance on 'find-and-shoot' tactics as opposed to dogfighting. To a certain extent, the problem is also offset by squadrons pitching their wraparound-camouflaged Phantoms against the glossy ADC or 'Hill Gray' machines in their unit, the

dissimilar paint schemes providing some visual differences between the combatants. An average air defence unit will clock up over 3,000 flying hours each year performing these various manoeuvres.

First-class live weapons training is sponsored by the Weapons Systems Evaluation Program (WSEP) crews, who fly follow-on test missions out of Eglin ADTC and Tyndall ADWC in Florida under the Combat Echo project. Over thirty drone kills are authorized each year – including expensive QF-100 and QF-106 aircraft conversions – allowing the unit to develop optimum tactics for Sidewinder and Sparrow missile use. The recent F-4 upgrade to AIM-9L missiles has doubtless seen the WSEP crews create a lot of scrap metal over the Gulf of Mexico!

Occasionally, live weapons are used against genuine

targets. On 11 August 1981 a USAF Seek Skyhook balloon broke loose from its 12,000ft tether and started to drift out to sea, towards Cuba. It was shot down by a 31st TTW F-4D, splashing 150nm off Cudjoe Key in Florida. This could hardly be called a challenging target (arguably, the balloon possessed hard-to-find 'stealth' characteristics), but it certainly provided a good opportunity to use a live Sparrow and see what it is capable of doing.

Fully integrated combat training takes place when air crews deploy to Tyndall ADWC, to participate in a 'William Tell' competition or 'Copper Flag' wargame – the respective air defence counterparts to Nellis TFWC's 'Gunsmoke' and 'Red/Green Flag' manoeuvres. Held at Tyndall every other October, 'William Tell' meets first started back in 1954 and, apart from a five-year lull at the height of the Vietnam War, have continued to provide the most stringent test of NORAD point interception capabilities based on team performance. As the USAF ADWC WT-82 news centre put it, ' "William Tell" is not like the World Series – it's not the final contest. It's a practice for a contest in which the teams would stake their lives – and ultimately the lives of many others – on their skill and equipment against the threat of enemy aircraft. That's a contest in which second place is unacceptable'. There are no losers at 'William Tell', just better teams. About fifteen carefully selected Phantoms have been participating at each meet since 1976.

The competition includes four mock combat profiles, each of which carries a maximum of 10,000 points, giving a possible total of 40,000, though the exact profile structure can, as at 'Gunsmoke', change from meet to meet. The structure gives a very good idea of the tactics employed by the Phantom crews. At WT-82, for example, Profile 1 required each unit to field four of its five aircraft, one at a time, in a point interception front cut-off attack against a manoeuvring target. Using live weapons with inert warheads, the Phantoms were vectored by ground controllers – giving heading, height and speed of the target – on to drones operating at between 30,000 and 40,000ft. Profile 2 tasked a pair of Phantoms at a time to hunt and kill PQM-102 Delta Dagger Pave Deuce drones. Here, live Sidewinders and Sparrows were used. One aircraft performed a front cut-off attack with AIM-7s while the other moved in to shoot from the stern with AIM-9 Sidewinders. The Phantoms were again vectored into a firing position by ground controllers and, following authorization, were allowed to 'kill' the target. If the first F-4 shot down the 'Deuce', then the mission would be re-flown to give the other Phantom crew a chance to fire off a live missile. Profile 3 again had the F-4s working in pairs, this time in a cut-off attack against other manned aircraft. This profile did not use live weapons, but did employ Sparrow and Sidewinder simulators with live seekers for lock-on practice. In true scramble style, the air crews were required to start off the session with a 300yd sprint to their Phantoms. After racing to the take-off pad, a longer-than-usual, twelve-minute margin was allowed

Above: A 32nd TFS F-4E about to launch with a TDU-10 aerial gunnery dart. The 347th TFW, from Moody AFB, Georgia, provide the 'towers' for 'William Tell'. (MAP)

in which to get airborne, provided so that aircraft could receive a full five-minute 'last chance' look-over before rolling – if a live missile strayed through the net, a tragedy could occur.* In live combat, this would be overruled and the launch time would be much tighter.

The fourth profile was the most integrated. Each participating unit was given a pre-defined piece of sky to defend, and was required to intercept, interrogate and 'destroy' all intruders in its airspace – including 'enemy' B-52 Stratofortresses and F-111 'Aardvarks', which used their onboard ECM to confuse the interceptors. This 'black-box warfare' provided valuable feedback for the bomber crews, who could work on their enemy airspace penetration tactics. One fighter pilot told the author that B-52 ECM was so effective that the 'Buff' 'just disappeared off my radarscope'. Fleeting high-speed RF-4Cs making high-mach dashes were also thrown into the game to make the fighter and GCI crews' jobs more challenging. For this leg of the meet, Tyndall's expensive Cubic Corporation ACMI range was used to its full. This range dictates that each participant carry an inert blue ACMI pod, about the size of a Sidewinder missile, a transmitter that allows ground receivers to keep track of individual aircraft and thus permits the judges accurately to deduce the performance of the competitors. The ACMI range is located just south-east of St. George Island in the Gulf of Mexico. Five unmanned solar-powered tracking stations, semi-submerged in the water in a ring of approximately 30 miles diameter, pick up the ACMI pod data then relay it to a master station in the town of Carabelle some 35 miles away. This station in turn re-transmits the information in microwave form to the Tyndall ADWC computers for processing.

Further sorties, in which Phantoms participated but did not compete, centred around 20mm gun intercepts. Here, F-4Es on detachment from the 347th TFW performed a target dart-towing mission. According to the 347th, there are several subvariants of the dart, all in widespread use with F-4 units. The first of these is a

16ft metal dart attached to a steel cable some 2,000ft long. This may sometimes be made of wood, but the flight characteristics remain the same. Once in flight over the range, the F-4E unleashes the cable, and then enters into a turn. The attacker then shoots at the dart and later joins up on it to assess the amount of damage. The second major type of towed target is a bright red styrofoam arrow shape. This has a cheap, integral, acoustic-scoring instrument which can 'hear' the shooter's bullets as they pass within a few feet. The number of 'hits' is then flashed up on a meter in the cockpit of the towing jet. 'The towing procedures are basically the same and are generally considered to be somewhat boring for the tow crews'. In all seriousness, this training is not without its hazards, despite the fact that stringent safety rules must be observed: in December 1976 an F-4E's cannon shells strayed on to a target-towing Marine Skyhawk, knocking the 'Scooter' down (fortunately the hapless A-4 driver managed to eject safely).

At the end of each 'William Tell' meet the scores are added and the winners presented with trophies at a formal ceremony; the others depart with at least a valid live weapons training session behind them. As a weary weapons builder (responsible for assembling weapons from their storage and transportation crates) concluded, the satisfaction of seeing hard work translated into a drone kill is the true climax of the event; 'home-drome' practice sorties never generate the same level of pressure and excitement. 'If it ever happened for real, there might only be the chance for one shot – a dud weapon would bring disaster'.

*In a recent accident in West Germany, an RAF F-4 crew accidentally shot down at Jaguar fighter-bomber in the mistaken belief they were practising their attack with an inert Sidewinder. Fortunately the Jaguar pilot escaped unhurt. Peacetime pre-flight weapons checks are an absolute 'must'.

'Copper Flag'

Continuing air defence wargames are conducted at Tyndall ADWC under the direction of the USAF Interceptor Weapons School (USAFIWS). This unit concentrates on integrated interception manoeuvres under the 'Copper Flag' programme. The meets are held in two-week blocks three times a year and usually involve 150 aircraft, made up from detachments from F-4, F-15, F-106 and E-3 AWACS units; battle staff from a NORAD Air Division act as primary ground controllers. Full use is made of the ACMI range's computerized 'scoring' as live weapons are not included – all combatant aircraft are manned, so the use of Sidewinders and Sparrows is out of the question! As under the 'Red' and 'Green Flag' battles, greater emphasis is placed upon the learning process than upon winning cups. One RAF exchange pilot summed up the value of the ACMI system: 'It cuts out all the bull. The pilots come in and watch a video replay of the mission they've just flown, see their mistakes and the things they did right. They see a real-time, as-it-happened, true picture of their mission . . . God's-eye-view'. This view can cover an area measuring anything from two to one hundred miles wide, and includes added horizontal, vertical, side and cockpit diagrams, with pertinent flight data comprising air speed, altitude, heading and a host of other facts. Qualitative

Above: This 'Shadow Demon' artwork belongs to F-4C-16-MC 63-7442, a Michigan Guard Phantom which carried three different variations on the 'Shadow Demon' theme before its retirement in 1986. (Mil-Slides)

Below: Air combat 'kill' marks adorn the splitter plate of Major Schnurr's 18th TFS, 21st Composite Wing F-4E. (Chris Williamson via Knowles).

analyses of the 'weapons firing' results are processed by the computer. How long was the pilot in a firing position? How often was he in the sights of his opponent? All this information is available for review on the big screen and in printed, hard-copy form for the students to take away for further perusal. Aircraft that are a full 40 miles apart when they fly into the ACMI range will likely be engaged in battle within two minutes, and a win, lose or draw situation should emerge within another 60 seconds. About 5,000 sorties are flown ach year under 'Copper Flag' and other USAFIWS-related flights.

CONUS-based strike Wings, most of which perform a secondary or back-up air defence support role, also have the opportunity to fight against 'Aggressors' and in other dissimilar multiple aircraft engagements at the Nellis TFWC and Canadian 'Maple Flag' manoeuvres. Although prohibited as a regular aspect of practice, crews are often tasked to identify private and commercial traffic, the supersonic Concorde, bound for New York, included. However, following an embarrassing near mid-air collision in 1979, this Anglo-French 'Backfire simulator' is now strictly out of bounds.

In the 1980s, the F-4 can no longer boast that it is the 'hottest' interceptor in the world; it can, however, claim with some pride that it forms the backbone (no less than 70 per cent) of dedicated air defence fire power for the North American continent. Two hundred Phantoms with the latest missiles and communications equipment, all integrated into a comprehensive, over-the-horizon early warning and surveillance network, provide a formidable opponent for any intruder.

Below: A 414th FWS, 57th TTW F-4E equipped with an AN/ASQ-T-13 ACMI pod for air combat training. These pods are carried by all participants at mock battles such as 'Red' and 'Green Flag', 'William Tell' and 'Copper Flag', permitting the ground computers to track and record the aircraft's manoeuvres. (Cubic Corporation)

Reconnaissance

Beneath the veneer of sleek metal the RF-4C houses many secrets, and even some twenty years after its service introduction much mystique surrounds the type. The popular label 'Photo-Phantom' is barely adequate to describe this variant's mission equipment – sensors tailored for pure information gathering, a task performed in both blatant overflight and in discreet stand-off modes. Aerial reconnaissance is a vital, unarmed and unsung job which provides as much as 95 per cent of all intelligence used by the services.

Ordered into production by the Air Force in the spring of 1962 under the original Phantom adoption contract, with the specifications, SOR 196, formalized two months later on 28 May, the prototype YRF-4C first took to the air on 8 August 1963. Incorporating a 33in nose extension to house the reconnaissance sensors, a beautifully streamlined ventral fuselage without wells and blisters for Sparrow missiles, and a clean appearance from the nose pitot to the fin-cap, the RF-4C model proved from the outset that it was capable of faster top speeds and offered better handling characteristics than the contemporary F-4B/C fighter variants. It was an immediate success.

USAF F-4 ACTIVE RECONNAISSANCE SQUADRONS

Unit	Wing	Base	Command	Tail-code
15th TRS	18th TFW	Kadena AB, Okinawa	PACAF	ZZ
16th TRS	363rd TFW	Shaw AFB, South Carolina	TAC	SW
38th TRS	26th TRW	Zweibrucken AB, West Germany	USAFE	ZR
12th TRS 91st TRS 45th TRTS 62nd TRTS	67th TRW	Bergstrom AFB, Texas	TAC	BA

AIR NATIONAL GUARD SQUADRONS

Unit	Wing	Base	Command	Tail-code
106th TRS	117th TRW	Birmingham, Alabama	TAC-ANG	BH
153rd TRS	186th TRG	Meridian, Mississippi	TAC-ANG	KE
165th TRS	123rd TRW	Louisville, Kentucky	TAC-ANG	KY
173rd TRS	155th TRG	Lincoln, Nebraska	TAC-ANG	'Nebraska'
189th TRTF 190th TRS	124th TRG	Boise, Idaho	TAC-ANG	'Idaho'
192nd TRS	152nd TRG	Reno, Nevada	TAC-ANG	'High Rollers'

Operational deliveries commenced in September 1964, the first examples going to the 33rd TRTS, 363rd TRW, at Shaw AFB, South Carolina. Further deliveries proceeded at a steady rate of about 70 aircraft each year through the 1960s, falling off after 1969. By January 1974, when the last example was handed over, the USAF had received no fewer than 505 of the type.*

In all this time there were no major design changes, no follow-on RF-4Ds or subsequent models – a reflection of the fact that, unlike the F-4 fighter variants, the RF-4C represented what the USAF had sought right from the start. Variations on the general theme, which included 46 predominantly 'thin-winged' RF-4Bs for the US Marines, and 146 J79-GE-17-powered RF-4Cs (re-dubbed RF-4Es by McDonnell) for export, incorporated different, or less-sensitive, onboard mission equipment.

So smooth was the USAF's transition to RF-4Cs that examples were made available for use by the Guard as early as 1971. The first such unit to fly Phantoms was the 106th TRS, 117th TRW in Alabama, achieving C1 status in the early months of 1973 under the command of Col. (now Brig. Gen.) Addison O. Logan. By 1974 the unit had logged 10,000hrs in the type.

In Vietnam the six RF-4C squadrons, split between Udorn RTAB, Thailand, and Tan Son Nhut, South Vietnam, gained an admirable reputation, proving time and time again the value of the Photo-Phantom as a dedicated, sophisticated, multi-sensor reconaissance platform. RF-4C missions would precede and follow the strike packages to, as the Udorn flight placard read, 'bring back the pictures . . .', for general intelligence gathering and target damage assessment purposes.† The motto was 'Alone, unarmed, and unafraid'. While the latter statement was subject to some debate (a McDonnell tech-rep recalled consoling an RF-4C crew who were ready to hand in their wings after drawing and evading no less than sixteen SAMs on their first combat mission over North Vietnam!), Photo-Phantoms accumulated an impressive tally of over 70,000 combat sorties in South-East Asia for the loss of only 72 aircraft to hostile fire.‡

---

*This total includes two YRF-4Cs converted from F-4Bs for development work.
†A companion placard read '. . . and Kill MiGs'. The 432nd TRW was a composite Wing flying RF-4Cs and F-4Ds, the latter accounting for at least 31 confirmed MiG kills in 1972 alone.
‡Four more were destroyed on the ground during the Tet Offensive in 1968, and a further seven were written off in operational accidents in SEA.

Training

To keep today's 227 active and Guard RF-4Cs fully crewed, two bases perform a continuing RTU function. Originally this was the sole responsibility of the 363rd TRW at Shaw AFB, which maintained two training and two operational RF-4C squadrons as 'TAC's home of reconnaissance'. From the start of operations in 1963 Shaw specialized in this role, putting USAF and several foreign RF-4C/E customer crews through an extensive basic course. The mission and Wing structure remained relatively static until September 1979, when one squadron was disbanded. Then, in 1981 the 363rd began to remould itself as a fighter Wing, ready for three new squadrons of F-16s. Training elements were transferred to Bergstrom AFB, Texas, to form the new training nucleus under the 67th TRW, boosting its strength by some 50 aircraft to 89 RF-4Cs, while just one squadron stayed behind at Shaw, dropping the Wing's long-time reconnaissance tradition and distinctive 'JO' tail-code (originally named after Jo Stopanian, the wife of a former 363rd pilot) in favour of the 'SW' designation. The entire process took just over six months, and was completed in September 1982.

The two training squadrons at Bergstrom, the 45th and 62nd TRTSs, help to fill the active USAF vacancies while also providing RF-4E transition for eighteen West German air crews each year. For ANG crews, who now fly 50 per cent of USAF RF-4C assets, training is accomplished at Boise International Airport, Idaho, under the direction of the 124th TRG, a large organization with 32 RF-4Cs pooled by the 189th Tactical Recon Training Flight and 190th TRS, and which includes all thirteen surviving Loran D 'towel bar' Photo-Phantoms. The active and Guard conversion courses are identical: both are designed to remould fighter-trained crews into recce flyers, using the basic-format, Vietnam-era sensors – the fundamentals. Newer technology is taught after the crews arrive at their operational bases, after having clocked up some 48 pilot or 30 WSO sorties spread out over six months, including an additional 80hrs of academics plus just under 20 simulator flights and check-rides.

Average instructor experience in reconnaissance, just as with the Wild Weasels, is higher than elsewhere in TAC Phantom circles. The same goes for the Guard crews. Air and ground crews tend to stay with the mission, particularly as the RF-4C provides better career opportunities for WSOs: a good number of SAC's SR-71 Blackbird Recce Systems Operators (RSOs) have come from the RF-4C, and a tour on the recce-Phantom is considered a good move. Pilots also generally like the mission – the crew is simply required to bring back the data, while how they do it is, within reasonable limits, entirely up to them.

Although a significant proportion of the training programme involves the same topics learnt at fighter bases – such as emergency procedures, visual and instrument navigation, aerial refuelling, and getting to grips with the 'hard-wing' Phantom itself – the conversion course centres around reconnaissance skills. The RF-4C mission is fundamentally different from strike; not only do the aircraft lack any sort of armament (other than the ability to carry a single nuclear bomb), but the job is a very solitary task. Indeed, whereas strike-fighter crews learn to fly in two- and four-ship tactical flights, reconnaissance missions are

Below: RF-4C-18-MC 63-7743, the fourth production Photo-Phantom for the USAF, at Edwards AFFTC in the early 1960s, wearing AFSC insignia and the old Phantom 'FJ' buzz code. (USAF via Lucille Zaccardi)

invariably a one-aircraft affair, so the crews must acquire very different habits from the outset of their training. There is little or no opportunity for a fledgeling to trail on the wing of an experienced crew before becoming fully qualified, though two-ship flights are sometimes used to help the new crews get over the hump of their initial 100hrs.

Descent to camera/sensor-operating heights usually takes the crew down to between 100 and 500ft above ground level (AGL), but the actual height flown varies with the clock (night missions are flown at 500–1,000ft AGL) and with the crew's own appraisal of the relative dangers involved – the intensity of anti-air defences and the hard terrain below them. Low-level routes usually include a long sweaty ride over a 200+ mile

course, a factor which requires the crews to maintain liaison with local civil authorities. Assisted by terrain-mapping radar, most pilots will push the throttles to the firewall and get over 600kts out of the jet. This is obviously intrinsically dangerous, but is made even more hazardous by unexpected obstacles, such as radio towers and power lines, together with the odd

Above: An 18th TRS, 363rd TRW RF-4C-30-MC, 66-0414, ready for take-off and with the pins out. (C.M. via Peter E. Davies)

Below: Spick-and-span RF-4C from the 33rd TRTS, 363rd TFW, based at Shaw AFB, South Carolina. (Via Peter E. Davies)

Above left: Boise, Idaho, is the home for the Guard's dedicated recce-training unit, the 124th TRG. (MAP)

Above right: RF-4C 66-0421 makes for the sky with afterburners glowing. The wheels are coming up and the altimeter needles are starting to rise. (MAP via P. Davies)

TYPICAL FLYING SCHEDULE, RENO NEVADA GUARD

Day	Time	No. of flights
Monday (one per month)	1.30 p.m.–3.30 p.m.	8
Tuesday–Thursday	1.00 p.m.–4.00 p.m.	4
Tuesday–Thursday	6.00 p.m.–8.30 p.m.	8
Friday	1.00 p.m.–3.30 p.m.	6
Saturday	3.00 a.m.–noon	8
Saturday	1.00 p.m.–3.30 p.m.	4

Note: There may be occasional deviations to this schedule, for mission requirements directed by higher command/authority.

Below: A flight-line of RF-4Cs at RAF Alconbury, England, in the mid-1970s. These days all forward-deployed jets are dispersed and sheltered in big, concrete and steel TAB-V hangars. (MAP)

light aviation plane straying into military training corridors; such mid-air collisions involving Phantoms do, unfortunately, occur far too often, the last such occasion being in June 1985 when a Beech aircraft strayed into restricted airspace and collided with an Alabama Guard RF-4C. The Guard crew managed to limp home in their damaged mount. Less fortunate were two crew members who died in a mid-air collision over Brownwood, Texas, on 21 January 1987, involving a pair of RF-4Cs. From the other angle, the sensors of the RF-4Cs have often located aircraft wreckage during training sorties, often after days or weeks of unsuccessful regular search and rescue operations. In April 1983 a B-52 took off from Robins AFB, Georgia, bound for a training session over the Nellis range and simply disappeared. Forty-eight hours later, an RF-4C on a low-level training flight discovered the wreckage in Utah. Other training sorties allow the RF-4C units to put their skills at the disposal of US Federal Agencies. Such flights have included detecting illegal sewage and waste disposal for the Environmental Protection Agency, and monitoring

melting snow so that warning of possible flooding can be given in good time, whilst radiation leaks and other potential hazards have frequently been detected early enough for safe preventative or remedial action to be taken. Well-publicized support has included flying emergency blood from state to state. Other, more clandestine work has seen RF-4Cs operating over Central America in recent months.

Overseas deployments and local manoeuvres form part of a typical recce squadron's annual itinerary. Reno Nevada's ANG, for example, completed what they termed a 'unique low-cost exchange programme with the Royal Air Force'. In October 1979 eight Reno air crews flew European theatre orientation missions in the rear seats of Jaguar GR.1 aircraft with the RAF Coltishall-based No. 41 Squadron (themselves long-time reconnaissance specialists); four months later RAF air crews came to Nevada for orientation flights in the rear seats of RF-4Cs. This was the first such exchange of its type, and has since been followed up with ANG RF-4C deployments to RAF Coltishall under the codename 'Coronet Mobile', as part of the 'Checkered Flag' programme. The only major difference between strike and recce Phantom flights and deployments is that RF-4C crews generally fly fewer sorties per month, generating a maximum of about two sorties per aircraft per day during surge drives, though the Birmingham Alabama Guard's recent 'Rapid Recce' effort generated an unprecedented 73 sorties with eighteen RF-4Cs in 7hrs 51mins, attracting national attention. On the other hand, the recce missions tend to be 30 or more minutes longer, and this trend in longer mission times is on the increase. Minimum training levels demand about 135 sorties per squadron each month; nevertheless, the Reno ANG claim that they burn up some six million dollars' worth of aviation fuel a year, equating to some 5,000 RF-4C 'events' – landings and take-offs. Active squadrons average nearer 400 sorties a month, while the whole fleet, active and Guard, amassed 78,000 flight hours in 1986, which works out to just under 350hrs per aircraft – a fairly vigorous flying schedule.

As a counterpart to the strike units' 'Fightcomp' meets, specialist 'mini-recce matches' are sponsored by the US and allied services, in which RF-4C teams can compete for top honours and which typically involve detachments from up to seven active and Guard squadrons: such events include 'Best Focus', 'Photo Meet' and 'Photo Finish'. Mission objectives provide each crew with a series of specific items to monitor, with points being awarded for target-acquisition, film usage, sensor coverage and the quality of the data retrieved, plus best time over target and back. The most prestigious event is TAC's new biennial Recon Air Meet (RAM), the first of which was hosted by the 67th TRW at Bergstrom in November 1976 – the recce equivalent of 'William Tell' and 'Gunsmoke'. During the course of seven reconnaissance profiles, the competitors had to tackle 'Aggressor' F-4Ds and F-15s, liaise with E-3 AWACs command posts, and get topped up with 'gas' by KC-10s. RF-4C units consistently came out top, beating recce-mod F-111s from Australia and Navy recon units, though the judges may have been a little biased: Maj. Gen. P. Hodges, the chief judge, flew 209 combat sorties in the RF-4C in South-East Asia and has some affection for the type! The next RAM is due in 1988.

'Red' and 'Green Flag' training manoeuvres conducted at Nellis TFWC are more challenging than the mini-meets, principally because of the decision-making demands placed on the recce teams: ground commanders have to allocate their scarce RF-4C resources carefully, while the air crews are heavily scrutinized for their use of ECM, communications, navigation and sensor equipment. This is what makes reconnaissance so different from strike: a bomb is a bomb, and despite newer and newer forms of guidance, 'hasn't changed much since World War One in terms of the hole it makes in the ground', as many recce flyers take pains to point out. Although premission planning of routes and ordnance or sensors is vital to any successful mission, in reconnaissance it is the post-launch decisions which can be the most important. It would be a waste of valuable time to film one gun emplacement with every onboard sensor, and equally wasteful to film a well-camouflaged SAM-radar installation on conventional film – infra-red imagery would help provide data as to its type and status. Additionally, objects of different sizes have varying minimum interpretation scales, and these must come in to the equation. The minimum scale for identifying a parked Foxbat-sized aircraft, for example, is 1:10,000, while to define it specifically as a MiG-25 would require an interpretation minimum of 1:3,000. Added to this, moving-target images need to be twice the size of stationary ones.

Self-defence is a vital skill that takes some time to master, particularly as RF-4C crews cannot call upon the same degree of back-up as their strike colleagues. RF-4Cs carry no Sidewinder missiles for self-defence, but rely solely on speed, evasive tactics and the effective use of ECM – mismanagement of ECM can cause one's position to be given away.* For this purpose, the Photo-Phantom employs the same package as that installed in the F-4E, combining Applied Technology ALR-69 or more recent -74 RWRs with Westinghouse ALQ-119 or -131 pods for co-ordinated radar disruption. The threat warning receiver antennae are fitted to the drag 'chute door and nose, the latter fitting comprising two buttons screwed into the forward-facing camera hatch. ECM pods are bolted on to inner wing pylons. The RF-4C uses the ALE-40 dispenser adapted to fit in the rear fuselage empennage photo-flash ejector compartments – a much more aerodynamic mode of carriage – with cartridge 'pop-out' at the command of the WSO. Full controls are being evaluated.

Missions assigned to the USAF RF-4C community, today embracing thirteen operational squadrons,

include general surveillance, pre- and post-strike target area coverage and an increasing amount of maritime cover. Since the rapid withdrawal of dedicated RF-8G and RA-5C fleet carrier recce jets, the Navy and Marines have been relying solely on a limited number of RF-4Bs (28 remaining) and F-14A pod-equipped 'Peeping Toms'. Consequently, USAF RF-4Cs are taking on an increasing number of over-water operations.

Basic sensors

There are many cameras, infra-red and radar sensors that the RF-4C can carry to perform its various tasks - so many, in fact, that it is rare to find a whole flight-line of jets fitted with a uniform package at any one time. Instead, RF-4C units will employ a number of different equipment configurations so that there is always at least one aircraft ready for any given task. The internal mix-and-match of equipment may even change from mission to mission. The more fastidious observer might also notice two distinct nose profiles – a flat-based type and another with more rounded ventral contours.† These have little bearing on internal equipment fitting, but rather the rounded version (introduced on Block 44 USAF, plus Greek, Israeli, Iranian, Japanese and Turkish machines and retrofitted to 26th TRW examples in the late 1970s) offer better optical characteristics and refined aerodynamics. It is also

*RF-4C Sidewinder Engineering Change Proposals (ECPs) are being studied by McDonnell Douglas. The Minnesota Guard considered the idea during their RF-4C to F-4D transition in 1983.
†'Peace Jack' RF-4X machines, three of which were supplied by General Dynamics to Israel in 1975–76 from converted FY 1969 F-4E airframes, featured entirely new noses, housing special high-resolution, high-altitude, long-range optical cameras. Special water injection tanks were experimented with for sustained high-mach, high-altitude flight. Little is known about their operational use or current status.

worth bearing in mind that while the devices described below form the bulk of Guard capabilities, they only contribute to the wider array of sensors available to active units, dealt with later.

Target run-in is assisted by the nose-mounted Texas Instruments AN/APQ-99 radar, which in the terrain-following mode provides a 25-degree vertical and 5-degree horizontal sweep of the terrain ahead of the aircraft on the pilot's left-hand scope to assist with his manual contour-hugging flying (by means of a pitch indicator); in the mapping mode both the pilot and WSO can monitor the radar imagery to help navigate to, line up with and cue sensors over the target on the reconnaissance pass. The pilot also has an additional right-hand scope, the LA-313A. Introduced on FY 64

Above: 'Hill Gray II' RF-4C 64-1044 approaches RAF Coltishall during the 106th TRS, Alabama Guard's 'Coronet Mobile' – 'Checkered Flag' – deployment conducted between 13 and 26 September 1986. The only concessions to colour (apart from some warning stencil data) are the red stars on the fin-cap and the Presidential Unit Citation ribbon on the nose. (Dave Robinson)

Below left: 'Royal Flush' 1975 markings adorn RF-4C-38-MC 68-0571. These markings are featured on Microscale decal sheet 48-108. (Udo Weisse via P. Davies)

Below right: The beady eyes of the AN/ALR-69 threat-warning system protrude from a Zweibrucken-based RF-4C in 1983. RF-4Cs of the 26th TRW carried several different variations on the 'sharkmouth' scheme at this time. (Author)

Block 20 machines, and retrofitted into earlier examples at Ogden, this ties through to the aft nose camera station to provide a direct look at the terrain beneath the aircraft, assisting in line-up during a high-altitude photographic session.*

Stabilized mounts and mirrors compensate for camera shake as the RF-4C thunders over enemy targets, while the WSO has a few small but important aids at hand to ensure that the quality of the film imagery remains good. These include buttons for window demist, compensation for cloud cover, operating altitude, day or night filming, infra-red sensor sensitivity and contrast, and range of sideways-looking airborne radar (SLAR) operation. A complete panel of counters showing the amount of film remaining in feet in each camera station and the quantity of cartridges left in the flash ejector bays assists sensor management. A 'special interest' switch enables the WSO to mark the film with a little arrow, highlighting a well-hidden target which may not show up very well after the imagery has been processed back at base.

Cameras are selected by pressing a series of buttons located on the right console, each of which denotes a specific sensor station; the WSO may have to cross-refer to his briefing and maintenance rosters in order to refresh his memory as to the whereabouts of a certain type of sensor and its lens fitting. This panel includes switches for infra-red and SLAR operation, together with a general master operate button, used to activate the pre-selected systems over the target. As can be seen from the accompanying tables, the cameras come in many shapes and sizes. The principal types used today include the KS-87, KA-56 and KA-91,

but the major point to note concerning these devices is that most come with an assortment of lenses. The KS-87, for example, may be fitted with a 3, 6, 12 or 18in lens. Each of these, because of their varying focal lengths, takes a series of snapshots covering an area of ground proportionate to the lens used and the altitude at which they are utilized. Accordingly, the 3in lens covers an area 1.5 times the aircraft height, the 6in lens an area .75 times the aircraft height, and so on, so that at 1,000ft, for example, the 3in lens will cover a tract of ground 1,500ft square while the 18in lens at the same height will produce a frame covering a piece of ground only 250ft square.

Complementing the cameras is the AAS-18A infra-red linescan set, fitted only to the special station aft of the wheel bay under the WSO's seat. This is used during an overflight manoeuvre. The equipment rapidly scans the ground in a series of sweeps, building up a picture by picking up heat radiation within the sensor's field of view and feeding the imagery on to a continuous-roll film, mirroring the ground as the RF-4C flies along its track. Because of the heat-sensing qualities of linescan, the AAS-18A can produce some remarkable intelligence: glowing aircraft parked on an enemy runway, for example, will reveal recent engine operation, in turn indicating how many fighters remain operational; bright images in a wood uncloak a well-hidden enemy ground force; and, at lower altitudes,

---

*The APQ-99 is being modified to APQ-172 standard with the addition of a digital scan converter and new cockpit displays to present the information in easier-to-digest form for improved safety and a reduced crew workload.

USAF RF-4 BASIC SENSORS

Camera	Mode	Focal length	Film frame
T-11	High altitude-mapping; non-stabilized	6in	9.4in square
KA-55	High-altitude panoramic	12in	4.5in×9.4in
KA-56	Low-altitude panoramic	3in	4.5in×9.4in
KS-72/87	High-speed camera (all stations) for day or night work, at high or low altitudes	3/6/12/18in	4.5in square
KA-1	Medium- to high-altitude day	12/24/36in	9in×18in
KA-91B	Medium-altitude (6,000–16,000ft)	18in f4	4.5in×18.8in (60°) 4.5in×29.2in (90°)

Infra-red line-scan	Mode	Film
AAS-18A/AAD-5	Low- to medium-altitude	4.5in wide, 350ft long

Radar	Mode	Film
APQ-102A	Sideways-looking stand-off sensor	5in wide, 150ft long

Note: Low altitude includes heights up to 1,000ft; medium altitude ranges from 1,000 to 20,000ft; high altitude is in excess of 20,000ft.

Below left: An RF-4C from the Nevada Guard 'High Rollers'. (Mil-Slides)

Below right: An RF-4C in the twilight. The revised, rounded nose shape was introduced on Block 44 aircraft and retrofitted to selected earlier examples. (USAF)

linescan can show up tank tracks, even footprints! Its performance, however, is severely degraded when it has to scan through cloud, rain or other adverse meteorological conditions, though it has better 24hr capabilities than cameras, which require less than ⅝ths cloud, and which can then only be usefully employed during daytime. Since 1977 the AAS-18 has been supplemented and gradually replaced by the Honeywell AAD-5 infra-red sensor. The new AAD-5 offers variable swath capabilities, so that scan-width can be adjusted to compensate for various operating heights and the degree of detail required. Its newer design also features much higher resolution imagery than the old linescan.

Finally, the basic format RF-4C comes with the Goodyear (bought up by the Loral Corporation in March 1987) AN/APQ-102 SLAR, a twin set of radars which 'fan-scan' an area 20 degrees wide, 90 degrees out from the sides of the jet in an all-round mode when both antenna arrays are used or from one side only when the aircraft flies in a pattern adjacent to the target area. The APQ-102 works by sending out X-band radar energy, and measuring, line by line, the returning reflected 'doppler phase histories' of terrain features and targets – radar-mapping the ground on roll film. The SLAR incorporates a Moving Target Indicator (MTI) facility, which enables the system to track targets moving as slowly as 8mph. All film is annotated with aircraft height and position to assist in post-mission interpretation. As with IR linescan, the SLAR drive motor unleashes the roll of film at a speed proportionate to aircraft velocity, so that a given length of film is always exposed for a given distance,

thereby freeing the pilot to play with the throttle controls. This ensures that the imagery remains at a constant scale for ease of analysis.

Extending through the production line to FY69 Block 44 aircraft was a film cartridge ejection system. This was designed to lob out exposed film cartridges while the RF-4C remained in flight, the general idea being to reduce the amount of time expended during the post-sortie 'down-loading' process. Finding the ejected film cartridges after release presented a new set of problems, so when production of the RF-4C picked up again in 1971 the system was dropped and the rounded nose profile adopted. Instead, ground crews gain access to the film and tape only after the RF-4C pulls up into its revetment or parking slot.

All films are processed on base, using a Loral ES-75 (for colour) or WS-420A/B Photo-Processing and Interpretation Facility (PPIF, for black-and-white shots). These are portable, and are routinely carried overseas in MAC cargo aircraft when squadrons perform 'Checkered Flag' deployments. Within PACAF and USAFE it is customary to slot the mobile shelters into a hardened hangar. The objective of the processing team is to get the film to the intelligence and debrief people as soon as possible, preferably within half an hour of engine shut-down, and 'wet' (not yet printed up) if necessary. Air-crew tape recordings, giving verbal descriptions of the target area, assist film interpretation – a process which may ultimately drag on for four or more hours and involve the consumption of several gallons of coffee! Air crews actively participate in interpretation because of their valuable first-hand knowledge, which is used to help point out things that film cannot pick up, such as the 'texture' of enemy fortifications – data on whether an enemy position is shielded by concrete or bricks, for example, may be vital to an Army or Marine Corps commander.

Newer developments have, however, greatly changed this 'bring back the pictures' routine. Two systems have been fielded operationally in recent years which are able to transfer their data in 'near real-time' or, in other words, almost instantaneously to ground interpretation centres. The impact on the RF-4C force structure has been substantial. The new systems are so much more effective that the resultant 'force multiplying' effect has enabled most forward-deployed active units to reduce by 50 per cent the numbers of Photo-Phantoms on standby. Moreover, the fact that the aircraft need not return to generate reconnaissance products has sparked off an increased awareness of the importance of self-defence within the recce community. The two sensors in question are the AN/ALQ-125 TEREC, and a brand new synthetic aperture radar (SAR) version of the AN/APQ-102 known as the AN/UPD-8.

TEREC

During the height of the air war over North Vietnam it was apparent that intelligence on the enemy anti-air defences was woefully inadequate. Radar, camera and infra-red systems were good at taking snaps and ribbon shots of anti-aircraft systems, and the special AN/ALR-17 ELRAC receiving set was able to pick up and spot-mark radars on the film, but little was available on the nature of the enemy defences. A radar dish might well show up, but in what frequencies was it operating? And was it a dummy with an infra-red emitter attached to the 'generator' to make it seem real? If tactical forces had access to such information, friendly strike aircraft could be routed around the worst 'hot-spots' of anti-aircraft activity, while on-board self-protection systems could be pre-programmed with specific 'jamming strategies' so that they were prepared to counteract radar threats anticipated

Left: A fine study of an 18th TRS, 363rd TRW RF-4C coming in to land at Shaw AFB in 1971. (MAP via Peter E. Davies)

Below: A beautiful study of an RF-4C from the Alabama Air Guard pulling in with its drag 'chute deployed. (USAF)

en route to the target and back. ECM pods can only cope with the complex act of jamming in a few radar bands, and while the Weasels' reputation in Vietnam was second to none, as hunter-killers they too could greatly benefit from prior knowledge on the disposition of hostile emitters.

Thus in 1970 Project 'Pave Onyx' was born, a programme which aimed to field an all-weather passive electromagnetic reconnaissance sensor, able to detect the position, operating frequencies and status of enemy radars at a safe stand-off distance. With this technology established in the works, in 1971 Litton Amecom came forward with a battle area device, the Tactical Electromagnetic Recon (TEREC) sensor. An R&D contract was issued to the manufacturers to supply seven prototype systems, each one a small, 450lb package that could fit snugly into the RF-4C's existing SLAR stations. Of the seven systems supplied for development work, two were assigned to the Eglin ADTC, while the remaining five kits were despatched to active units, to be tested under operational conditions.

Using TEREC, 26th TRW crews on detachment to Zaragoza, Spain, flying over the Mediterranean, found that they were not only able to map the location and structure of 'enemy' land-based radar networks, but were also capable of identifying and classifying naval traffic, thus providing a complete picture of radars over land and sea, around the clock. In 1980, with tests complete and all milestones met, a contract worth in excess of $30 million was issued to Litton Amecom for 23 advanced production TEREC systems, newly designated the AN/ALQ-125. One was assigned for follow-on trials at Eglin, four were kept as spares back-up at Warner-Robbins avionics logistics centre and the remaining eighteen sets were deployed to the active forces, though principally Kadena and Zweibrucken. Including the updated prototype systems, 24 TEREC RF-4Cs achieved their IOC in 1982.

Below: A Lincoln, Nebraska Guard RF-4C in flamboyant exercise markings, comprising yellow and blue fuselage stripes and a brown bulldog. (MAP)

TEREC 'tactical ferreting' provides complete radar detection, or as a junior officer from Zweibrucken graphically demonstrated with a jubilant sweep of his arms, 360-degree coverage. In practice, the navigator may either choose all-round coverage, or elect to look left or right only, as would be the case when flying along the FEBA in a stand-off mode. TEREC is pre-programmed before take-off to 'sniff out' ten types of enemy radar, any five of which can be assigned a high-priority status; the WSO may change the priority status during the course of the mission. When TEREC detects signals from any of the five priority radar types, it tracks them long enough so that it gets a series of directions of arrival (DOAs), or bearings relative to the Phantom. By matching the relative aircraft position at each DOA (calculated by the onboard ARN-101), the TEREC triangulates the co-ordinates of the enemy radars. During this 'auto search', the WSO uses two displays to monitor the proceedings – not PPIs as in the rear cockpit of the F-4G Weasel, but 'control' and 'location' panels. The 'control' panel has a series of fruit machine-style, push-button lamps, each of which relates to a pre-programmed priority radar type. When one shines up, TEREC has picked up and is listening to an emitter in that category; if the WSO then pushes the button, a complete report on the enemy radar will be flashed up on the 'location' display. This other panel shows all pertinent information – bearing, estimated range in miles and latitude/longitude co-ordinates – in easy-to-read digits. Working through all the lit-up buttons on the 'control' unit, one at a time, the navigator can relay all available data on the priority emitter types over secure radio to friendly C³I, electronic support and strike aircraft, while the crew, if they desire, can single out one or more of the enemy radars and use their onboard camera and infra-red sensors for closer examination.

More importantly, 'real-time' data-link transmission is built into TEREC. At the push of the 'DL' button, TEREC automatically passes on all available information on the five priority radars to friendly ground stations. This is done by using a data-link broadcast through the RF-4C's standard UHF or longer-range

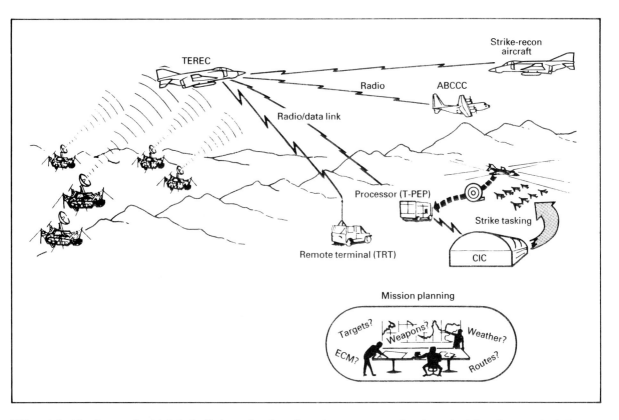

Labels in diagram:
TEREC, Strike-recon aircraft, Radio, ABCCC, Radio/data link, Processor (T-PEP), Strike tasking, Remote terminal (TRT), CIC, Mission planning, Targets?, Weapons?, Weather?, ECM?, Routes?

HF aerials (the latter of which is built into the dorsal fin). The importance of this capability is speed. During operations in South-East Asia using conventional photography, infra-red and radar-film imagery, it took anything up to four hours after landing before the ground commanders could handle the interpreted data. As the TEREC data-link feeds the information straight to the ground, it may be processed virtually instantaneously by ground-based T-PEPs (TEREC Portable Exploitation Processors) or TRTs (TEREC Remote Terminals) while the RF-4C remains in flight. T-PEPs and TRTs are provided with TEREC priority collection objectives prior to the RF-4C sortie, so that they can decode and pass on the information directly to commanders in a matter of minutes. Commanders, in turn, may use it for any number of purposes, gaining tactical advantages from the immediacy of the intelligence.

Coupled to near 'real-time' intelligence transmission the WSO may elect to press the 'EOB' button, directing TEREC to go into full spectrum search, to 'sniff out' all enemy radars it can pick up and not just those accorded priority before the mission. This data is recorded on a nine-track recorder, the tape of which can be processed in a T-PEP after landing to provide a complete picture of the enemy's electronic order of battle.

Israel is known to operate a similar 'radar-sniffing' package on its hunter-killer F-4Ps and RF-4Es, these jets having taken part in the highly successful 1982 raids on Syrian SAM sites in the Beka'a Valley.*

Above: Diagram showing principles of F-4 Tactical Electronic Reconnaissance (TEREC) system. (Litton Amecom)

Twenty-two SAM sites – nineteen in one day – were knocked out by a combination of radar-detection gear, anti-radar missiles and decoys – unquestionable proof of the value of Ferret and Weasel Phantoms.

UPD radars

Complementing the ALQ-125 TEREC is the UPD-SLAR, a brand-new version of the APQ-12 sideways-looking airborne radar. This update originates from January 1970, when a $21 million contract to design, develop and fabricate an improved side-looking radar was awarded to the Arizona Division of the Loral Corporation. Occupying essentially the same space in the sensor bays as the routine APQ-102A, the new units, just like TEREC, were designed to be installed without the need for extensive modification to the RF-4C. With fabrication of the prototypes complete, the 'black boxes' were deployed to USAFE in the late autumn of 1973, giving enough time for the 26th TRW to work up to operational status prior to the 1974 NATO 'Reforger' exercises – the big operational test.

The technology represented a major breakthrough in radar-mapping techniques. This was because it introduced synthetic aperture radar, working much like the APQ-102 but building up a picture by

---

*The F-4P is otherwise known as the RF-4X, a special reconnaissance rebuild of the RF-4E.

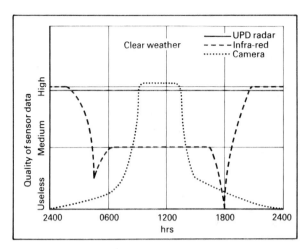

Above: Graph showing comparative quality of UPD radar, infra-red sensor and camera data in clear weather.

Far right, top: A 26th TRW RF-4C displays its 'top hat' data-link antenna used in conjunction with the 'real-time' UPD SLAR. (McDonnell Douglas)

Far right, bottom: The new RF-4C SLAR pod. The UPD-8 systems may be carried in these pods. (McDonnell Douglas)

recording a series of neat synthetic portions of the returning reflected radar energy on to roll film, via a sophisticated laser-optical correlation-processor. Films were processed back at base on a companion ES-83 correlator-processor, which decoded the raw material to produce exceptionally high quality, photograph-like radar pictures. The initial results were very pleasing, and in comparison with conventional camera and infra-red sensors the new UPD-4 SLAR showed many advantages. First, there was virtually no weather or time of day that disrupted the mission – the imagery remained just as good, no matter when it was collected. Second, unlike cameras, which introduce perspective when used for oblique shots (making target images difficult to interpret because of the absence of a constant sense of scale), the new SLAR imagery was filmed at a constant scale of 1:100,000 across and along the roll film. The imagery was then magnified to produce fine details of ground targets, even when SLAR passes were made at low altitude and at stand-off ranges of up to 30nm! With cameras, this detail and ease of interpretation could only be achieved if the film were exposed during vulnerable overflight, and only then under optimum weather conditions. With the operational evaluation nearly complete, Dr. Malcolm R. Currie, from the DDR&E, before the first session of the Congressional Appropriations Committee in February 1975, stated:

These systems demonstrated the great potential of this unique sensor which permits detection and location of trucks, tanks, aircraft and similar-sized targets at night and under all weather conditions. During the Reforger '74 exercise, in which extremely poor weather conditions

were encountered, these systems obtained virtually *all* of the reconnaissance products that were generated.

Army commander Lt. Gen. G. S. Blanchard wrote to the 26th TRW to say:

For the first time in six Reforgers we consistently got the data to commanders in time for them to respond. The imagination and commitment of the RF-4C air crews was especially noteworthy. They refused to allow a marginal communications environment to discourage them, or prevent the information reaching those who needed it. The importance of this work is underlined by the fact that ground commanders were frequently able to fire artillery on targets reported (radioed in) by recce crews before the aircraft landed.

The impressive results obtained from the UPD-4 during the 'Reforger' exercise had also attracted much interest from other RF-4 operators: a five-year, $4.2 million contract was awarded to Loral to field the package on USMC RF-4Bs, Japan joining the league soon after and buying fourteen kits for its RF-4EJs. But that was not the end of the story. The USAF decided to go one better and, in December 1975, the Aeronautical Systems Division of AFSC awarded a further contract to Loral to add a data-link for instant transmission of the radar imagery back to the ground. Defined under QRC 76-01, this quick-reaction capability requirement stipulated that the system be fielded in time for the 1976 series of NATO autumn exercises. Flight-tested in July 1976 at Luke AFB, Arizona, the new black boxes got the all-clear and were passed on to the 26th TRW at Zweibrucken that August. One aircraft was re-rigged with the 'top hat' data-link capability and, just one month later, flew all-out in the 'Reforger' and 'Coldfire' manoeuvres. The results were outstanding. How the system was put to use best answers why.

Prior to the actual exercise, a 'radar data base' was laid down. This essentially split the V and VII Corps areas (just east and 50nm south of Frankfurt respectively) into strips 30nm long and 10nm wide. The 26th TRW then directed its 'real-time' UPD-4 Phantom to fly along each strip and map the territory with the SLAR, one strip at a time, to form a composite picture of the entire area. (Presumably, in much the same way, most of Europe and much of the Pacific has already been mapped.) During the exercise, the 38th TRS acted in support of US Army 'Blue Forces', and was 'fragged' to overfly and re-map parts of the radar data base, as directed. This called for a 4.30 a.m. take-off and, with two air-to-air refuellings, meant a gruelling, non-stop, six-hour sortie each day, comprising up to twelve SLAR runs. While making each of the SLAR passes the radar data was transmitted back to the ground; the incoming signals were then fed on to roll film back at base, so that within twelve minutes of a start of a SLAR run processed film was being churned out from the ground correlator-processor equipment, providing a continuous record of the RF-4C's scan that could be analyzed on the spot for potential targets.

To unearth better-camouflaged targets, further detailed examination took place in four special interpe-

tation shelters. Two of these had been acquired as part of the bumper QRC 76-01 package, and featured extensive time-saving automation; these mobile ground support shelters later became standard operational equipment under the name MARRES (Manual Airborne Real-time Reconnaissance Exploitation Systems). In these, SLAR films were fed into viewing machines, TV screens which offered between 5× and 50× magnification, producing scales ranging from 1:20,000 up to 1:2,000, the former magnification showing enough detail to classify a ship or detect the presence of a SAM-radar complex, the latter sufficiently large not only to show individual 'enemy' trucks and tanks but to do so with such clarity that interpreters could ascertain the exact model of the object under scrutiny! Ease of interpretation of the targets that were more difficult to find was made possible by the ability to compare old and new pictures of the same piece of ground, effected by comparing fresh SLAR strips with pictures taken during the establishment of the radar data base. New features in the imagery which seemed to have sprouted from nowhere probably indicated the presence of 'enemy' hardware. All target information was passed on to the Mission Controller, including vital UTM, 'lat/long' and Loran TD co-ordinates; this was in turn despatched to allied 'Blue Force' air units via a TIPI (Tactical Information Processing and Interpretation) shelter, which directed F-4s and F-111s on to the opposing 'enemy' ground forces. Other reports were made down the hot-lines to Army commanders for immediate up-to-date news on the disposition of the 'Red Force', and was used to

Below: UPD-8 SLAR operation (diagrammatic).

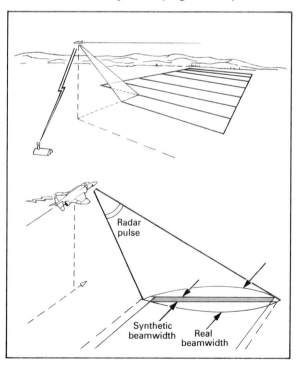

help pin-point impact points for rocket and artillery fire. In all, it was discovered that just under 60 lucrative targets could be identified within an hour of RF-4C time-over-target (TOT), and no fewer than 75 could be identified within two hours of TOT.

From the USAF point of view, the near 'real-time', data-linked SLAR showed four supreme advantages over the old systems. First, whereas regular aircraft were film-limited, the new RF-4C was merely fuel-limited. This meant that, as long as aerial-refuelling support was available, the data-link aircraft was able to continue to provide vital information, crew fatigue being the major limitation. Second, areas of high- or low-ground activity were identified early in the mission, thus enabling optimum target-area coverage. Third, the data-linked RF-4C had the flexibility to launch and recover at different airfields and still transmit target imagery back home; by contrast, the regular RF-4Cs had to be recovered at their home base in order for the film to be processed. Finally, the near 'real-time' data could be fused with other data-linked information, such as TEREC, in good time for it to be useful: mobile enemy anti-aircraft systems could be stopped in their tracks.

Following the successful QRC 76-01 demonstration, some eighteen USAF RF-4Cs were re-equipped with the package, which was dubbed the AN/UPD-8 in October 1982. Suitably impressed, the Luftwaffe fielded a derivative model called the UPD-6 on several of its AKG-51 and -52 RF-4Es, and the USMC fitted the UPD-9 variant to its VMFP-3 RF-4Bs, as part of both services' Photo-Phantom improvement programmes. Furthermore, to bolster its own numbers, the USAF is purchasing nine podded UPD-8s for 'strap-on' to regular RF-4Cs, while even more advanced ground-based support equipment has entered service for yet faster and more comprehensive data processing. One such aid is Loral's complementary ABLE network. This Advanced Building Block for Large Area Exploitation device, tested during NATO's 1981 'Reforger' exercise, uses four shelters able to handle information ten times faster than the QRC 76-01 system, and includes automatic comparisons between fresh and old film strips for rapid target identification; furthermore, the scene being mapped by the RF-4C gets flashed up on a 4ft square 'Star Trek' type bridge screen for an immediate look at the battle area under observation!

Going digital
In addition to TEREC and the UPD-8, the USAF has been working on near 'real-time', data-linked cameras and infra-red sensors as part of the Compass Sight effort, due to come to operational fruition in 1993 as the ATARS (Advanced Tactical Aircraft Recon System). This will introduce 'real-time', film-less, electro-optical sensors generating imagery from digital charged coupled devices (CCDs) rather than celluloid. Forerunners to the ATARS include a special electronic wide-angle camera system (EWACS), built by Chicago Aerial Industries, which has demonstrated a near all-

weather capability to cover large tracts of territory. This is made possible by under-the-weather, low-level flying and a CCD married to a lens with a 140-degree FOV. A zoom facility is available at the crew's discretion, while companion ground-based controllers use a light pen on a near 'real-time' TV image to expand selected areas being stored on tape, for close-up examination on a second display. More recently, in early 1987, the Control Data Corporation flight-tested an integrated package comprising a pair of electro-optical panoramic cameras and IR sensors in an RF-4C at Eglin ADTC, with promising results. The technology is maturing. Using the production ATARS system the WSO will be able to view and edit the imagery on his scope as it is being collected, then relay it to ground interpretation facilities.

The importance of these integrated near 'real-time' systems cannot be overemphasized. They have given the Photo-Phantom a much extended lease of life. Plans are being drawn up to keep 244 ATARS-modified RF-4Cs in service through to the end of the century, and involve combining recce Phantom assets with RPV mini-craft, as mother-ships for the remotely piloted vehicles. But that is another five years away. Much more decisive has been the impact of the superb ARN-101.

Concurrent with the F-4E digital refit, selected RF-4Cs from production Blocks 37–53 were equipped with the Lear-Siegler ARN-101. Sixty-one aircraft were flying at the time of writing, of which 39 had also been wired up to accept the versatile Ford Aerospace AN/AVQ-26 Pave Tack pod. The primary operational ARN-101 RF-4C bases are Bergstrom, Shaw, Zweibrucken and PACAF – the loose term PACAF is used

here because although the 15th TRS officially operates from Kadena AB, Okinawa, the squadron maintains a permanent detachment of seven aircraft as Osan AB, South Korea, while the balance of the force fly from either Clark Field in the Philippines or the home-base, Kadena, but rarely both. Foreign customers of the ARN-101 recce modification are confined to Israel, which has bought and fielded fifteen kits for use on RF-4Es – three as spares, and a dozen for operations.

As in the ARN-101-equipped F-4E, RF-4s received a Loran C/D receiver and a new inertial measurement unit, replacing the old INS and several other 'black boxes'. However, rather than employing the system for ground attack, the RF-4C/Es use the DMAS in conjunction with their extensive range of onboard sensors and support equipment, namely the Pave Tack, ASQ-154 film annotation set (used to put interpretation marks on film), TEREC, AAD-5 infra-red sensor, UPD-SLAR and APQ-99 radar cursors. The ARN-101 can automatically activate any of these items over pre-selected co-ordinates, or assist in manual operation, by cueing selected sensors on to points being tracked by the WSO.

The navigation procedure is identical to the process used in the F-4E, with the ability to insert up to 60 waypoints at the insertion of a data transfer module and a push of a button. Recce crews, however, will use one of three flight profiles, 'route' point-to-point, 'patterned' race-track, or an adjacent parallel coverage

Below: Glossy RF-4C-25-MC, 65-0850, assigned to the 6512th Test Squadron, Edwards AFFTC, California. RF-4Cs are used primarily by the Test Pilot School to demonstrate dissimilar aircraft chase techniques. (Mil-Slides)

Left, top: RF-4C-43-MC 69-0369, with photoflash/chaff/flare ports open, rolls along the runway at Alconbury. The 'AR'-coded 10th TRW flew three squadrons of RF-4Cs until 1976, when two were disbanded; the remaining unit, the 1st TRS, was disbanded in 1987. (MAP)

Left, centre: A pair of ARN-101 modified RF-4Cs from the 67th TRW, based at Bergstrom AFB, Texas, await clearance for take-off. (USAF via Robert Scott)

Left, bottom: A 1st TRS, 10th TRW RF-4C climbs with a Ford Aerospace AN/AVQ-26 Pave Tack deployed. (Ford Aerospace)

Right: Pave Tack close up. The rear sensor head rotates and swivels to provide complete ventral coverage. The large red window is the zinc sulphide FLIR; the two smaller windows hide the laser transmitter/receiver and marked-target receiver. This RF-4C, 69-0378, performed all of the 'recce-Tack' integration trials after 1976. (Ford Aerospace)

mode. Point-to-point is exactly what it sounds like, a rally-like, roller-coaster mode of travel taking the crew and their jet through hostile terrain, up over and down and around undulating topography with sensor operation over pre-selected points. 'Race-track' is simply a flight pattern composed of neat circuits over or near enemy-held ground, while parallel coverage provides up to twenty consecutive straight paths and is used with systems such as the SLAR so that specific strips of a radar data base can be mapped or re-mapped in perfect co-ordinated lines.

Pave Tack, if available, can be used to assist in checking on route waypoints, just as on the ARN-101 F-4E. 'Data freeze' may also be employed. The press of this button will store the current aircraft position into the ARN-101 memory and can be used to spot-mark opportunity targets along the navigation track or, when used in conjunction with Pave Tack or radar, to store offset co-ordinates. ARN-101 lateral steering commands are used in conjunction with the AFCS for automatic piloting to take the aircraft along the intended route or pattern, while the aircraft commander monitors the manual terrain-following indicator, prepared to jump in for necessary override to take the jet up and down over the terrain. The navigator uses radar and Pave Tack during these possibly contour-hugging manoeuvres to call out dangerous obstacles, such as electrical wires, transmitter towers or smoke stacks.

For command and control tie-in with other aircraft, the WSO can press one of two buttons, 'up-link' or 'down-link'. Down-link is used to report aircraft position and altitude plus any other pertinent information to C^{3}I; up-link works the other way, providing the ARN-101 with fresh target information, again all part of the modern 'netted' command, control and intelligence system. To deal with high-value, high-risk targets, positional information can be despatched over a secure radio link to Ravens and Weasels, who will 'knot' or 'chew up' the opposition.

Flying in the Quick Strike Reconnaissance (QSR)

mode, using 'real-time' sensors and a Pave Tack pod, RF-4C crews can locate enemy targets and direct strike forces accordingly. Using their Pave Tack pods to mark the enemy targets, friendly fighter-bombers equipped with LGBs can run in and lob their Paveways, a tactic which reduces their exposure to enemy defences and which permits extra pylon space for more bombs. Amazingly, Pave Tack RF-4Cs can also help 'dumb' bomb equipped support aircraft. This is made possible because, alongside the Pave-podded Phantoms and F-111s, a similar reception-only device, Pave Penny, is fitted to A-7D/Ks and A-10As, enabling these strike machines to pick up the reflected laser energy from a marked spot, navigate to the target and compute the weapons release point.

With the mission nearly over, the crew report on the condition of their twenty-ton jet. The ARN-101 now assists in automatic approach to landing. This furnishes precise runway approach information, based on the Loran co-ordinates of the touch-down point, approach heading, touch-down ground height and the desired glidescope – between 2 and 5 degrees. Unlike normal ARN-101/AFCS-assisted flight, the landing aid works in the vertical as well as lateral axis, providing safe automatic approach even when the cloud ceiling is as low as 300ft with visibility less than one mile. Approach angle, heading and height are all supplied on the instruments, leaving the pilot to watch the AFCS gently bring the aircraft towards the runway threshold. Having of course remembered to lower the flaps and undercarriage, the pilot then resumes control of the RF-4C as the runway looms into view, and places the Phantom on to the concrete with typical, effortless style. The 16ft diameter ring-slot drag parachute pops out, decelerating the jet before disengaging. Still playing with the throttle controls and nosewheel steering, the pilot eases the aircraft back into its assigned parking slot. This procedure has, to date, been safely accomplished several million times – a testimony to a truly great aircraft and to the expert crews who fly and maintain them.

5. THE FUTURE

Phantom Plus

As the US Navy embarks on another conversion programme of QF-4 target drones, and replacement 'Teenage' fighters roll out from the factories in increasing numbers, many people are beginning to eye the growing stock of surplus F-4s as an attractive investment. Some have scrap metal in mind, others a bank balance healthy enough to envisage a flight of privately owned F-4s growling across the skies of the Confederate Air Force Base at Harlingen, Texas, forming part of the immortal Colonel Culpepper's historic air arm. Although it may be an old dog, however, the Phantom has a proven record of being able to adjust to brand-new requirements, so much so that in the future it may be flown by combat pilots who have not yet been born.

Over the past five years there has grown up a school of thought which is expounding the economic virtues of keeping 1,000 or more of the 3,000 Phantoms still in service worldwide operational into the twenty-first century. New production fighters cost in excess of $20 million a copy, whereas an upgraded F-4, incorporating some 1980s-style improvements, offers a virtually brand new machine for a mere fraction of that price. Even if such modernized Phantoms are not deemed suitable for countering the emerging generation of Soviet-built fighters and air combat missiles such as 'Flanker' and 'Alamo', the US could still recoup several billions of dollars by selling surplus refurbished aircraft overseas to its allies, or use them solely for strike or point interception work – a far more attrac-

tive proposition than letting otherwise capable aircraft rot in the American sun-belt in one of the many aeroplane graveyards.

At the same point in time that these thoughts were gathering momentum in the Defense Department, Israel decided to embark on a totally new, indigenous fighter to replace its Kfirs in the 1990s. Leaning heavily on US industrial and political support to get the Lavi (as the new fighter was named) airborne, Pratt & Whitney Aircraft came forward with the P&WA 1120 afterburning turbofan powerplant, a thrusty, modular engine, based on, and sharing no less than 70 per cent commonality with, the successful F100 which powers the Eagle and Fighting Falcon. By little coincidence, this new engine was also found to slot neatly into the Phantom. With this in mind, P&WA decided to look into the possibilities of marketing an upgraded F-4 worldwide.

Right, top: An unidentified Phantom serving as gate guardian in the Vietnam-era markings of the 557th TFS, 12th TFW, complete with 750lb bombs. (MAP)

Right, bottom: Ex-'Green Mountain Boys', Vermont Guard F-4D-29-MC 66-0266 serves as a battle damage repair article in USAFE, along with numerous other F-4C/Ds. (MAP)

Below: F-4C-16-MC 63-7421, an ex-San Antonio, Texas Guard Phantom, serving as a battle damage repair ship. (MAP)

Consequently, in the spring of 1983, Pratt & Whitney put out feelers to find a companion for the project, able to manage F-4 airframe-avionics refurbishing, while they in turn could concentrate their efforts on the production of new engines to slot into the reworked jets. The company to join them was BMAC at Wichita, Kansas, due, thanks to enthusiasm, to prior experience with a number of developments relevant to an upgrade – dealt with below – and an ace up their sleeve: that October, BMAC won a contract from the USAF Logistics Command to overhaul and incorporate TCTOs into the F-4C fleet, lending them the vital airframe know-how. By that October, P&WA had already spent four months working on designs for the upgraded F-4, dubbed 'Super Phantom'. Although the project was subject to severe criticism from some quarters in the USAF, within weeks of establishing the partnership the group had US-allied F-4 operators knocking at the door to get a closer look at the proposals, spurred on by the attraction of a fighter

carrying a modest price-tag. The most enthusiastic of these was Israel, which has since teamed up with P&WA.

Super Phantom

The refit proposals encompass three major, optional elements. The first part of the package is to re-engine the Phantom with the 20,000lb P&WA 1120, to 'take advantage of over twenty years of propulsion technology improvements since the J79 was developed', as P&WA said. An Israeli F-4 took to the air with a J79 and 1120 installation for the first time on 31 July 1986, and since 24 April 1987 has been 'sucking air' with a double installation, in time for an impressive public début at the Paris Air Show that June. According to the latest calculations, the engines give the F-4 15 per cent more sea-level thrust, but at the same time weigh 26 per cent less than a pair of J79-GE-17s; the net result improves the F-4's thrust-to-weight ratio from 0:76 to 1.04:1. With this much extra energy, the Phantom can

Above: A P&WA 1120 engine being test-fitted to an Israeli F-4E. (Israel Aircraft Industries)

Below: A 'Jayhawks' F-4D tries out a P&WA 1120 engine for size at the BMAC in Kansas. (P&WA)

Right: P&WA 1120 benefits. In the air-to-ground role, the Phantom's speed/load capabilities are increased (upper left) and its manoeuvrability is improved (right); in the air defence mission, take-off distance is cut by 21 per cent (lower left) and climb rate improved by 31 per cent (right).

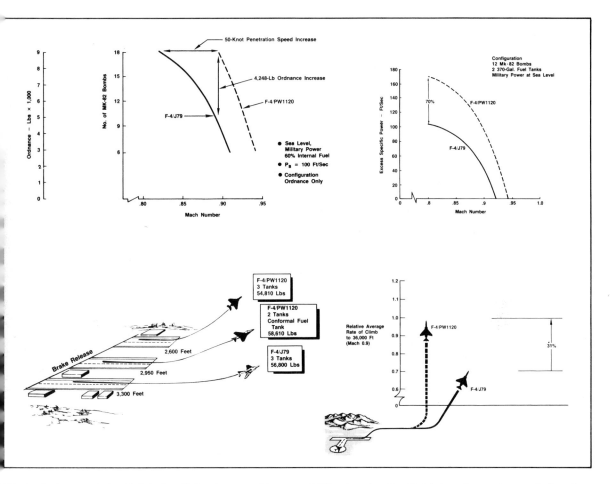

climate faster, sustain tight dog-fight turns without falling from the sky and respond to the pilot with, depending on altitude, 18–25 per cent better acceleration.

The second key element of the upgrade on offer is a 1,100 US gallon Conformal Fuel Tank (CFT) which can be bolted on the F-4's belly. This is proven technology. In 1970, after some four years of privately funded studies by BMAC, the USAF/USN awarded a joint-service development contract to Boeing to design and supply such a pallet. Flight trials commenced in August 1972 on an F-4B at China Lake, California. Before the test data had been fully processed the following summer, it was clear that the performance gains were remarkable.

Configured with full internal fuselage and CFT fuel (thereby deleting the requirement for the 'draggy' external tanks), the F-4B was rigged to carry a number of munitions in a low-drag conformal mode under the pallet; these weapons loads included up to twelve 500lb or 750lb bombs, of five different types. Compared to a comparatively crude TER/MER ejection rack-toting bomber, the CFT F-4B provided significant improvements – 75 per cent less drag, 43 per cent more range, an increased loiter capability and, very importantly, a safe higher-speed weapons separation cap-

ability, turning the F-4 into a true supersonic bomber. Normal TER/MER 'iron' bomb equipped Phantoms are limited to Mach 1, but the CFT F-4B performed safe weapons release at speeds ranging between Mach 1.25 at 10,000ft and Mach 1.8 at 30,000ft. Most remarkable of all was the test data that showed that even when weighed down with the bombs the CFT Phantom actually performed better than a 'clean' F-4! Flight-test crews at China Lake anticipated that they could perform SAM avoidance manoeuvres without having to jettison their external loads. With such positive results, it seems absurd that no CFTs were deployed on operational Phantoms, but there were some policy hiccups in the project. First, the USAF were anxious to replace their Phantoms with the undoubtedly higher performance F-15. Money was short, and TAC HQ's initial plans were to withdraw most F-4s from front-line service by 1980. For the short life-time expected for the CFT, the pay-off was considered too marginal. The second factor was that the CFT blocked off the F-4's Sparrow missile wells, thereby confining the aircraft to guns and Sidewinder missiles for air combat. Pending the introduction of the sophisticated AIM-7F Sparrow, the F-4s were required to hold the air defence fort as the F-15s were suffering from some very complex interface problems with the

Above: An Israeli F-4E takes to the air with Pratt & Whitney 1120 powerplants. Israel plans to upgrade its Phantoms under two phases – engines and pallet, followed by high-lift canards reminiscent of the CCV YRF-4C. The plans are subject to budget authorizations. (Israel Aircraft Industries)

Sparrow models then in service. By the time the F-15 achieved IOC with the AIM-7F the F-4 would be due for retirement, and the high cost of the pallets could not be justified. The possibility of extending the service life of the F-4 well into the 1990s and beyond as a pure strike or interceptor machine has now given much new impetus to the BMAC pallet concept. Furthermore, as an added bonus, Boeing has redesigned a slimmer CFT compatible with a great number of Weasel and recce stores, bombs, AGMs, LGBs and AIMs, including a full complement of Sparrow or AMRAAM missiles.

The third part of the upgrade on offer involves an airframe re-work plus revamped or additional avionics, estimated to provide more than a ten-fold increase in Mean Time Between Failures (MTBF). McDonnell Douglas are offering a similar avionics package, and are still striving in whatever way they can to improve safety as well as reliability. Most noteworthy in both proposals is the Westinghouse F-16 radar, so reliable that Japan has already begun to embark on a replacement programme: a special APG-66-modified F-4EJ took to the air on 17 July 1984, from the Gifu Test Centre. Ninety-six F-4EJs are to be upgraded, creating a four-squadron strong force that will be operational into the 1990s (of the remaining 27 F-4EJs, seventeen will be converted to the reconnaissance configuration). The West German

Air Force is looking forward to similar integration trials under their ICE improvement programme. ICE centres around the Hughes APG-65 (F/A-18 Hornet) radar system, and 75 F-4Fs are destined to be upgraded by 1992. The APG-66 and -65 come complete with a number of attack options, including the vital air-to-air automatic acquisition of aerial targets, and bombing in visual CCIP, 'dive–toss' and continuously computed release point modes.

Within the USAF, where a potential upgrade market for up to 1,000 Phantoms exists, the views remain split. Some within the Air Force see the upgrade as an opportunity to provide highly capable, modestly priced jets for use by the reservists into the early twenty-first century. Others are fiercely opposed, saying that the programme would eat deeply into the budgets of LANTIRN and similar systems: even if such projects are not affected, this lobby argues, sales of reworked surplus F-4s overseas would reduce sales of newer F-16s and other American fighters, subsequently causing USAF unit prices to escalate. Besides, they claim, the Phantom is simply too long in the tooth to justify a total refit. While the USAF remains split between two camps, the Defense Department is pressing for some sort of tests to proceed, mainly on the basis that, even without USAF involvement, Japan, West Germany and Israel will go ahead with improvements of their own, leaving the Americans out in the cold. Tests are starting in 1987, all the same, with a BMAC nav-attack avionics upgrade kit – the first positive step.

The USAF stand is further complicated by another controversy. In recent moves, Congress mandated that the USAF evaluate the General Dynamics F-16 and

Northrop F-20 in a competitive fly-off with a view to procuring some 270 of one type to replace all air defence-assigned F-4C/Ds by 1991. The F-16 was declared the winner in November 1986, and selected Block 15 aircraft will receive an air defence kit while undergoing scheduled PDM at Ogden, giving them Sparrow/AMRAAM capability. However, there are opponents: commanders, test pilots and weapons and tactics officers, all experienced men, have publicly stated that the F-16 is the 'least desirable' of all available options or, more bluntly, 'the wrong choice for the strategic defence mission', unable to engage cruise missiles and limited in air-to-air ordnance capacity. Given the realities of budget restraints, and the consequent lack of funds for F-15 Eagles for the job, many in this school firmly believe that the North Dakota ANG's proposal for Hughes to refit 180 selected F-4Ds with IRSTS, the APG-63 (F-15) radar, and possibly a BMAC pallet for around $3.5 million a copy is the right choice. The lobby is gathering momentum.

USAF upgrades

Whether or not the USAF will proceed with the Phantom refit proposals in any shape or form to take advantage of the large numbers of F-4s available for extended service will not affect a number of other improvements which are in prospect. The bulk of these are minimal changes, reflecting the usual evolution of electronic warfare and avionics systems, while others are aimed, only now, at solving some of those old design 'glitches' that continue to nag the Air Force.

Probably the two most noteworthy elements are a new windshield and a smokeless engine. Standard J79 powerplants, equipping the entire USAF fleet in both GE-15 and GE-17 form, are very very smoky, but a small modification kit developed under Project 'Seek Smoke' provides the answer. Redesignated J79-GE-15E and -17C/E, the modified engines simply generate a slightly higher jet-pipe temperature which, without grossly affecting the F-4's infra-red signature, causes the carbon soot to dissipate, dissolving the give-away dirt trail that has so often caused the demise of F-4s in combat. Originally designed for use by Iran, after the fall of the Shah the 'liberated' kits were diverted for use by the USAF, principally for ARN-101 F-4Es and F-4Gs. Since then, many more Phantoms have gone

Below: F-4D-30-MC 66-7635 went on from being the Advanced Wild Weasel V test-bed to serve as a trials machine for the Westinghouse APG-66 radar system. Japan is retrofitting the APG-66 to selected F-4EJs. (Westinghouse)

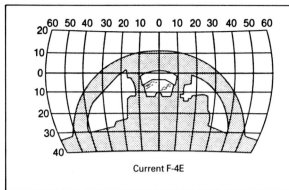

Current F-4E

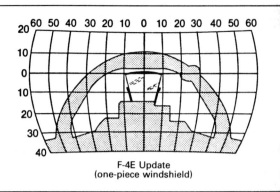

F-4E Update
(one-piece windshield)

smokeless, and all F-4s with the exception of the F-4C are to be so modified, under T.O. 2J-J79-1241. Related work is being performed under the Pace Frugal programme, which aims to increase the time between major engine strip-downs.

The other bonus for existing models is a newly developed, one-piece windshield, similar to those found on the F-15 and F/A-18. The F-4's windshield plate, some 1.3in thick, provides fairly good protection, but the side panels do not – they are thinner, less well supported, and screwed into a comparatively weak aluminium frame. F-4s worldwide have been involved in some forty serious windshield-related bird-strike incidents, at least a dozen of which have claimed the loss of both crew and aircraft. With high-speed, low-level flying forming the bulk of modern Phantom

Above: As well as being lighter, less complex and more resistant to bird-strike, the new windshield for the F-4 offers substantially improved visibility, as illustrated in these drawings. (McDonnell Douglas)

operations, the problem has grown more acute. The new Loral windshield, reinforced by a titanium bow frame, slots into place in the existing fuselage supports, protecting the pilot from a 4lb bird hitting the screen at speeds of up to 500kts, while having 31 per cent fewer parts and being 20lb lighter. At present, F-4s are vulnerable to extensive bird-strike damage at a mere 200kts.

The new transparency also offers vastly improved clarity. Phantom 'jocks' often comment that they quite easily lose track of an aircraft they are chasing if it becomes shadowed behind the support frames for any length of time. The new windshield eliminates this problem, while, with several canopy bow frame and console coaming-mounted devices moved further down on a reorganized main instrument panel, the pilot will be able to enjoy an even better forward view. Five new windshields are being tested by the USAF, two for impact trials and three for flight-test work with the Missouri ANG (F-4Es 68-0345, 0351 and 0448). All pilot response indicators suggest that the new acrylic-polycarbonate-sandwich transparency is a major innovation that would be a great bonus to safety. Fleet-wide refit contracts are possible.

Below: The improved one-piece windshield aboard F-4E-37-MC 68-0345, Brig. Gen. Rick Layman's jet. Three Missouri ANG F-4Es are configured with the new windshield, with fleet-wide upgrades in prospect. (McDonnell Douglas)

Finale
Whatever the outcome of these upgrade proposals, it appears highly unlikely that the F-4 will totally disappear from the skies for a long while yet, even though numbers will start falling as attrition continues to take its toll and more and more airframes clock up and expend their effective fatigue lives. Indeed the Super Phantom, and many similar ventures, may give the F-4 a dramatic lease of life, taking the type through to the next century in considerable numbers. The key lies in decisions which will be taken in high places over the next few years. One thing is certain: even when measured up against the more svelte high-technology fighters of the 1980s, the Phantom continues to command the greatest admiration and respect.

APPENDICES

APPENDIX I: GLOSSARY OF ABBREVIATIONS AND ACRONYMS

AAA   Anti-aircraft artillery. Usually radar-directed.

AB   Air Base. Not USAF-owned, and usually located outside the USA.

AD   Air Division. Part of an Air Force, e.g. 831st AD, 12th AF, TAC.

ADTAC   Air Defense Tactical Air Command. HQ Langley AFB, Virginia, Now known as 1st AF.

ADTC   Armament Development Test Center. Eglin AFB, Florida.

ADWC   Air Defense Weapons Center. Tyndall AFB, Florida.

AF   Air Force. Subordinate to a Command, e.g. 12th AF, TAC, and made up from two or more Wings.

AFB   Air Force Base. USAF owned.

AFFTC   Air Force Flight Test Center. Edwards AFB, California.

AFLC   Air Force Logistics Command. HQ Wright-Patterson AFB, Ohio.

AFRES   Air Force Reserve. HQ Robins AFB, Georgia.

AFSC   Air Force Systems Command. HQ Andrews AFB, Maryland.

AGM   Air-to-ground missile. For example, AGM-65 Maverick.

AIM   Air intercept missile. For example, AIM-9 Sidewinder.

ANG   Air National Guard. HQ Andrews AFB, Maryland.

ARM   Anti-radiation (radar) missile. Usually designated AGM.

ASD   Aeronautical Systems Division. HQ Wright-Patterson AFB, Ohio.

CAS   Close air support. Conducted in support of friendly ground forces along the forward edge of the battle area (FEBA).

CBU   Cluster bomb unit. A bomb made up from a large number of anti-personnel or anti-radar bomblets, e.g. CBU-24.

C³I   Command, Control, Communications and Intelligence. 'See-three-eye'.

CEP   Circular Error Probable. Average projected circular miss from a desired impact point by a given weapon or weapons release system.

CRT   Cathode ray tube. TV screen. When using radar the WRCS-generated crosshairs are moved across and along track over the target or identification point imagery. When an electro-optical sensor or seeker is selected, the video crosshairs remain stationary in the centre of the TV image and the image underneath is slewed about, as the sensor or seeker is swivelled on to target.

CW   Continuous Wave. Radar energy (cf. pulsed emissions).

DACT   Dissimilar Air Combat Training. Used to familiarize F-4 crews with the very different flying characteristics of Soviet jets.

DDR&E   Directorate of Defense Research and Engineering.

DoD   Department of Defense.

ECM   Electronic counter-measures. Designed to foil enemy electronic defences. ECCM, for counter-countermeasures, are systems designed to work through ECM disruption.

EWO   Electronic Warfare Officer (or 'Bear'). Skilled in the art of enemy radar analysis, defence-suppression tactics and advanced navigation.

Ferret   An air crewman or aircraft honed or optimized to 'sniff out' and judge the status of hostile radars, for electronic intelligence-gathering purposes.

FLIR   Forward-looking infra-red. Sensor able to see through darkness.

FOT&E   Follow-on Operational Test and Evaluation. Usually carried out at Nellis TFWC or Tyndall ADWC.

FOV   Field of view (of an optical sensor or seeker). The smaller the FOV, the greater the magnification of an object under scrutiny.

FWIC   Fighter Weapons Instructor Course. Held at McConnell AFB, Kansas.

FWS   Fighter Weapons Squadron. Usually associated with the FWIC, TFWC or TAWC.

GBU   Guided bomb unit. For example, Paveway laser-guided GBU-10.

GC   Gigacycle. 1GC=1,000 million Hertz or cycles per second.

GCI   Ground Control Intercept. Used to vector air defence fighters on to enemy air intruders.

HAWC   Homing and Warning Computer. Used by the Advanced Wild Weasels.

IFF   Identification Friend or Foe. A military transponder used to identify an aircraft as friendly.

IOC   Initial Operational Capability. Refers to the status of a new system at combat-ready squadron level.

IOT&E   Initial Operational Test and Evaluation. Usually carried out at Eglin ADTC.

I²R   Imaging infra-red. Sensor or seeker which sees hot on cold or cold on hot to provide a TV image despite darkness or haze.

LCOSS   Lead Computing Optical Sight System. F-4D/E/G servoed gunsight.

LGB   Laser-guided bomb.

LIFT   Lead-In Fighter Training. Conducted at Holloman AFB, New Mexico, on Northrop AT-38Bs.

Loran   Long-range hyberbolic radio navigation aid.

LOS   Line of sight. Direct target sighting.

LRU   Line replaceable unit. A module which can be unplugged from the aircraft for servicing.

MAC   Military Airlift Command. Flying C-5, C-130 and C-141 cargo aircraft; HQ Scott AFB, Illinois.

MiGCAP   MiG combat air patrol; patrolling against enemy MiG aircraft in support of strike aircraft.

nm	Nautical mile. 6,076ft; cf. one statute mile (5,280ft).
NORAD	North American Air Defense. Embraces Canada and the USA.
PACAF	Pacific Air Forces. HQ Hickam AFB, Hawaii.
PDM	Programmed Depot Maintenance. Conducted on F-4Cs every 36 months, on F-4Ds every 48 months and on RF-4Cs, F-4Es and F-4Gs every 54 months.
QRC	Quick-reaction capability. Refers to the speed with which a new system is put into operational service rather than its ability to perform the job rapidly.
Raven	The dedicated Grumman-converted EF-111A jamming platform, otherwise known as the 'Spark Vark' or 'Electric Fox'.
RHAWS	Radar homing and warning systems. Now known as radar warning receivers (RWR).
RTU	Replacement Training Unit. Responsible for training new crews, RTUs are typically Tactical Fighter Training or Tactical Reconnaissance Training Squadrons.
SAM	Surface-to-air missile. Either radar or optically guided. Soviet-built systems are prefixed 'SA' by NATO.
SEA	South-East Asia. Term used to embrace Vietnam, Thailand, Laos and Cambodia (Kampuchea).
SLAR	Sideways-looking airborne radar. Used for reconnaissance. SAR is an advanced synthetic aperture radar, which may perform in the SLAR mode.
TAC	Tactical Air Command. The biggest user of the Phantom in the world. HQ Langley AFB, Virginia.

TAS	Tactical air support. See CAS.
TAWC	Tactical Air Warfare Center. Eglin AFB, Florida. The Eglin complex is run by two organizations: TAC operates the TAWC, and AFSC the ADTC.
TES	Test and Evaluation Squadron.
TFS	Tactical Fighter Squadron. Flying 20–26 mission-ready F-4s.
TFW	Tactical Fighter Wing. Composed of 2–4 TFS, TFTS or TTS.
TFWC	Tactical Fighter Weapons Center. Nellis AFB, Nevada. Home of 'Red' and 'Green Flag' wargames, 'Gunsmoke' competitions, etc.
TRS	Tactical Reconnaissance Squadron. Flying 18–20 RF-4Cs.
TRW	Tactical Reconnaissance Wing. Composed of 1–4 TRS and TRTS.
USAFE	United States Air Forces Europe. HQ Ramstein AB, West Germany.
USN/MC	United States Navy/Marine Corps.
WGAF	West German Air Force. Otherwise known as the Luftwaffe.
WRCS	Weapons-Release Computer System. The automatic bombing package used by most F-4D/E/G Phantoms.
WSO	Weapons Systems Operator. Rear-seat crewman in an F-4 or RF-4. Originally dual-qualified pilots and radar operators, after 1969 'Wizzos' came mainly from non-pilot, navigator schools, though many back-seaters have attained basic handling proficiency on simulators and a few have full pilot skills.

APPENDIX II: USAF F-4 DELIVERIES

F-4C

Block Nos.	Serials	Built	Notes
F-4C-15-MC	62-12199	15	
	63-7404–7420		
F-4C-16-MC	63-7421–7442	22	
F-4C-17-MC	63-7443–7468	26	
F-4C-18-MC	63-7469–7525	58	
F-4C-19-MC	63-7527–7597	71	
F-4C-20-MC	63-7598–7662	65	
F-4C-21-MC	63-7663–7713	70	
	64-0654–0672		
F-4C-22-MC	64-0673–0737	65	
F-4C-23-MC	64-0738–0817	80	
F-4C-24-MC	64-0818–0881	64	
F-4C-25-MC	64-0882–0928	47	
	Total	583	

F-4D

Block Nos.	Serials	Built	Notes
F-4D-24-MC	64-0929–0937	9	6 remaining
F-4D-25-MC	64-0938–0963	26	19 remaining
F-4D-26-MC	64-0964–0980	49	32 remaining
	65-9580–0611		
F-4D-27-MC	65-0612–0665	54	29 remaining
F-4D-28-MC	65-0666–0770	105	70 remaining
	65-0771–0801		
F-4D-29-MC	66-0226–0283	139	79 remaining
	66-7455–7504		
F-4D-30-MC	66-7505–7650	146	78 remaining
F-4D-31-MC	66-7651–7774	138	84 remaining
	66-8686–8698		
F-4D-32-MC	66-8699–8786	88	43 remaining
F-4D-33-MC	66-8787–8825	39	23 remaining
	Total	793	

F-4E

Block Nos.	Serials	Built	Notes
F-4E-31-MC	66-0284–0297	14	3 remaining
F-4E-32-MC	66-0298–0338	41	19 remaining
F-4E-33-MC	66-0339–0387	56	21 remaining
	67-0208–0219		
F-4E-34-MC	67-0220–0282	63	21 remaining
F-4E-35-MC	67-0283–0341	59	21 remaining
F-4E-36-MC	67-0342–0398	57	33 remaining
F-4E-37-MC	68-0303–0365	63	47 remaining
F-4E-38-MC	68-0366–0409	44	36 remaining; total includes 4 supplied to Israel (68-0396–0399)
F-4E-39-MC	68-0410–0451	42	28 remaining; total includes 8 supplied to Israel (68-0414–0417 and 68-0434–0437)
F-4E-40-MC	68-0452–0494	43	24 remaining; total includes 12 supplied to Israel (68-0454–0457, 68-0469–0472 and 68-0484–0487)

Right: A line of ARN-101 F-4E tails from the 37th TFW. The aircraft were previously assigned to the 52nd TFW, at Spangdahlem, West Germany. (USAF photo by SSgt. M. Dugre)

Designation	Serials	Qty	Notes
F-4E-41-MC	68-0495–0547	53	28 remaining; total includes 20 supplied to Israel (68-0499–0502, 68-0519–0525 and 68-0539–0547)
F-4E-42-MC	69-0236–0303	68	8 remaining; 43 converted to F-4G, 37 remaining
F-4E-43-MC	69-0304–0307 69-7201–7260	64	2 remaining; 36 converted to F-4G, 31 remaining
F-4E-44-MC	69-7261–7273 69-7286–7303 69-7546–7578	64	8 remaining; 28 converted to F-4G, all remaining
F-4E-45-MC	69-7579–7589	11	2 remaining; 9 converted to F-4G, 6 remaining
F-4E-48-MC	71-0224–0247	24	8 remaining
F-4E-49-MC	71-1070–1093	24	14 remaining
F-4E-50-MC	71-1391–1402 72-0121–0138	30	9 remaining
F-4E-51-MC	72-0139–0144 72-0157–0159	9	7 remaining
F-4E-52-MC	72-0160–0165	6	4 remaining
F-4E-53-MC	72-0166–0168 72-1407	4	All remaining
F-4E-54-MC	72-1476–1489	14	8 remaining
F-4E-55-MC	72-1490–1497	8	3 remaining
F-4E-56-MC	72-1498–1499	2	0 remaining
F-4E-57-MC	73-1157–1164	8	3 remaining
F-4E-58-MC	73-1165–1184	20	13 remaining
F-4E-59-MC	73-1185–1204	20	13 remaining
F-4E-60-MC	74-0643–0660 74-1038–1049	30	26 remaining
F-4E-61-MC	74-0661–0666 74-1050–1061 74-1620–1637	36	31 remaining
F-4E-62-MC	74-1638–1653	16	13 remaining
F-4E-63-MC	75-0628–0637	10	Purchased by Luftwaffe for training at George AFB; 8 remaining

Total 1,003

RF-4C

Designation	Serials	Qty
RF-4C-16-MC	63-7740–7741	2
RF-4C-17-MC	63-7742	1
RF-4C-18-MC	63-7743–7749	7
RF-4C-19-MC	63-7750–7763	14
RF-4C-20-MC	64-0997–1017	21
RF-4C-21-MC	64-1018–1037	20
RF-4C-22-MC	64-1038–1061	24
RF-4C-23-MC	64-1062–1077	16
RF-4C-24-MC	64-1078–1085 65-0818–0838	29
RF-4C-25-MC	65-0839–0864	26
RF-4C-26-MC	65-0865–0901	37
RF-4C-27-MC	65-0902–0932	31
RF-4C-28-MC	65-0933–0945 66-0383–0386 66-0388	18
RF-4C-29-MC	66-0387 66-0389–0406	19
RF-4C-30-MC	66-0407–0428	22
RF-4C-31-MC	66-0429–0450	22

RF-4C-32-MC	66-0451–0472	22	
RF-4C-33-MC	66-0473–0478	21	
	67-0428–0442		
RF-4C-34-MC	67-0443–0453	11	
RF-4C-35-MC	67-0454–0461	8	
RF-4C-36-MC	67-0462–0469	8	
RF-4C-37-MC	68-0548–0561	14	
RF-4C-38-MC	68-0562–0576	15	
RF-4C-39-MC	68-0577–0593	17	
RF-4C-40-MC	68-0594–0611	18	
RF-4C-41-MC	69-0349–0357	9	
RF-4C-42-MC	69-0368–0366	9	
RF-4C-42-MC	69-0367–0375	9	
RF-4C-44-MC	69-0376–0384	9	
RF-4C-48-MC	71-0248–0252	5	

RF-4C-49-MC	71-0253–0259	7
RF-4C-51-MC	72-0145–0148	4
RF-4C-52-MC	72-0149–0152	4
RF-4C-53-MC	72-0153–0156	4
	Total	503

Note: All direct foreign buys are excluded, as are two YRF-4Cs converted from Navy F-4Bs on the production lines. If one includes the two YRF-4Cs, the USAF, for its own use, took a grand total of 2,830 Phantoms of various marks between 1963 and 1976; this equates to 54 per cent of all Phantoms built! Numbers of F-4Cs remaining cannot be provided due to the wholesale disposal of the type being carried out at the present time; numbers remaining for the F-4D/E/G variants are correct as of April 1987.

APPENDIX III: USAF F-4 MAIN DIFFERENCES

Item	RF-4C	F-4C	F-4D	F-4E	F-4G
Engines	J79-GE-15	J79-GE-15	J79-GE-15	J79-GE-17	J79-GE-17
No. 7 fuel cell	No	No	No	Yes	Yes
Ram air turbine	Yes	Yes	Yes	No	No
Hydraulic wing-fold	Yes	Yes	Yes	No	No
Internal gun	No	No	No	Yes	No
Radar set	AN/APQ-99	AN/APQ-100	AN/APQ-109	AN/APQ-120	AN/APQ-120
Intercept computer	No	AN/APQ-157	AN/APQ-157 or -165	AN/APQ-120, LRU-1	AN/APQ-120, LRU-1
Optical sight	No	Fixed	AN/ASG-22	AN/ASG-26	AN/APQ-30
TISEO AN/ASX-1	No	No	No	71-0237 and up	No
Radar receiving set	AN/ALR-17 or AN/ALQ-125	No	No	No	AN/APR-38A, upgraded to AN/APR-45
Radar warning receivers	AN/ALR-69	AN/APR-25 or -26 or AN/ALR-46	AN/APS-107 or AN/ALR-69	AN/ALR-69 or -74	AN/ALR-69 or -74
Radar mapping set	AN/APQ-102 or AN/UPD-4 or -8	No	No	No	No
Weapons Release Computer System	No	No	AN/ASQ-91 (+ AN-ARN-92)	AN/ASQ-91 or AN/ARN-101	AN/ASQ-91 Mod or AN/ARN-101
Inertial navigation set	AN/ASN-56 or AN/ARN-101	AN/ASN-48	AN/ASN-63	AN/ASN-63 or AN/ARN-101	AN/ASN-63 or AN/ARN-101
Navigation computer	AN/ASN-46A or AN/ARN-101	AN/ASN-46	AN/ASN-46A	AN/ASN-46A or AN/ARN-101	AN/ASN-46A or AN/ARN-101
Boundary layer control wings	Yes	Yes	Yes	No	No
Leading-edge slats	No	No	No	Yes	Yes
Slotted tail	No	No	No	Yes	Yes
Length	62.9ft	58.2ft	58.2ft	62.9ft	63ft
Wingspan	38.4ft	38.4ft	38.4ft	38.4ft	38.4ft
Height	16.5ft	16.5ft	16.5ft	16.5ft	16.5ft
Max take-off weight	58,000lb	59,689lb	59,483lb	61,795lb	61,795lb
Max landing weight	46,000lb	46,000lb	46,000lb	46,000lb	46,000lb
Empty weight	28,546lb	28,539lb	28,873lb	30,328lb	30,300lb
Total fuel (US gallons) with external tanks	3,229	3,312	3,229	3,333	3,333
Sidewinder AIM-9 missiles	Being evaluated	Up to 4	Up to 4	Up to 4	Up to 4
Sparrow AIM-7 missiles	No	Up to 4	Up to 4	Up to 4	Up to 4
Maverick AGM-65 missile	No	No	Selected, Block 30+	Selected, Block 36+	Yes
Pave Spike AVQ-23/ ASQ-153 laser	No	No	Selected, Block 30+	67-0342 and up	No
Pave Tack AVQ-26 Laser	Selected, Block 37+	No	No	Selected, Block 48+	Yes
ECM pod	Yes	Selected, Blocks 16–24	Yes	Yes	Yes
AN/ALE-40 chaff/flares	Yes	No	Yes	Yes	Yes

APPENDIX IV: USAF F-4 POWERPLANTS

Designation Details

J79-GE-15 Standard engine (10,900lb s.t. military, 17,000lb s.t. afterburner).

J79-GE-15A J79-GE-15 with T-Duct 1st stage nozzle and R80 first-stage blades.

J79-GE-15E J79-GE-15A with low smoke combustor and high-energy ignition.

Inventory (August 1985) 2,058 J79-GE-15s installed; 541 spares.

J79-GE-17A Standard engine (11,870lb s.t. military, 17,900lb s.t. afterburner).

J79-GE-17C J79-GE-17A with low smoke combustor and low energy ignition.

J79-GE-17E J79-GE-17C with low smoke combustor and high energy ignition.

J79-GE-17F J79-GE-17A with Pacer Frugal (reliability) enhancements.

J79-GE-17G J79-GE-17E with Pacer Frugal enhancements, low smoke combustor and high-energy ignition.

Inventory (August 1985) 1,216 J79-GE-17s installed; 254 spares

Below: A WGAF RF-4E banks to port to reveal its Westinghouse ALQ-101 ECM pod. Two Luftwaffe Groups fly the RF-4E, the AKG-51 'Immelmann' at Bremgarten AB and the AKG-52 at Leck AB. (Westinghouse)

APPENDIX V: FOREIGN USERS OF USAF F-4 MODELS AND DERIVATIVES

Country	Type(s)	No. acquired	No. in service	Notes
Australia	F-4E	24	–	Loaned 1970–73 pending deliveries of F-111Cs; 23 survivors flown home to Hill AFB, Utah.
Egypt	F-4E	36	36	Ex-USAF 31st TFW aircraft supplied under Camp David agreement as Project 'Peace Pharaoh'.
Greece	F-4E	56	52	All new aircraft from McDonnell Douglas. Possible acquisition of 40 surplus
	RF-4E	8	7	USAF F-4Es in pipeline.
Iran	F-4D	32	5	Two F-4Es loaned by the USAF, one of which was later returned; others all
	F-4E	179	30	new-builds.
	RF-4E	16	3	
Israel	F-4E	164	110	All RF-4Es and some 102 F-4Es were factory-fresh. Balance supplied during
	RF-4E	12	11	October 1973 emergency resupply effort.
Japan	F-4EJ	140	127	25 supplied in kit form from McDonnell Douglas; remainder built under
	RF-4EJ	14	14	licence to Mitsubishi Heavy Industries. RF-4EJs all McDonnell Douglas-built.
Spain	F-4C	40	34	All ex-USAF stocks, reworked by CASA Getafe and redesignated C12 (F-4C)
	RF-4C	4	4	and CR12 (RF-4C).
South Korea	F-4D	66	58	All F-4Ds ex-USAF stock; 37 F-4Es delivered from McDonnell Douglas
	F-4E	41	37	production stock, 4 from USAF stocks.
Turkey	F-4E	97	91	80, including all RF-4Es, delivered fresh from McDonnell Douglas; balance
	RF-4E	8	8	ex-USAF F-4Es supplied under Peace Diamond III and IV. 40 more F-4Es have been offered from USAF stocks.
West Germany	F-4E	10	8	F-4Es stationed at George AFB, California; F-4Fs are F-4Es specially designed
	F-4F	175	159	for Luftwaffe. All Phantoms acquired from production lines at McDonnell
	RF-4E	88	79	Douglas.

Note: All figures courtesy of the McDonnell Douglas Corporation. Iranian figures are manufacturer's estimates.

APPENDIX VI: USAF F-4 PERFORMANCE

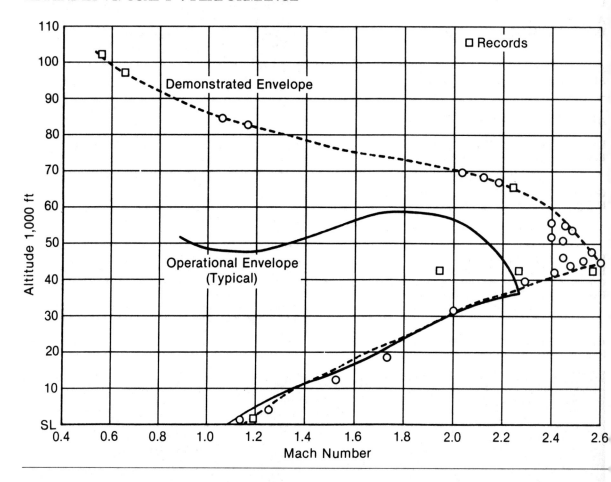

APPENDIX VII: USAF F-4 MUNITIONS

'Iron' bombs

Designation	Type	Charge weight
Mk.82	Conical low-drag bomb	500lb
Mk.82	Snakeye high-drag bomb	500lb
Mk.83	Conical low-drag bomb	1,000lb
Mk.84	Conical low-drag bomb	2,000lb
M117	General-purpose bomb	750lb
M118	General-purpose bomb	3,000lb

Cluster bombs

Designation	Type	Approx. all-up weight
CBU-52		800lb
CBU-58		750lb
Mod II	Mk.20 Rockeye	500lb
CBU-87	'Spin up' dispenser	1,000lb
SUU-54		2,000lb

Guided bombs

Designation	Name	Origin	Charge weight
GBU-12	Paveway II	Mk.82 adaptation	500lb
GBU-16	Paveway II	Mk.83 adaptation	1,000lb
GBU-10	Paveway II	Mk. 84 adaptation	2,000lb
GBU-24	Paveway III	Mk.84 adaptation	
GBU-2B/B	Pave Storm	SUU-54 adaptation	2,000lb
GBU-8	Hobos	Mk.84 adaptation	2,000lb
GBU-15	'Cruciform' or 'Short-Chord'	Mk.84 adaptation	2,000lb

Guided missiles

Designation	Name	Type	Approx. range
AGM-45	Shrike	Anti-radar missile	15nm
AGM-65	Maverick	TV or imaging IR-guided	12nm
AGM-78	Standard ARM	Anti-radar missile	35nm
AGM-88	HARM	Anti-radar missile	40nm
AGM-130		Rocket-assisted GBU-15 glide bomb	12nm

'Special weapons'

Designation	Type	All-up bomb weight
B-28	Nuclear	2,170lb
B-43	Nuclear	2,060lb

B-57	Nuclear		500lb	AIM-7E2	Sparrow	Semi-active radar	28 miles
B-61	Nuclear		708lb	AIM-7F/M	Sparrow	Semi-active radar	60 miles

Air intercept missiles

Gun pods

Designation	Name	Type	Approx. max. range	Designation	Name	Type	Calibre
				SUU-16/A	Vulcan	'Gatling' gun	20mm
				SUU-23/A	Vulcan	'Gatling' gun	20mm
AIM/9J/N/P	Sidewinder	Heat-seeking	9 miles	GPU-5/A	Gepod	'Gatling' gun	30mm
AIM-9L/M	Sidewinder	Heat-seeking	11 miles				

APPENDIX VIII: USAF TRAINING COURSES

Undergraduate Pilot Training (UPT) Course

Bases: Columbus, Mississippi; Laughlin, Reese and Sheppard, Texas; Vance, Oklahoma; and Williams, Arizona.

Ground: 17 pre-flight days and 386hrs academics.

Flying: Cessna T-37: 57 sorties or 74.4hrs (62 dual, 12.4 solo)
Northrop T-38: 80 sorties or 101.1hrs (71.1 dual, 29.9 solo)

Undergraduate Navigator Course

Base: Mather AFB, California.

Ground: 391hrs academics and 101 in simulator trainers.

Flying: Cessna T-37: 6 sorties or 24.6hrs
Boeing T-43: 14 sorties or 124hrs

Below: Northrop T-38 pilot students get to grips with formation flying. (USAF)

Advanced Tactical Navigation Training Course

Base: Mather AFB, California.

Ground: 78hrs academics plus 22hrs in simulator on low-level weapons delivery; 36hrs on electronic warfare (RWR and ECM pod) systems and electro-optics.

Flying: Cessna T-37: 9 sorties or 36.9hrs

Lead In Fighter Training (LIFT) Course

Base: Holloman AFB, New Mexico.

Ground: F-4 pilots follow 'C Track' course, which includes 70hrs academics on tactics and general airmanship ('C Track' is also followed by F-16 and A-7 pilots).

Flying: Northrop AT-38B: 28 sorties spread over 38 flying training days. Sorties embrace air-to-air, air-to-surface and advanced fighter manoeuvres. No-notice search and rescue survival training may be performed.

APPENDIX IX: THE F-4E TO G 'SEX CHANGE'

Summary
Two conversions, 1975–76, by McDonnell Douglas, Missouri; 114 conversions, 1977–81, at Module A, Hangar 3, Ogden OOALC, Utah. Total refit cost: $325 million ($2.8 million per copy). Average man-hours of work: 14,420 per F-4G. Length of job: 110 days per aircraft. (Note: Eighteen more F-4Gs to follow, 1987 on.)

Conversion kit
Seven crates containing 3,100 line items grouped into 161 assembly packs.

Work on nose
Three people in two shifts working for two weeks. Remove gun and ammunition drum, install a two-shelf avionics stack, including a mission recorder and self-destruct, nose antennae and new laminated fibreglass chin pod fairing. Remove the gun gas purge scoop and cover the gas vents. Add a 3in extension to the nose pitot.

Tail re-work
Two-man crews in two shifts for fourteen days. Strip off the metal skin from the starboard side of the tail-fin, install new wiring and a sheet metal fin-cap pod, then reskin the tail within a period of 12hrs to avoid moisture accumulating in the black boxes.

General work
Add dorsal spine and APR-38A and communications equipment, re-work the cockpits and install new wiring for Weasel ARMs, as part of 5,500 new wire terminations, 125 new wire bundles and 56 antennae. General airframe re-work. Add provisions for the McDonnell Douglas Tulsa/Fletcher F-15 type centreline fuel tank for 6g manoeuvring. Dismantle 100 'black boxes' and mission items for inspection and TCTO modifications in the 25 support shops. Repaint the aircraft, then test-fly it prior to delivery/acceptance.

Below: All out! An F-4E cockpit is re-worked to F-4G standard at Ogden OOALC. (USAF)

INDEX

Above: A 'Euro One'-painted F-4G assigned to the CO of the 561st TFS. The tail logo is shadowed in white and reads '561st TFS/AMU'; the fin cap is golden yellow. (USAF)